HEBREW TEXTS WITH PALESTINIAN VOCALIZATION

NEAR AND MIDDLE EAST SERIES

1 *The Mosaic Tradition*
F.V.Winnett

2 *Safaitic Inscriptions from Jordan*
F.V.Winnett

3 *History and Chronology of the Eighteenth Dynasty of Egypt: Seven Studies*
Donald B.Redford

4 *Oral Formulaic Language in the Biblical Psalms*
Robert C.Culley

5 *Jewish and Mandaean Incantation Bowls in the Royal Ontario Museum*
W.S.McCullough

6 *Ancient Records from North Arabia*
F.V.Winnett and W.L.Reed

7 *Hebrew Texts with Palestinian Vocalization*
E.J.Revell

Hebrew Texts with Palestinian Vocalization

E. J. REVELL

University of Toronto Press

Printed in Belgium for
University of Toronto Press,
Toronto and Buffalo

ISBN 0-8020-5215-0

TO MY WIFE

אשת חיל עטרת בעלה

Proverbs 12:4

Preface

The present work began as a study of a number of non-biblical Hebrew texts with Palestinian vocalization which were discovered by Dr. Manfried Dietrich in the boxes of the New Series of the Taylor-Schechter Collection of the Cambridge University Library. As a result of our introduction by Professor Kahle, Dr. Dietrich very kindly agreed to my collaborating with him in the study and eventual publication of these texts. After we had worked together for some time, however, Dr. Dietrich found that the pressure of his work in assyriology would not allow him the time necessary for the study of these manuscripts. With great generosity, therefore, he relinquished his interest in the work, and suggested that I continue alone with the publication we had planned. The texts of mss 1, 4, 4a, 5, 7, 8, and 9 published here are the result of our collaboration. They were prepared by Dr. Dietrich and myself together, from our independent readings of the mss. Besides this direct benefit, I have had the use of the notes made by Dr. Dietrich on the vocalization of the other texts he had discovered, and of his study of the biblical texts with Palestinian vocalization[1] which he very kindly lent to me. In addition to this, my own insight into the problems of the Palestinian vocalization has benefited much from many discussions with him.

My own studies, however, have eventually led me to adopt views rather different from those we both entertained during our collaboration. As a result, the present work differs considerably from the book we had planned together. The chief cause of this difference was the fact that I found at Cambridge some thirty texts with previously

[1] See M. Dietrich, *Neue palästinisch punktierte Bibelfragmente* (Thesis, Tübingen, 1960).

unpublished Palestinian pointing. The study of this large number of texts together gave me a new outlook on the problems of Palestinian pointing, and led to my disenchantment with commonly accepted theories. I also began to realize that, if the Palestinian pointing system as a whole was to be studied, some method of classifying the texts had to be found. There are several quite different methods of vocalizing a text with Palestinian signs, so that without a general classification, there can be no basis for the evaluation of different pointings of the same form, and no grammatical study of the dialect as a whole can be made.

The main purpose of this work, therefore, is not the study and publication of texts, as it was for the study planned by Dr. Dietrich and myself, but the analysis and classification of the pointing of the known Hebrew texts with Palestinian vocalization. Such analysis has been carried out before, but never in detail over a large number of manuscripts, as is done here. While I am certain that Palestinian texts remain to be found, I consider that the number now available for study (see chapter VI) is sufficiently large that a classification based on these is likely to be comprehensive.[2] The study of the details of the use of vowel signs permits secure establishment of the similarities in the pointing of related manuscripts, and therefore provides a firm basis for classification. It also makes possible a detailed survey of the extent to which phenomena considered typically 'Palestinian' are common to texts with Palestinian vocalization, and the extent to which Palestinian forms resemble, or differ from, those of related dialects. It therefore provides a firm basis for grammatical study.

Classification is not, of course, an end in itself. The purpose of this classification is to permit easy comparison of the written, and

[2] This book is based on the mss of which I knew in the spring of 1966, when the writing of the book was finished. In 1967–68, I was able to spend a year in England, where I found many more mss with Palestinian pointing. These do not, however, contain any features which would necessitate changes in the classification presented here. Many of them contain only a few vowel signs, and even those with more pointing fit the classification already established and present few features not found in the texts already treated. The incorporation of these new texts in the book would have required many changes in almost every page, but would have added only minor details to the information contained in it. Much material still remains to be searched for texts of this sort, so that even with the inclusion of the new texts the list in chapter VI could not claim to be complete. Consequently, I have included, from the new texts, only fragments of mss already mentioned in the book, with a few references to significant features in other texts.

ultimately of the spoken, forms of words, both within Palestinian Hebrew and outside it. This, in turn, will permit a proper appreciation of the place of the Palestinian pronunciation in the history of the Hebrew language.[3] An attempt to fulfil this purpose by suggesting a basis for phonological comparison, together with a discussion of the historical position of the Palestinian pronunciation, follows, and depends on, the classification of the texts. These two connected features form the first, and major, part of the book.

Because of the evident importance of the classification of Palestinian texts, the publication of new texts has been subordinated to it. One text has been chosen and published as an example of each type of vocalization, so that the details of each type of vocalization can be studied and compared. For the same reason, photographs of a portion of each published text have been included. Adoption of this plan has meant that some of Dr. Dietrich's texts, which we originally intended to publish together, are not printed here. It has also meant that all the texts published are non-biblical. However, this emphasis on the study of non-biblical texts is justified from the point of view of a grammarian, since biblical texts exhibit certain characteristic differences from non-biblical mss.

The texts chosen for publication are, of course, selected primarily on the basis of their pointing. However, in cases where a choice was possible, texts were also chosen on the basis of their content. The poems printed here include some of considerable literary and liturgical interest. One extra text, 4a, containing *qerobot* by Yannai, was included for this reason. Dr. Dietrich and I had intended, in our joint work, to give translations of all the texts we published if they were not too fragmentary. This plan was abandoned, since, as is explained in the introduction to chapter VII, the value of the translations did not seem commensurate with the space required.

In many parts of this work – the classification and its interpretation, the texts and their translation – I have received help from other scholars, to whom I offer my thanks. I think first, in this connection, of the late Professor Paul Kahle, who gained my interest in this subject with his books, and fed it, when I later met him in Oxford, with lengthy discussions and with books which, with his accustomed generosity, he lent me from his library. Most help has come, of course,

[3] It is with this grammatical aim in mind that I have ignored the Aramaic texts vocalized with Palestinian signs.

from Dr. Dietrich, to whom, as I have explained, this work owes its inception and a great deal more. Dr. Meir Wallenstein of Manchester gave generously of his time at a busy period to a discussion of my translations, and to him I owe many ideas and insights in them. Professor N. Allony and Professor A. Díez-Macho were kind enough to tell me of texts unknown to me which they had found, and so allowed me to make my list of texts as complete, and my classification as comprehensive, as possible. Dr. S. A. Birnbaum very kindly commented on my interpretation of the palaeography of some of the texts. To these, and to others of my colleagues with whom I discussed my problems, I wish hereby to express my gratitude.

I would also like to express my gratitude to the librarians in charge of the various collections in which the texts here studied are kept. I owe them deep thanks, since they have provided me with photographs of all the mss used. In several cases they went to considerable trouble to trace for me texts which had been published or described under the wrong accession number, or under no number at all. I owe particular thanks to the Library Syndicate of the Cambridge University Library, who very kindly gave me permission to publish twelve of the thirteen texts published here, and to the Manuscript Committee of the Jewish Theological Seminary of America in New York, which gave me permission to publish text no. 5. The acquisition of photographs of all these texts was made possible by a grant from the University of Toronto 'President's Fund for Research in the Humanities and Social Sciences,' which also supplied me with funds for my trip to Cambridge in 1964. Earlier grants for travel in connection with this work, and a fellowship in 1967–68, came from the Canada Council. I am very grateful to these organizations, without whose help the study could not have been carried out.

This book has been published with the help of grants from the Humanities Research Council of Canada, using funds provided by the Canada Council, and from the Publications Fund of the University of Toronto Press.

Toronto, 1968 E.J.R.

Contents

List of Plates

HEBREW TEXTS WITH PALESTINIAN VOCALIZATION

I

Introduction

The first part of this work is concerned with the classification of Hebrew texts with Palestinian vocalization on the basis of the number of vowel signs used, and the manner of their use. Chapter II contains a detailed description of the vocalization of some dozen non-biblical texts. Chapter III shows that these texts use eleven different types of vocalization, and that every other non-biblical text known uses the vocalization signs in one of these eleven ways. Chapter IV classifies the biblical texts in the same way. Chapter V attempts to explain the eleven classes of vocalization as recording the existence of two major divisions or 'dialect groups' of Palestinian Hebrew, each of which was written and pronounced in a number of different ways. The present chapter deals with the assumptions basic to this study, and the principles according to which it is carried out.

Previous studies of the Palestinian pointing system have suffered, in my opinion, from two major defects: the use of the vowel signs was never studied in sufficient detail, and the texts were normally studied individually, with no real attempt at comparison or classification. These faults are interconnected, arising from the scarcity of Palestinian texts and from the prevailing assumptions about those texts. The only basis of classification used has been similarity to the standard 'ben Asher type' (bA, see 3 below) pointing of Hebrew. The traditional view that forms deviant from this standard are due to error or ignorance was rightly rejected, but the reaction against this view led to the idea that the forms most deviant from the standard represented 'true Palestinian' Hebrew, while those similar to the standard forms resulted from a process of 'Tiberianization.' Forms whose vocalization placed them between these two poles were considered as accidents of the artificial process of assimilation to the standard, and therefore not worth cataloguing. As a result no attempt was made to discover whether the deviant forms might follow a pattern, or to seek a grammatical reason for the various spellings of the same form possible in the Palestinian texts, or to ascertain whether the Palestinian *naqdanim* might not have used the vowel signs at their disposal according to a pattern totally unrelated to that in which the signs were used in the standard pointing of Hebrew. All was seen as 'true Palestinian' or 'Tiberianized.'[1]

The present study is concerned with the language of the texts, not with any hypothetical spoken form of Hebrew which may have been contemporary with them. It should not be necessary to justify the treatment of any text as a record of language in its own right. The fact that the language of the text may contain elements originating in different periods and in different localities does not mean that it is degenerate and perverted. No literary language with any history behind it can be expected to display the homogeneity of a spoken idiolect. The fact that a language is recorded in written form shows that it was in use among a number of people. It is therefore a fitting subject for linguistic research *in the form in which it was recorded.*[2] Few of the authors of previous studies of Palestinian vocalization have viewed their texts in this light. Similarly, the present study is based on assumptions about the history of the Hebrew language somewhat different from those which lie behind earlier studies. These historical assumptions do not affect the classification, which is based on linguistic facts. They do, however, affect the interpretation of this classification, and they have also affected the choice of methods used in the analysis of the texts. Consequently it seems advisable to state these assumptions, and the principles according to which the texts have been studied.

1 *Hebrew never fell out of use for literary composition.* The common assumption that Hebrew went out of use for literary purposes (being already dead in spoken usage) after the close of the Mishna has always seemed to me rather difficult to defend. Various arguments can be

[1] This is not true of some recent studies, particularly those by Israeli scholars, but these do not normally attempt any comparative evaluation of the forms at all.

[2] Judaeo-Arabic is an excellent example of a literary language heavily influenced by the language of other periods and localities; yet its study is not only of great interest linguistically, but is also of great importance for the historical study of Arabic. See Blau, 1965, chapter 9.

raised against it. None is absolutely conclusive, but, in my opinion, those based on the *piyyuṭim* are virtually so. These compositions were written for the enjoyment and edification of congregations. The difficult language of these poems could not have been understood by the members of a congregation unless they had a real grasp, not only of the traditional literature to which they constantly allude, but also of the use of Hebrew as a living medium of literary composition. These poems are definitely not stereotyped copies of traditional cultic forms, but employ innovations in morphology, syntax, and figures of speech which would have been impossible if they were not part of a living literary language. After the Arab conquest, when literary history can be traced with reasonable continuity, Hebrew never went out of use for this purpose, although Arabic was used in all other areas of literary composition.[3] The use of Hebrew in this situation cannot have been an innovation of the end of the Byzantine period.[4] Continuity in morphological change can be traced from biblical Hebrew to that of the *piyyuṭim*.[5] There is every reason to suppose that Hebrew was always in use as a medium of literary composition. For my part, it does not seem at all unlikely that it should have continued in use in common speech among Jews in many localities.

2 *Palestinian Hebrew texts represent a traditional pronunciation of the literary language.* This statement alone would probably be accepted by all scholars. When it is taken with the assumption that Hebrew was still in living literary usage when the Palestinian pointing was produced, however, it has connotations which may not be so readily accepted. It is assumed that Palestinian vocalized texts are records, as accurate as the system of pointing permitted, of the pronunciation of literary texts traditional among certain communities. This pronunciation is assumed to have changed over the years during which it was used, but to have developed naturally, and to be a direct descendant of the pronunciation used in mishnaic times and earlier. In some cases allowance must be made for the influence of other

[3] I have no doubt that, besides the reasons adduced in Blau, 1965, pp. 22f., a major reason for the retention of Hebrew in *piyyuṭ*, at least at first, was the fact that allusion to biblical or midrashic passages simply by the choice of significant words would have been impossible in Arabic. The fact that a large proportion of midrashic lore was recorded in Hebrew is an additional reason for seeing that language as a continuing medium of literary composition.

[4] See Schirmann, 1954.

[5] See Revell, 1970, I, no. 39, and note there. Also Spiegel, 1960, p. 874.

systems of pointing (see 4 below). There is no reason, however, to suppose that, on the whole, any particular method of using the available vowel signs was not determined by the pronunciation the *naqdan* wished to represent. To put the same assumption more cautiously: if any method of sign usage was a direct attempt to copy some other pointing system, no examples of that system of pointing are known.[6] The various methods of using the Palestinian vowel signs are, then, due to differences of locality or time, of the type of ms to be pointed, or of the use to which it was to be put. An attempt to explain these differences is made in chapter v. Here, however, it is important only to note that different vocalizations are considered to represent phonological differences due to normal processes of linguistic change, not to the attempt of a provincial to give his work a sophisticated polish.

3 *The 'ben Asher' system of pointing* (bA) *also represents a traditional pronunciation.* The term 'ben Asher system' (bA) was chosen to avoid the inexact use of the terms 'Tiberian' and 'masoretic.' In this context it includes not only the model codices produced by the members of the ben Asher family and their immediate disciples, but also the much less polished works of all *naqdanim* who used the Tiberian signs according to the ben Asher principle – even though they might point some forms differently from the Aleppo codex.[7] This system of pointing is also assumed to be the record of a pronunciation of the literary language used in some communities. Unlike the 'Palestinian' communities, however, where no standard form of pointing was ever produced, variations between individual speakers or recorders of the 'bA pronunciation' were by degrees harmonized, and the pointing system perfected, until it reached the stage with which we are familiar, and which we ascribe to the ben Asher family.[8] This harmonization was not carried out by arbitrary rules, as witness the numerous

[6] Even those Palestinian texts with pointing most similar to that of ben Asher are obviously not copies of his system (see III.1 and IV.1). On the arguments of bA influence on other features, see Revell, 1970, I, no. 4.

[7] It thus includes the ben Naftali of the '*ḥillufim*' lists, but not the 'so-called ben Naftali' texts described in Díez-Macho, 1963b, which consistently confuse *qameṣ* with *pataḥ* and *ṣere* with *segol*. Goshen-Gottstein's term 'receptus type' seems to me to include too many features besides phonology to be of use in this context. The term bA is certainly not ideal, but seems better than the other possibilities I have considered.

[8] This is certainly true for biblical pronunciation. It would be of great interest to know to what extent this pronunciation was used for non-biblical literature during the early period.

illogical exceptions in the masoretic lists. Divergent vocalizations were also retained, and accepted, according to the freedom of choice between respectable traditions always allowed, even in halakic matters. For a long time after the death of Aaron ben Asher, no necessity for absolute standardization was felt.[9] There is no reason to suppose that the bA pronunciation was the product of a conscious speech reform, or of any other artificial process.[10] It is to be taken, as is the Palestinian, as the result of normal processes of linguistic development.

4 *The Palestinian and bA pronunciations are different dialects of the same language.* Following the assumptions made in 2 and 3 above, we are forced to assume that these two pronunciations of Hebrew are simply different dialects of the same language. As far as we can tell, they were in use in the same general area at the same time.[11] Neither is 'better' or 'truer' Hebrew, except in so far as it was so regarded by its speakers and the fashion of their times. Ultimately, as we know, the bA pronunciation came to be regarded as best. We may therefore expect to find that it had some influence on other dialects with less prestige. It is well known that some users of the Palestinian dialect began to write it with Tiberian signs. The pronunciation which these signs represent is, however, still recognizably Palestinian, and only becomes harmonized with the bA pronunciation after a considerable development.[12] It is in this stage of the Palestinian dialect, when Tiberian signs were used to write it, that the real influence of the bA system is shown. Texts with Palestinian signs show little evidence of bA influence (see III.1, IV.1). Consequently, the Palestinian and bA pointing systems can be regarded as representing independent dialects of Hebrew.

5 *Study of the Palestinian vocalization can only be carried out by comparison against a single standard.* The individual Palestinian mss differ considerably from each other in their use of the signs. For example, some use two 'a' signs, some only one. Obviously the value of the signs will differ in the various mss depending on the number used and the manner of their use. The purpose of the present study

[9] Orlinsky, 1966, pp. xxxiii f.
[10] See Goshen-Gottstein, 1963, pp. 89f., 94.
[11] For an attempt to define their relationship, see Revell, 1970, I, nos. 31f.
[12] See Díez-Macho, 1963b, p. 18.

is to gain an over-all view of the Palestinian vocalization system. This is impossible unless a single standard is used against which all the different mss can be compared.

6 *The best available standard is the bA pointing system.* The ideal standard against which to compare the mss would, of course, be a complete description of the Palestinian dialect, but that is, in fact, what we are working towards. Failing this, a single ms could be selected as a standard on some arbitrary basis.[13] However, no ms is large enough for this use. Other texts would certainly contain forms not found in the standard, and these could not be evaluated. A further possibility would be the evaluation of Palestinian forms on the basis of some 'proto-Semitic' or 'proto-Hebraic' morphology. However, in my opinion, the study of comparative Semitic grammar is not sufficiently advanced to make any such reconstructed morphology of value to a study of this sort. Consequently some related dialect of Hebrew must be used as a standard against which the texts are compared. The ben Asher system early became the accepted standard of literary Hebrew, and is familiar to all students, and so is the obvious choice. It is regarded here, as stated in 3 above, as a natural product of linguistic development in no way resulting from artificial reconstruction. Since it is assumed to have developed in the same area, and been in use at the same time, as Palestinian Hebrew, it is to be expected that considerable similarities between the two dialects will appear. While this expectation rests only on assumptions which cannot be fully proved,[14] it is specifically stated here to show that, where Palestinian forms are interpreted as similar to or identical with those of bA, this is not because I cannot free my mind from the influence of my early training.[15] Since the two dialects must have the same system of morphemes (see 8 below), it would be astonishing if many phonological similarities did not appear.

7 *The categories in which the vocalization is analysed must be derived from the Palestinian texts.* The categories into which the elements of a dialect are classified must be those imposed by that dialect and not by the features of any other dialect, however similar. This prin-

[13] As in Murtonen, 1958.

[14] Unless my argument in Revell, 1970, part I, can be taken as proof.

[15] See the charges against ben David in Murtonen, 1964, p. 14, and cf. Revell, 1970, part II.

ciple, which should be basic to all descriptions of language, should guarantee freedom from undue influence from the bA system on this analysis. It cannot be assumed, simply because a Palestinian text uses two 'a' signs, that these correspond to the *qameṣ* and *pataḥ* of bA, and that differences of use are due to error or ignorance. Similarly, it cannot be assumed, if the Palestinian text uses either of these signs indiscriminately in a position where bA uses only *qameṣ*, that the Palestinian signs are allographs of the same grapheme, and that that text "has only one 'a' vowel." This can only be stated if it can be definitely shown that the two Palestinian 'a' signs are never used distinctly in any way.

8 *The morphemes of the Palestinian dialect are the same as those of the bA dialect.* This assumption has been made by all students of the Palestinian texts, and so scarcely needs to be stated. However, its implications are of importance. Where the consonants of a particular grammatical form are vocalized with Palestinian signs, the same morphemes are represented as where they are vocalized with Tiberian signs according to the bA system. The morphemes are represented by different graphemes. These may represent different phonemes, but the morphemes represented are the same. The justification for this is that the same text can be pointed with Palestinian signs, or with Tiberian signs in the bA (or other) system. The meaning of the text is not affected. Therefore, if the Palestinian and bA vocalizations represent two dialects of the same language, it can be stated that there is some relationship between the sounds represented by the Palestinian and bA signs used to vocalize a particular morph. The nature of this relationship can only be suggested after a considerable process of interpretation (see 9 below). However, the existence of the relationship permits the use of the morphological categories standard in Hebrew grammar as a means of classifying the positions in which Palestinian signs are used.

9 *A language must be studied in the medium in which it is recorded.* In the case of spoken languages, this medium is, of course, sound. However, written texts must be studied in terms of graphemes. When the graphemic system of a language is thoroughly understood, an attempt can be made to interpret the graphemic phenomena in terms of the sounds represented. At this point only can the techniques and information gained from the phonological analysis of spoken language

be of use. Consequently, comparison between Palestinian and bA forms is made in terms of graphemes. The Palestinian vowel signs are given in graphemic transcription as follows: ‗̈ (in one ms ‗̤̇) ⟨u⟩, ∴̲ ⟨o⟩, ˌ̲ ⟨a⟩, ‗̄ ⟨a′⟩, ⋰̲ ⟨e⟩, ⋱̲ ⟨e′⟩, ∶̲ ⟨i⟩.[16] The typical comparative statement ⟨o⟩ ≑ *ḥolem* is to be read "where bA has *ḥolem*, the Palestinian pointing has ⟨o⟩." In this way the positions in which the signs are used are compared. The sounds represented by the Palestinian signs can only be guessed at on the basis of comparison with the phonology of better-known dialects. There is admittedly danger here that familiarity with the bA system will influence the interpretation. There is equal danger that the desire to avoid bA influence will lead to the opposite extreme (see 11 below and note 17). However, such comparison is the only available method of determining the sounds represented by the signs. Arguments based on the number of signs, such as "each grapheme must represent a phoneme," or "each phoneme must have been represented by a single grapheme," are absurd, as comparison with other written languages will show. The *naqdanim* doubtless could have produced a phonemic transcription, but the purposes for which the texts were vocalized did not require it.

10 *Non-linguistic features of the texts are also of use in the analysis.* A few non-linguistic features, such as the shape of the ⟨a′⟩ sign, and the shape and frequency of occurrence of the 'Palestinian *dagesh*' sign, are characteristic of certain types of pointing. They are, however, considered of secondary importance, and are only used to support classifications made on other grounds. Their use is justified on the assumption that the various forms of Palestinian pointing are due to differences in the locality, period, etc., in which the text was pointed. Such differences may be expected to be reflected in the form of signs, as well as in their use. In so far as I am able to interpret it, however, the palaeography of the texts does not indicate that all the texts using the same type of pointing were written at the same period. The general palaeographic features of texts are not, therefore, used in the initial classification. They are, however, discussed in connection with the historical significance of the various classes of pointing.

[16] Other vowel signs occasionally occur. These, and diacritical signs, are normally given in the form in which they occur in the text, not in transcription.

11 *Standard, not unique usage is important.* This is a commonplace observed by all who introduce students to a language. It should equally be observed by all who describe languages. The standard, or typical, usage gives the general character of a language or dialect. Unique forms may always be due to individual idiosyncrasy or scribal error. Unique forms can, of course, be of significance as indicators of the local or temporal relations of a dialect. However, their significance can only be appreciated in the context of normal usage, and can never be greater than that of the normal form.[17] Consequently unique forms found in the texts studied here are sometimes ignored. Such forms are not considered as errors, but are ignored because no connection has been noticed between their unique features and comparable phenomena within the texts studied. On the same principle, many of the statements on the use of vowel signs in the various classes of pointing are general, not absolute. Thus even if sporadic uses of ⟨a'⟩ are found where bA has *qameṣ*, a class will still be described as using only ⟨a⟩ in this position. The few cases in which ⟨a'⟩ is used are probably grammatically significant, and are therefore noted in the detailed descriptions of the mss, but for purposes of classification, the primary aim of this work, such minor deviations must be ignored.

[17] The assumption of overwhelming Tiberian influence on Palestinian texts was felt, by some, to create a special situation which justified the interpretation of anomalous forms as 'genuine Palestinian.' Admittedly it is necessary to take all forms at face value in the initial study of a ms, but if analysis shows them to be unique they must either be treated as without much significance for the grammar of the text or explained otherwise than as normally vocalized forms. It may not be out of place to recall the comments of scholars such as Goshen-Gottstein (1958, nos. 1–6) on the 'eclectic' study of the grammar of the Qumran Scrolls.

II

The Vocalization of Selected Palestinian Texts

This chapter contains descriptions of thirteen texts with Palestinian vocalization, which are intended to serve as typical examples of the classes of Palestinian pointing set up in chapter III. The number given to each text (1, 2, etc.) indicates the class of pointing which it exhibits. Two mss have been given for class 4 (4 and 4a), because they were both judged to have content of sufficient interest to justify their publication (see VII.4, 4a). Moreover, the detailed description and publication of two mss from one class is of value to this study also from the grammatical point of view, as it serves as an illustration of the variation in the minor details of pointing which is to be encountered within any class.

To facilitate comparison, the mss have all been described under the same headings: A, physical characteristics; B, palaeographical characteristics (excluding date; see introduction to chapter III); C, normal use of vowel signs; D, exceptional uses of vowel signs; E, diacritical signs; F, pointing other than Palestinian. The text of (or the vocalized words in) each ms is given in chapter VIII, and a photograph of a part of each ms in the plates at the end of the book. The content of each text is described in chapter VII.

1 TS NS 249:2

A Part of a single leaf of parchment. The outer part of the leaf, and much of the lower part, is broken away. The maximum height of the fragment is 10¼ inches and the breadth 6 inches. The recto contained 29 lines, traces of the 29th still being visible. Nearly half of the width of the text has been lost. The fragment has various holes and tears, but the text is generally well preserved.

B The script is a Syriac square hand of a rather formal type. Text and pointing are in a brown ink.

C The pointing is sparse. Seven vowel signs occur, used normally as follows: ⟨u⟩ ≑ *shureq*, ⟨o⟩ ≑ *ḥolem*, ⟨a⟩ ≑ *qameṣ*, ⟨a′⟩ ≑ *pataḥ* and *ḥaṭef pataḥ*, ⟨e⟩ ≑ *segol* and *shewa*, ⟨e′⟩ ≑ *ṣere*, ⟨i⟩ ≑ *ḥireq*.

D The following exceptional uses of vowel signs should be noted:

⟨a⟩ ≑ *qameṣ ḥaṭuf* פֹּעלך r12.
≑ *pataḥ* בֹּזה r24, שֹׁחת v6 (אֹני, r17, is presumably a 'pausal' form).

⟨a′⟩ ≑ *shewa* כ̄איין v11. This usage is probably determined by the following sounds (cf. Revell, 1970, II, nos. 11, 12).

⟨e⟩ ≑ *shewa* r5, 5, 11, 17, 22, v4, 14, 16.

⟨i⟩ ≑ *shewa* before *yod* v22.

E The following diacritical signs are used in this ms:

_<_ ≑ *dagesh forte* r20.

_∩_ ≑ *rafe* r17.

שׂ marks ⟨ś⟩.

F A Tiberian *shewa* appears to be used in v13.

2 TS NS 118:38

A Part of a leaf of parchment; probably the upper outside corner. Maximum height 5 inches, breadth $5\frac{3}{4}$ inches. Parts of 19 lines are visible. The fragment contains several holes, but the text is generally well preserved.

B The script is a Syrian square of formal type. Fragmentary notes, in different hands, appear in the left-hand margin of the recto, and in the upper and right-hand margins of the verso. The ink of the text is brown, that of the pointing black.

C It is presumed that the pointing was normally used as follows: ⟨u⟩ ≑ *shureq*, ⟨o⟩ ≑ *ḥolem*, ⟨a⟩ ≑ *qameṣ*, ⟨a′⟩ ≑ *pataḥ*, ⟨e/e′⟩ ≑ *ṣere/segol*, ⟨i⟩ ≑ *ḥireq*. However, owing to the small size of the fragment, and the fact that the pointing is sparse, this pattern cannot be fully demonstrated.

D The vowel signs actually found in the fragment are used as follows:

⟨u⟩ ≑ *shureq.*

⟨o⟩ does not appear in the fragment.

⟨a⟩ ≑ *qameṣ* 8 times, including שתוליך v9.

⟨a′⟩ ≑ *pataḥ* twice.

≑ *shewa* in כנם] r16.

⟨e⟩ ≑ *ṣere* 3 times.

⟨e′⟩ ≑ *segol* in עיתר v2. Since in the Palestinian pointing ⟨e′⟩ normally ≑ *ṣere* and ⟨e⟩ ≑ *segol*, the use of the 'e' signs in this ms is taken as indicating that they were used indiscriminately.

⟨i⟩ ≑ *ḥireq.*

E No diacritical signs are used in this text.

F Tiberian *shewa* appears to be used in v5.

3 TS NS 119:42 + TS NS 301:66

A Part of a scroll, now consisting of two fragments of a strip of parchment to the lower of which the corner of a second strip is sewn. Maximum height 13¼ inches, breadth 5½ inches. The text is written in a single column down the length of the scroll. Parts of 30 lines are visible. The fragment contains a number of holes. Much of the writing is poorly preserved, particularly on the verso.

B The script is a Syriac square of a formal type. The text and the pointing are in a brown ink.

C The pointing is sparse. Seven vowel signs occur, used normally as follows: ⟨u⟩ ≑ *shureq*, ⟨a/a′⟩ ≑ *qameṣ/pataḥ*, ⟨e/e′⟩ ≑ *ṣere/segol*, ⟨i⟩ ≑ *ḥireq.*

D The following exceptional uses of vowel signs should be noted:

⟨o⟩ does not occur in this fragment.

⟨a⟩ ≑ *qameṣ* v3, 5, 20.

≑ *pataḥ* v23, 34.

⟨a′⟩ ≑ *pataḥ* r4, 7, v6, 7.
⟨e⟩ ≑ *segol* 6 times.
≑ *ṣere* 11 times, of which 3 are questionable.
⟨e′⟩ ≑ *ṣere* r9, 20.
≑ *segol* r8 (?), 10, v42.

E ‹ v19 and ∩ v23 are presumably equivalent to Tiberian *dagesh* and *rafe*, but they are not used according to bA rules.
⟨ś⟩ is marked in the Tiberian manner throughout the text.

4 TS NS 249:7 + TS NS 301:28

A (i) A sheet of parchment folded to form two leaves, each of which is *ca.* 10 inches high and 8½ inches broad, and contains 29 lines. A piece was torn from the bottom of the sheet. Part of this is preserved as TS NS 301:28, but the lower outside corner of fol. 1 and some text adjacent to the inner margins of both leaves are still missing. There are other holes and tears in the leaves, but the text is generally well preserved.

(ii) This sheet formed the inner two leaves of the fascicle of which Hebrew Union College MS 1001[1] formed the outer. The 'Levias' ms[2] formed the outer leaf of the adjoining fascicle. The description of the pointing in C, D, and E below covers all three fragments, save that TS NS 249:7 contains two poems in Aramaic, the pointing of which is not taken into consideration, since this is a study of Hebrew grammar.[3] The pointing of the 'Levias' fragment given in the original publication (Levias, 1899) appears to be typical of the ms save in minor points, and so has been treated as an exact record. Sonne's transcription of the pointing of H.U.C. MS 1001 (Sonne, 1944) is quite inadequate. The reading of the pointing on which these notes are based is therefore taken from a photograph. There are so many differences between Sonne's reading and that used

[1] Partly published in Sonne, 1944, pp. 205–20, with a photograph.
[2] Published in Levias, 1899, pp. 161–4. The ms itself was subsequently lost. The text was republished in Kahle, 1927 (Hebrew), pp. 24–27 (with one or two printer's errors).
[3] ⟨e′⟩ ≑ *shewa* is much more common in the Aramaic poems than in the Hebrew, but this appears to be the only real difference.

here that I have thought it best not to take the space to discuss them.[4]

B The script of the ms is a Syriac hand of a free type. The ink of the script is a dark brown; that of the pointing is a somewhat lighter colour.

C The pointing is consistent and thoroughgoing, but does not mark the vowel of every syllable. The normal use of the signs is as follows: ⟨u⟩ ≑ *shureq*, ⟨o⟩ ≑ *ḥolem*, ⟨a⟩ ≑ *qameṣ*, ⟨a′⟩ ≑ *pataḥ*, ⟨e⟩ ≑ *segol*, *ḥaṭef segol*, and *ṣere*, ⟨e′⟩ ≑ *shewa*, ⟨i⟩ ≑ *ḥireq*.

D The following exceptional uses of vowel signs should be noted:

⟨u⟩ Conjunctive *waw* is pointed with ⟨u⟩ where bA would use *shureq*. No other sign is used in this position. (⟨u⟩ may be used in a number of cases where bA has *ḥolem* but all are doubtful.)

⟨o⟩ ≑ *qameṣ ḥaṭuf* e.g. TS NS 249:7 1r7, 19, 27; 19 cases in all.

≑ *shureq* המרוחק H.U.C. MS 1001, 1r21; also probably יונשב Levias, 1899, p. 164, l. 6.

⟨a⟩ ≑ *qameṣ* in the ך-form of the 2ms pronoun. This form either follows a (bA) 'full vowel' or occurs in a biblical quotation (e.g. TS NS 249:7 1r4).

≑ *pataḥ* 29 times in the following types of syllables: Stressed, closed final, 17.[5] Unstressed, open, 8, all before a laryngeal; closed, 4, two before a laryngeal, one before a doubled letter.

≑ *shewa* H.U.C. MS 1001 נשכחה 1r18, כאיש 1v9, כבבת 2r16, גלותו 2r24, בדבריו 2r27, ומגינך 2v29; TS NS 249:7 שולחו 1v15, זומנו 2v12, ישולמו 2v24, שבועו Levias, 1899, p. 162, l. 17.

≑ *ḥaṭef qameṣ* H.U.C. MS 1001 פעלו 1v9, אוהלי 2r25; TS NS 249:7 אוהלי 1r8.

[4] The reading of H.U.C. MS 1001 used here was prepared jointly by myself and Dr. Dietrich as was that of TS NS 249:7 (see introduction to chapter VIII). We had originally planned to publish this text in full for the sake of the pointing, but when I expanded our joint work, I decided that the space required did not warrant republication.

[5] Other forms which occur at the end of a stich may be 'pausal,' and so are not included. Note that syllables are classified according to bA stress patterns. The Palestinian were not necessarily the same.

⟨a⟩ ÷ *ṣere* e.g. ניתחכם TS NS 249:7 2r5, and similar forms, H.U.C. MS 1001, 1r12, 13, Levias, 1899, p. 162, l. 6, p. 163, l. 5 (all but the first possibly pausal), also לעניו H.U.C. MS 1001 2r3(?).

÷ *ḥaṭef pataḥ* 2 cases.

⟨a′⟩ ÷ *qameṣ* 15 cases in the following types of syllables: Stressed, open final, 1; closed final, 13, three of which are closed by laryngeals. Unstressed, open, 1, before a laryngeal.

÷ *shewa* 15 cases, e.g. מכפרים TS NS 249:7, 1r14.

÷ *ḥaṭef pataḥ* 3 cases.

÷ *ṣere* H.U.C. MS 1001 בירך 2v23; Levias, 1899, ניתמלל p. 163, l. 5.

⟨e⟩ ÷ *ḥireq* 11 cases in the following types of syllables: Stressed, open, possibly טעינו TS NS 249:7 1r14. Unstressed, open, 7 cases, before a laryngeal, ייחוד H.U.C. MS 1001 1r3, 2v2, and nouns of the same form, *ibid.* 1r5, 29, 1v10, Levias, 1899, p. 162, l. 9, elsewhere מיתת Levias, 1899, p. 162, l. 12. Unstressed, closed, 3 cases, two before doubled letters.

⟨e′⟩ ÷ *shewa* 40 cases, e.g. להרפותו TS NS 249:7 1v29.

÷ *ḥaṭef pataḥ* H.U.C. MS 1001 2r18; Levias, 1899, p. 161, l. 4, p. 162, l. 24. Cf. such forms as הֶעֱבַרְתָּ (Josh. 7:7) and הֶעֱלָה (Hab. 1:15) with the normal bA pointing. But ⟨e′⟩ here probably only indicates a 'simple *shewa*' sound. See Revell, 1970, 1, no. 36. Also in הנחה H.U.C. MS 1001 2r5, where the double pointing presumably indicates variant readings ÷ הַנּחה and הֶנחה.

÷ *qameṣ* לכן Levias, 1899, p. 162, l. 21.

÷ *segol* נענשה Levias, 1899, p. 162, l. 22. The value of ⟨e′⟩ is here uncertain (see III.4.1).

⟨i⟩ ÷ *shewa* before *yod* 8 cases; elsewhere Levias, 1899, p. 161, l. 1, p. 162, l. 20. (These last two cases may well be misreadings of ⟨e′⟩ by Levias, although ⟨i⟩ is occasionally used in this position in other mss.)

÷ *ṣere* עירבנו H.U.C. MS 1001 1v17.

E The following diacritical signs are used in the ms:

_<_ 1 ÷ *dagesh forte* 87 cases in all.

2 ÷ *dagesh lene* perhaps בדמדום H.U.C. MS 1001 2r3, and נעתקה Levias, 1899, p. 162, l. 11, but these instances may better be taken with the following group.

3 Marks the beginning of a syllable following a medial laryngeal, e.g. רחמה, לחשה, H.U.C. MS 1001 1r7, similarly Levias, 1899, p. 162, l. 16, also p. 162, l. 11 (see above, no. 2), probably also after *nun* תונקב Levias, 1899, p. 162, l. 15, תונשב Levias, 1899, p. 164, l. 6, and possibly after *mem* (see above, no. 2). In these cases the sign may also be said to indicate that the consonant above which it is placed is not preceded by a vowel.[6]

4 Marks *'alef* as consonantal. E.g. אאשימך TS NS 249:7 1r10, also *ibid.* 1v16, Levias, 1899, p. 163, l. 12. Cf. the sporadic use of *dagesh/mappiq* to mark consonantal *'alef* in Tiberian mss.

5 Marks *waw* as consonantal. בגויו H.U.C. MS 1001 2r26, also ולא 2v23 (?).

6 Corresponds to *dagesh forte* 'conjunctive,' ניכפלה לו ניכללה לו Levias, 1899, p. 162, l. 25, probably[7] חנה בה *ibid.* p. 163, l. 19, and טובו TS NS 249:7, 1r8.

7 ÷ *mappiq*, marking final *he* as consonantal. (See examples in no. 3 above.) 26 cases in all. צירירה H.U.C. MS 1001, 1r6, which appears to mark medial *he* as consonantal, is probably an error induced by the surrounding '*mappiqs*.'

ˆ ÷ *rafe* e.g. TS NS 249:7 1r9, 13. 11 cases in all.
Marks a consonant as preceded by a vowel (cf. *dagesh* no. 3) האזין H.U.C. MS 1001, 1r2.

שׂ marks ⟨ś⟩ e.g. TS NS 249:7, 1r13, 13, 27. The position of the dot varies somewhat. This sign does not occur in the Levias fragment. This may be due to an oversight of Levias, as the dot, being sublinear and small, is easy to pass over as insignificant.

[6] It would then be used as is the '*dagesh* = *shewa*' of the Masoretes, as described by Ginsburg, 1897, pp. 123f.; i.e. really marking that the laryngeal closes the syllable.

[7] In these two cases the placing of the sign is unusual. In Levias, 1899, p. 163, l. 19, it could have been written in error owing to the other *mappiqs* in the context (as suggested for another case in no. 7 below, but cf. 6.E below). In 249:7 1r8 the position of the sign (clearly over the *bet*) has no Palestinian parallel in this usage, but the sign seems difficult to explain other than as 'conjunctive.'

ש̊ marks ⟨ś⟩ Levias, 1899, p. 162, ll. 16, 16.

ש (with ש above) marks ⟨š⟩ Levias, 1899, p. 162, ll. 21, 22.

The last two signs both appear only on the recto of the Levias fragment.

F Tiberian *qibbuṣ*, appears in H.U.C. MS 1001, 1r28.

4a TS NS 117:6 + TS NS 123:2

A Five small fragments forming parts of two leaves of text. Two fragments of TS NS 117:6 belong to each leaf, on which parts of the inner and lower margins are preserved. TS NS 123:2 forms the outer bottom corner of fol. 2. The maximum height of the largest fragment is 6 inches, probably between one-half and two-thirds of the original height of the leaf. Parts of 19 lines are preserved on this fragment. The original length of each line can be estimated at *ca.* 6¾ inches. The fragments are much damaged, and the writing is often obscure, particularly at the edges of the fragments.

B The script is a neat, fairly formal, Syriac square hand. Both text and pointing are in a brown ink.

C Vocalization is fairly thorough, although many syllables have no vowel sign. The normal use of the vowel signs is as follows: ⟨u⟩ ≑ *shureq*, ⟨o⟩ ≑ *ḥolem*, ⟨a⟩ ≑ *qameṣ*, ⟨a′⟩ ≑ *pataḥ*, ⟨e⟩ ≑ *segol*, *ḥaṭef segol*, and *ṣere*, ⟨e′⟩ ≑ *shewa*, ⟨i⟩ ≑ *ḥireq*.

D The following exceptional uses of vowel signs should be noted:

⟨u⟩ ≑ *qameṣ ḥaṭuf* קודשך 1v10. This is perfectly clear in the ms, but is unique in Palestinian Hebrew. It may, therefore, be an error for ⟨o⟩.

⟨o⟩ ≑ *shureq* זועמו 1r18, רועגן 2r3 (?) presumably a verbal form.

⟨a⟩ ≑ *qameṣ* in אליך 2r14.

≑ *pataḥ* in 6 cases in syllables of the following types: Stressed, closed final, 4 cases.[8] Unstressed, open, before a laryngeal, 2r16, also 2r6 (?).

≑ *ḥaṭef pataḥ* 2r8.

≑ *shewa* ניפצם 1r7, נוסחו 1r13, and similar forms, 1r18, 18.

[8] Also in other forms which occur at the end of a stich, and so may be 'pausal.'

⟨a⟩ ≑ *ṣere* בוחן 1r15.

⟨e⟩ ≑ *shewa* 'silent' להזכיר 1v10. וימהרו 2r16 may be a 'pausal' form.

≑ *ḥaṭef pataḥ* הלל 2r8.

⟨e′⟩ ≑ *shewa* 1r16, 1v12, 14, 17, 2r5.

E The following diacritical signs are used in this ms:

_<_ ≑ *dagesh forte* 1r9, 2r9, 14 (?), 2v6, 11.

_ⁿ_ ≑ *rafe* 1r17.

שׂ marks ⟨ś⟩, e.g. 1r10.

5 J.T.S. MS E.N.A. 2020 f. 23

A This fragment was discovered by Dr. A. Díez-Macho, and has been described by him in *Supplements to 'Vetus Testamentum' IV* (1957), p. 30.[9] It is part of a leaf of parchment, badly preserved and difficult to read.

B The script is a Syriac square hand of a free type. The ink of the text is a dark brown, that of the pointing a lighter colour. The form of ⟨a′⟩ is remarkable in this ms, being a dot, only slightly elongated horizontally.

C The pointing is consistent and thoroughgoing, but many syllables have no vowel sign. The vowel signs are normally used as follows: ⟨u⟩ ≑ *shureq*, ⟨o⟩ ≑ *ḥolem*, ⟨a/a′⟩ ≑ *qameṣ/pataḥ*, ⟨e⟩ ≑ *segol*, *ḥaṭef segol*, and *ṣere*, ⟨e′⟩ ≑ *shewa*, ⟨i⟩ ≑ *ḥireq*.

D The following exceptional uses of vowel signs should be noted:

⟨o⟩ ≑ *qameṣ ḥaṭuf* קרבן v10.

'a' vowels: ⟨a⟩ ≑ *qameṣ* 65, *pataḥ* 32 times.
⟨a′⟩ ≑ *qameṣ* 24, *pataḥ* 25 times (see also in E below).

⟨a⟩ ≑ *ṣere* לבקש v14.

⟨a′⟩ ≑ *shewa* 10 times; e.g. דמות v13.

⟨e⟩ ≑ *shewa* ליישר r17.

≑ *ḥireq* אילים v10 (?).

⟨e′⟩ ≑ *shewa* יכבדנני v7, גדי v16.

[9] See also Díez-Macho, 1956, p. 7.

E The only diacritical sign used in this ms is ש, which marks ⟨ś⟩ in v7. The sign ש in ותלשתה (r12) could be a unique marker of ⟨š⟩ but is more probably a case of ⟨a⟩ corrected to ⟨a′⟩.

6 TS H2:30

A A sheet of paper folded to form two leaves, each *ca.* 6 inches high and 4¼ inches broad. The number of lines per page varies: 1r has 16; 1v, 17; 2r, 21; 2v, 22. The variation is largely due to the different styles of writing used on fol. 1 and fol. 2. The bottom outside corner of both leaves has been slightly damaged, but the preservation is good and the script clearly legible.

B The writing is in an Egyptian square hand, in three different styles ranging from formal towards cursive. The text and the pointing are both in a black ink.

C The pointing is almost completely confined to fol. 2. Both Palestinian and Tiberian signs are used, but the one system complements the other, so that no syllable has its vowel marked by both systems. The signs of both systems are used rather sparsely. Six Palestinian signs occur, used normally as follows: ⟨u⟩ ≑ *shureq*, ⟨o⟩ ≑ *ḥolem*, ⟨a⟩ ≑ *qameṣ*, ⟨a′⟩ ≑ *pataḥ*, ⟨e⟩ ≑ *segol* and *ṣere*, ⟨i⟩ ≑ *ḥireq*.

D The following exceptional uses of vowel signs should be noted:

⟨u⟩ is used where bA would point conjunctive *waw* as *shureq*, 2r18.

⟨o⟩ ≑ *qameṣ ḥaṭuf* בחשבו 2r1.

⟨a⟩ ≑ *pataḥ* גל 2r8.

⟨a′⟩ ≑ *ṣere* אפס 2v9.

⟨e⟩ ≑ *qameṣ* שיעורם 2v1.

≑ *ḥireq* ביעור 2r13, שיעורם 2v1.

E The following diacritical signs are used:

ᵕ ≑ *dagesh forte* and *lene*. The form of the sign varies considerably. Note the double use corresponding to 'conjunctive *dagesh*' in מה לי 2r13.

ᶺ ≑ *rafe*, e.g. 2r18.

F The Tiberian pointing uses the seven vowel signs and *shewa*. They are used, on the whole, according to the bA system, but the following uses are notable:

Qibbuṣ in הַמְרִירֻונוּ 2v16.

Ḥireq in חִילּוּיִ 2v1. Cf. both Palestinian usage (e.g. III.2.N, IV.3.N) and Tiberian (e.g. Ginsburg, 1897, pp. 558, 637).

Shewa in תְצוּד (2v15) replaces expected *qameṣ*, possibly a mark of 'Palestinian' usage (see Revell, 1970, I, no. 23).

Shin is marked in the Tiberian manner.

The Tiberian *rafe* sign is used in 1r3, 2v5.

The Babylonian sign ⸗ appears to be used in 2r5.

7 TS NS 249:1

A (i) A fragment of the upper part of a leaf of parchment. The maximum height is 3 inches, breadth 6½ inches. The fragment is very badly preserved, so that much of the text is almost illegible, particularly on the verso.

(ii) The lower part of this leaf is formed by TS H16:1, published by Edelmann in *Zur Frühgeschichte des Maḥzor* (Stuttgart, 1934) as MS F, and briefly described on p. 13. The number of lines on the verso of the completed leaf can be established as 32. The following description of the pointing covers both fragments.

B The script is a Syrian square hand of a free type. Both text and pointing are written in a brown ink. The form of ⟨a'⟩ is remarkable in that it is usually a dot only slightly elongated horizontally.

C Only six vowel signs are used in this text. ⟨e'⟩ may appear (see D below), but, if so, it is to be considered abnormal (see III.7.O). The normal use of the vowel signs is as follows: ⟨u⟩ ≑ *shureq*, ⟨o⟩ ≑ *ḥolem*, ⟨a/a'⟩ ≑ *qameṣ/pataḥ* and *ḥaṭef pataḥ*, ⟨e⟩ ≑ *segol*, *ḥaṭef segol*, and *ṣere*, ⟨i⟩ ≑ *ḥireq*.

D The following exceptional uses of vowel signs are to be noted (the figures in brackets after references to H16:1 refer to the (Hebrew) page and line of Edelmann's edition):

⟨o⟩ ≑ *qameṣ ḥaṭuf* NS 249:1 r3, v10, H16:1 v9, 18 (30:2, 10).
≑ *shureq* הוּא H16:1 r13 (29:8).

'a' vowels: ⟨a⟩ ÷ *qameṣ* 85, *pataḥ* 20 times.
⟨a′⟩ ÷ *qameṣ* 37, *pataḥ* 52 times.

⟨a⟩ ÷ *shewa* זווית H16:1 r22 (29:17).

⟨a′⟩ ÷ *qameṣ ḥaṭuf* אהליבה H16:1 r20 (29:15).
÷ *shewa* 7 cases; e.g. פאיר H16:1 r11 (29:6).
÷ *ṣere* לחיי H16:1 v5 (29:21).

⟨e⟩ ÷ *shewa* 6 cases; e.g. בחילו NS 249:1 v9.
÷ *ḥireq*. In an open syllable before a laryngeal or *resh* ייחוד H16:1 r8 (29:3), also r17 (29:12), NS 249:1 v7. Before a doubled letter פיצח H16:1 v12 (30:5).

⟨e′⟩ ÷ *ḥaṭef pataḥ*. So Edelmann in אקדש H16:1 v19 (30:11), but my photograph suggests that the reading אקדש is more probable (i.e. *nif'al* not *pi'el*?). The context is broken.

E The following diacritical signs are used in this ms:

ᴸ marks *ḥeth* as consonantal according to Edelmann's transcription of H16:1 r22 (29:17). In my opinion this sign is ⟨a′⟩.

שᴸ marks ⟨ś⟩ H16:1 r17 (29:12).

8 TS NS 249:14 + TS 12:210

A TS NS 249:14 is a single leaf of parchment *ca.* 11 inches high and 8½ inches broad. The original text contains 30 lines on the recto, 28 on the verso. A second text (TS NS 249:14[a]) was written in a different hand in the lower margin in two lines on the recto, five on the verso. There are many holes in the leaf, but the text is otherwise well preserved. TS 12:210 is the lower part of a leaf of the same ms. The full original width is preserved at the bottom (8½ inches), and the lower and outer margins are intact. Most of the inner margin and much of the adjacent text are, however, torn away. The maximum height is now *ca.* 5¼ inches. Parts of 19 lines are preserved on both sides. A second text (TS 12:210[a]) is written in the lower margin, as in TS NS 249:14, in two lines on the recto and one on the verso. There are no holes in this fragment, but the writing is not so well preserved as in the other, especially adjacent to the torn edges.

Both fragments are palimpsest, the lower writing being Syriac in a Western hand. It now appears to be almost completely illegible. The following information covers both fragments.

B The main text is written in a Syrian square hand of a formal type, in a brown ink. The pointing is in a darker brown ink. It is a peculiarity of this text that a sign indicating a vowel following *lamed* is often placed to the left, rather than to the right, of the upper stroke of that letter. Several layers of addition to this text can be discerned. A second hand wrote the word בססאה in the outer margin of the recto of NS 249:14 at line 20, and placed a circle above the final consonant of the word in the text to which it referred. This could have been the pointing hand. If it was not, it is possible that it was responsible also for some of the uses of vowel signs which are common in Palestinian pointing, but unusual in this text (e.g. ⟨a′⟩ ÷ *pataḥ*, ⟨e⟩ ÷ *shewa*).

A third hand wrote the second text (TS NS 249:14[a] + TS 12:210[a]) in a rather free square hand of Egyptian style in the wide lower margins left by the first hand. This was probably done not long after the writing of the main text. The ink used is darker than that of the main text. The pointing, which is in a similar ink, is quite different from that of the main text, and is described in 9 below.

A fourth hand wrote two annotations in the margin of the verso of NS 249:14, at lines 24 and 26. The annotations are in a dark brown, almost black ink. They are pointed with Tiberian signs in the same ink. The word in the text to which they refer is indicated by the sign < above its first consonant.

C The pointing of the main text is a consistent and thoroughgoing Palestinian type, which vocalizes most syllables, but leaves some unpointed. Only six vowel signs occur. Their normal use is as follows: ⟨u⟩ ÷ *shureq*, ⟨o⟩ ÷ *ḥolem*, ⟨a⟩ ÷ *qameṣ/pataḥ*, ⟨a′⟩ ÷ *shewa*, ⟨e⟩ ÷ *segol*, *ḥaṭef segol*, and *ṣere*, ⟨i⟩ ÷ *ḥireq*.

D The following exceptional uses of vowel signs are to be noted:

⟨u⟩ Conjunctive *waw* is pointed with ⟨u⟩ in most cases where bA would use *shureq* (but cf. ⟨a′⟩ ÷ *shewa*).

⟨o⟩ ÷ *qameṣ ḥaṭuf* e.g. גפרית, NS 249:14 r1, and 12 other cases.

⟨a⟩ ÷ *qameṣ ḥaṭuf* צהרים 12:210 v7.
÷ *ḥaṭef qameṣ* צהרים 12:210 v7.

⟨a⟩ ∸ *pataḥ* is repeated in the first person singular pronominal suffix on a plural noun ישישיי, ידועיי NS 249:14 v15.[10]

∸ *ḥatef pataḥ* 8 cases; e.g. וערפל NS 249:14 r9.

∸ *pataḥ furtive* דיע NS 249:14 v17 (cf. III.2.G).

∸ *shewa* in third person plural *pu'al* or *hof'al* verb forms; NS 249:14 r3, 4, 23, 23. Possibly silent *shewa* חצצתה *ibid.* r29.[11]

⟨a'⟩ ∸ *shewa* 56 cases in all. These include an apparent case of silent *shewa* (נ]שפטו NS 249:14 r3), and the pointing of conjunctive *waw* where bA would have *shureq* in NS 249:14 r25, and perhaps 12:210 v19 (cf. ⟨i⟩ ∸ *shewa*).

∸ *pataḥ* in a total of 14 possible cases, many in such words as עד (NS 249:14 v18, 25), טל *ibid.* v22, 12:210 r15, על *ibid.* r15, בל *ibid.* v7, where the first hand might be expected to have omitted the vowel sign. The two ⟨a'⟩ signs in אפתח (NS 249:14 v20) appear definitely to be the work of a secondary hand.

∸ *ḥatef pataḥ* 7 cases.

∸ *segol* בעשר NS 249:14 r13, also לגישת *ibid.* v6, where the sign might possibly have the value of a '*shewa* vowel.'

⟨e⟩ ∸ *pataḥ* possibly מעל NS 249:14 r27, but unlikely.[12]

∸ *ḥireq* גבריאל NS 249:14 r30.

∸ *shewa* possibly טללי 12:210 r6, טללם *ibid.* v4, but the position of the sign could be due to lack of space between the two *lameds*. Cf. לים ∸ לְיָם TS H16:6 2r19 (see Edelmann, 1934, [Hebrew] p. 4, note 1, and note 47 to chapter III, and note 114 to chapter VIII below).

∸ is used to denote the prefix vowel of a first person singular imperfect verb form in NS 249:14 v7 and v12 (∸ *segol*

[10] I have not noted a similar pointing in any Palestinian text; however, one does occur in a ms with Tiberian pointing in a Palestinian tradition, נוֹהֲרַיי (∸ נְהוֹרָאי) TS E1:95 1r22, 25.

[11] More likely the sign is misplaced, and הצצתה should be read. The form could be an example of the -V*t* ending of the 2ms. perfect verb form which occasionally occurs (see Revell, 1970, II, no. 17), but the rhyme is against this as well as the orthography.

[12] The modern texts which I have seen read מַעַל, but our pointing is perfectly intelligible. It was probably intended as a word-play, so that both מֵעַל as a preposition and מַעַל as a noun meaning 'heaven' (cf. Ps. 50:4) should be understood here.

and *ṣere*). It may possibly denote an 'e' vowel coloured by 'a.' However, the stroke is probably not due to the original pointing hand, and the sign cannot in any case be considered characteristic of this pointing.

⟨i⟩ ≑ *shewa* before *yod* 8 cases. After *yod* יְבַטֵּל NS 249:14 v10. Elsewhere perhaps וְלִתפארת 12:210 v19, but the pointing is probably misplaced.

E The following diacritical signs are used in this ms:

< ≑ *dagesh forte*. Note the exceptional use on *ṣade* NS 249:14 r19, 19.

ᐢ ≑ *rafe* NS 249:14 r14.

Consonantal pronunciation of *'alef* is indicated by a dot beneath the letter in NS 249:14 r27 (cf. III.1.N).

שׂ (with ° above) marks ⟨ś⟩.

שׁ (with ν above) marks ⟨š⟩.

The last two signs occur only on the verso of NS 249:14. E.g. ⟨ś⟩ l. 13, and six other times, ⟨š⟩ l. 16.

9 TS NS 249:14[a] + TS 12:210[a]

A, B This number refers to the pointing of the text written in the lower margins of TS NS 249:14 and TS 12:210. The description of these mss is given in 8 above.

C This pointing is of great interest as it employs a unique combination of Palestinian and Tiberian signs. All the signs appear to derive from the same hand. A vowel may be indicated by a supralinear sign, by a sublinear sign, or by both. The supralinear signs are all Palestinian. The sublinear signs are Tiberian in those cases in which Tiberian has a sublinear sign. Where Tiberian has no sublinear sign *(shureq, ḥolem, dagesh)*, the Palestinian sign is used below the line. The significance of this pointing is discussed in V.15. In terms of Palestinian vowel signs, the normal usage of this text can be said to be five signs used as follows: ⟨u⟩ ≑ *shureq*, ⟨o⟩ ≑ *ḥolem*, ⟨a⟩ ≑ *qameṣ/pataḥ*, ⟨e⟩ ≑ *segol/ṣere*, ⟨i⟩ ≑ *ḥireq*. The Tiberian *shewa* sign occurs with no Palestinian equivalent.

D The vowel signs are used as follows:

Corresponding to ⟨u⟩: [sign] or [sign]. The dots of the subscript form may be more or less slanted down to the left, but are indistinguishable from the subscript ⟨e⟩ sign (*ṣere*) save from the context. ≑ *shureq* e.g. לֵוד NS 249:14 v29, צרֵו *ibid.* v31, קוטלֵו *ibid.* v32, also *ibid.* v32, v33, 12:210 r20.

Corresponding to ⟨o⟩: [sign] or (inverted) [sign] or [sign].

≑ *ḥolem* e.g. ריעֹו NS 249:14 r31, חמֹורים *ibid.* v32, תֹוכו 12:210 r20, also *ibid.* r20, NS 249:14 r31, 32, v29, and presumably שֻׁולחֹון *ibid.* v33.

Corresponding to ⟨a⟩: [sign] or [sign] or [sign]. ≑ *qameṣ* e.g. כָשל NS 249:14 v29, פָרס *ibid.* v31, רמָסָם *ibid.* v32. Also *ibid.* v31, 31, 31, 32, 32, 32, 32, 33, 33, 12:210 r20, 20, 20, v20, 20, 20.

≑ *pataḥ* כהופָעָת NS 249:14 r31, רָוות *ibid.* v29. Also *ibid.* v29, 29, 31, 31, 31, 31, 32, 12:210 r20, v20. (The form [sign] is not used ≑ *pataḥ*.)

≑ *ḥaṭef pataḥ* עָרבות 12:210 r20.

≑ *shewa* קוטָלו NS 249:14 v32.

≑ *ṣere* רָד NS 249:14 v33.

Corresponding to ⟨e⟩: [sign] or [sign] or [sign]. The dots of the subscript sign may be slanted down to the left. ≑ *segol* e.g. בשֶׁילֶך NS 249:14 r32, לֶכם 12:210 r20. Also NS 249:14 v29, 29, 32, 32.

≑ *ṣere* e.g. רֶיעו NS 249:14 r31, חֶילך *ibid.* r31, קֶירה 12:210 r20. Also NS 249:14 v31, 33, 12:210 r19, 20, 20, v20. In חילֶך NS 249:14 r31 the final syllable is the 2ms. pronominal suffix. Normal Palestinian usage would require חילָך but the 'e' vowel here is presumably used to fit the rhyme, and is not, therefore, grammatically significant (but cf. לזרעֶך Bod. Heb. d55, f. 4r1; see III.5.D).

Corresponding to ⟨i⟩: [sign] or [sign] or [sign]. ≑ *ḥireq* e.g. שנִינת NS 249:14 v29, בִיכה *ibid.* v31, רִיהב 12:210 r20. Also NS 249:14 v30, 31, 32, 32, 12:210 r19, 20, 20.

The Tiberian *shewa* sign is used ≑ *shewa* in שְׁנינת NS 249:14 v29, also *ibid.* v31, 32, also marking the vowel of the first syllable of a word.

≑ *ḥaṭef pataḥ* עְזור NS 249:14 r32.

E The only diacritical grapheme used corresponds to *dagesh*. The forms used are _ᶜ_ or ÷ᶜ: e.g. רוּות NS 249:14 v29, כגּת *ibid.* v32. Also *ibid.* v31, and לדורות *ibid.* v32, where the '*dagesh*' sign probably indicates the presence of the definite article (see 11.E below) as its occurrence seems otherwise inexplicable.

10 TS NS 117:7 + TS H6:51

A Two fragments, originally adjacent parts of a strip of parchment forming a scroll *ca.* 7 inches wide. Together, the two fragments have a maximum length of 19 inches. The text is written in a single column down the length of the scroll. Of the text preserved, TS NS 117:7 carries parts of lines 1–20, TS H6:51 lines 18–66. Both fragments have a number of holes. The text on the hair side of the skin (verso) is well preserved; that on the flesh side is worn, and often difficult to read.

B The script is a square Syrian/Egyptian hand of a formal type written in red-brown ink. The ink of the pointing is black, faded in some places to brown.

C The vocalization is very sparse. Five vowel signs occur, used normally as follows: ⟨u⟩ ≑ *shureq*, ⟨o⟩ ≑ *ḥolem*, ⟨a⟩ ≑ *qameṣ/pataḥ*, ⟨e′⟩ ≑ *segol/ṣere*, also *shewa*, ⟨i⟩ ≑ *ḥireq*.

D The following exceptional uses of vowel signs should be noted:
⟨a⟩ ≑ *shewa* תמימים v64.
⟨e′⟩ ≑ *shewa* בקרן v57, also r7 (?) and v30 (?).
In להגיהם r40, the apparent ⟨i⟩ sign is presumably a broken ⟨a⟩ sign.

E The only diacritical sign used is a dot which marks ⟨ś⟩ in the Tiberian manner. This could be due to the Palestinian hand, or to the author of the few other Tiberian signs which occur (see F below). In r49 the scribe omitted from the poem a stich which he afterwards wrote in above the line. He placed a circle after the addition, and another below the line at the place at which it was to be inserted.

F A few Tiberian signs occur in the ms. E.g. *pataḥ* r62, 63, 64, *ṣere* r39, 41, 43, *ḥolem* v18 (?). They appear to be used according to the bA system.

11 TS H2:29

A A sheet of parchment folded to form two leaves, each *ca.* 10¼ inches high and 8¼ inches broad. The number of lines per leaf varies from 30 to 35. The upper margin of both leaves has been slightly damaged, and their outer margins are more seriously broken, so that some of the adjacent text is lost. Otherwise the text is generally in a good state of preservation.

B The script is a Syrian square hand of a free type, written in a red-brown ink. The ink of the pointing is of a rather lighter colour.

C The vocalization is sparse. Five vowel signs occur, used normally as follows: ⟨u⟩ ≑ *shureq*, ⟨o⟩ ≑ *ḥolem*, ⟨a′⟩ ≑ *qameṣ/pataḥ/ḥaṭef pataḥ*, also *shewa*, ⟨e⟩ ≑ *segol/ḥaṭef segol/ṣere*, ⟨i⟩ ≑ *ḥireq*.

D The following exceptional uses of vowel signs should be noted:

⟨u⟩ Conjunctive *waw* is pointed with ⟨u⟩ where bA would have have *shureq* 1r15.

⟨o⟩ ≑ *shureq* חמוס 2r18.

≑ *qameṣ ḥaṭuf* ויוזעם 2v21.

≑ *ḥaṭef qameṣ* עוני 2r6. (See III.4 and note 39 there.)

⟨a′⟩ ≑ *qameṣ* in the 2ms. bound pronoun form ־ך 1r8, 20, 2r18. This form is possibly also used in באפך 1v23, since the following *bet* is marked with _>_, but see E below.

≑ *shewa* 13 cases, e.g. פוררו 1r16, 2v26.

⟨e⟩ ≑ *ḥireq* וויעודיך 1r20, כנעימה 2r28, מיליל 2v1.

⟨i⟩ ≑ *shewa* before *yod*, 5 cases. Elsewhere לבניי 2r2.

E The following diacritical signs are used in this ms:

_<_ ≑ *dagesh forte* 30 cases.

≑ *dagesh lene* possibly כנהר 1v24, also 2r29, 2v18, but more likely the sign here indicates the presence of the definite article (see below). In לשקעו 1v11, and אגנ[ו]ן 1v24 the sign is presumably misplaced, and should stand over the *qof* or *nun*. If so, the latter was corrected.

_>_ ≑ *rafe* in a total of 18 cases. Among these its use on *qof* (2v24) and on initial *bet* (2r6, 32, 2v3, 6, 32, also possibly 1v23, see under ⟨a′⟩ ≑ *qameṣ* in D above) should be noted. The use on *bet* would contrast with the use of ‹ in 2r29, if that is taken as equivalent to '*dagesh lene*.' The sign › here, then, probably indicates the absence of the definite article. This use of the '*dagesh*' and '*rafe*' signs on prepositional *bet* and *kaf* corresponds to Tiberian masoretic terminology noted by Elias Levita, who states that the *shewa* with which prepositional *bet*, *kaf*, or *lamed* was pointed was called '*rafe*,' and that the same letters, when pointed with *patah* (the article), were called '*dagesh*ed.'[13] I know, however, of no ms in which the Tiberian signs *dagesh* and *rafe* are used according to this terminology, as the corresponding signs appear to be in this ms. Presumably the other exceptional uses of the signs ‹ and › in this ms are to be explained according to similar differences in their value from the value of bA *dagesh* and *rafe*, although the majority of their uses correspond to that of bA.

∩ appears to mark final consonantal *he* 1v24.[14]

שׂ° marks ⟨ś⟩ 1r17, 1v5, 32, 2v32.

12 TS H7:7

A, B This ms was described by Zulay in *Meḥqere Yannai* (Zulay, 1936), p. 323. The text was published by him in *Piyyuṭe Yannai* (Zulay, 1938) as text no. 3 (p. 342). The pointing, however, has not been published.

C The vocalization is thoroughgoing, although many syllables have no vowel marked. The form of ⟨a'⟩ is remarkable in that it is often a dot, only slightly elongated horizontally. Seven vowel signs occur, used normally as follows: ⟨u⟩ ÷ *shureq*, ⟨o⟩ ÷ *ḥolem*, ⟨a/a'⟩ ÷ *qameṣ/pataḥ*, ⟨e⟩ ÷ *segol/ṣere*, ⟨e'⟩ ÷ *shewa*, ⟨i⟩ ÷ *ḥireq*.

D The following exceptional uses of vowel signs are to be noted: ⟨u⟩ ÷ *ḥolem* בוֹ r7, v1.

[13] See Ginsburg, 1867, pp. 199f. Examples of this terminology are easily found in Tiberian masoretic lists. Other Palestinian examples of this usage are noted in 9.E above and IV.7.N.

[14] It is not certain that this mark is due to the pointing hand. If it is, it is to be compared to the use of the ∩ (÷ *rafe*) sign to indicate consonantal pronunciation of *waw*, *yod*, and laryngeals (see III.2 and IV.3).

⟨o⟩ ≑ *qameṣ ḥaṭuf* 5 cases, e.g. פעלם v4.

'a' vowels: ⟨a⟩ ≑ *qameṣ* 77, *pataḥ* 39 cases.

⟨a′⟩ ≑ *qameṣ* 49, *pataḥ* 53 cases.

⟨a⟩ ≑ *qameṣ*. Note the form לך r13 (in a biblical quotation).

≑ *qameṣ ḥaṭuf* לאהליהם v2, 8, גדלך v22.

≑ *ḥaṭef pataḥ* r4, 8.

⟨a′⟩ ≑ *qameṣ ḥaṭuf* לאהלם v3.

≑ *ḥaṭef qameṣ* לאהליהם r12.

≑ *ḥaṭef pataḥ* v26.

≑ *segol* קבע v19.

≑ *shewa* r5, 6, v1, 13 (?), 16.

⟨e⟩ ≑ *qameṣ* לארץ v17.

≑ *pataḥ* הדרת v5.

≑ *ḥireq* before a doubled consonant r2, 11, v13, elsewhere בקהל v4. The instances at r11 and v4 were later corrected (see below).

≑ *shewa* r7, 9, 11, 20, 25, v1, 4, 14, 19, 28.

⟨e′⟩ ≑ *shewa* יגלה v24.

⟨i⟩ ≑ *pataḥ* למשלישי v10, no doubt a broken ⟨a⟩ sign.

≑ *shewa* before *yod* r13, v14.

In addition to these, a sign ⟨e⟩ (i.e. a correction of ⟨e⟩ to ⟨e′⟩) is found, as follows: ≑ *ṣere* ריח r2, ימי r8, שם r11, זיר v2, תפלג v16, נדובב v22, לחדש v28. Other corrections are found, e.g. שבחו, בירכו r11 (perfects corrected to imperatives), בקהל v4 (≑ בקהל not בְּ). In some cases vowel signs were rewritten, e.g. ישמיענה v29. Presumably all this was done by the same correcting hand.

E The following diacritical signs are used in this ms:

⌒ ≑ *rafe* v19, 21.

⟨ś⟩ is marked as follows: שׁ e.g. r8, 8, 8, ש e.g. r10, 13, 28, שׁ e.g. v2, 6. The use of the dot within the letter presumably also derives from the 'correcting hand.'

Dots occasionally appear within other letters but do not appear to be significant (see III.1.N).

F Tiberian *qibbuṣ* appears in v27, *mappiq* possibly in r7.

III

The Classification of Non-biblical Texts

The mss described in chapter II differ considerably in their use of the vowel signs and diacritics. This has come to be expected of Palestinian mss. It may even be true to say, when the smaller details are considered, that no two Palestinian mss have identical pointing. However, if only the broad characteristics of each ms are taken into account (those characteristics termed 'normal,' and listed in section C of the description of each ms) it will be seen that that the differences in the mss are well defined. These differences, which are most clearly shown in the use of the 'a' and 'e' signs, can serve as a basis for a classification into which the pointing of any known ms will fit. When the Palestinian mss are classified in this way, a number of less noticeable details of pointing seem to fall into a meaningful pattern. This suggests that this classification is not merely a convenient system of arrangement, but does actually reflect some chronological, local, or other division of the Palestinian pointing system.

Table I shows the Palestinian use of signs corresponding to the bA vowel signs. This gives the basic characteristics by which the mss are classified. In this chapter some 60 non-biblical mss with Palestinian vocalization are classified in this way. In addition to these I have studied a number of other fragments in which the vocalization is too sparse to permit classification (see chapter VI). These together represent the total number of non-biblical Hebrew mss with Palestinian pointing known to me in the spring of 1966. More mss are now known, but almost certainly more remain to be found.[1] However, I feel that sufficient

[1] Professor Allony, Professor Díez Macho, and Dr. Yeivin have very kindly informed me of mss with Palestinian pointing which were not included in my lists. However, they also, I believe, have not yet exhausted the possible sources.

TABLE 1

Palestinian class	*qameṣ**	*pataḥ*	*segol*	*ṣere*	*shewa*
1	⟨a⟩	⟨a′⟩	⟨e⟩	⟨e′⟩	⟨e⟩
2	⟨a⟩	⟨a′⟩	⟨e/e′⟩	⟨e/e′⟩	⟨a′/e⟩
3	⟨a/a′⟩	⟨a/a′⟩	⟨e/e′⟩	⟨e/e′⟩	⟨a′/e⟩
4	⟨a⟩	⟨a′⟩	⟨e⟩		⟨e′⟩ *et al.*
5	⟨a/a′⟩	⟨a/a′⟩	⟨e⟩		⟨e′⟩ *et al.*
6	⟨a⟩	⟨a′⟩	⟨e⟩		—
7	⟨a/a′⟩	⟨a/a′⟩	⟨e⟩		⟨a′/e⟩
8	⟨a⟩		⟨e⟩		⟨a′⟩
9	⟨a⟩		⟨e⟩		⟨a/e⟩
10	⟨a⟩		⟨e′⟩		⟨e′⟩
11	⟨a′⟩		⟨e⟩		⟨a′/e⟩

* Not including *qameṣ ḥaṭuf*.

mss have been used to make it likely that any further texts which turn up will fit this classification.

Since the classification is based on general usage rather than on details, unique phenomena, which may in any case be due to accident or error, are sometimes ignored. Few examples of the less common uses of vowel signs are given, since it is spelling, and not morphology as such, which is the chief concern here. Some aspects of these unusual spellings are dealt with in chapter v. Complete references to examples of a particular uncommon usage are given if their number is small. Where this is not done, the number of cases is noted, together with the type of syllable in which the usage occurs, if this seems significant. The syllable types are classified – as is of course inevitable – according to the syllables of the bA form corresponding to the Palestinian form in question. This is done for purposes of comparison. It is not suggested that Palestinian stress patterns and syllable divisions were necessarily the same as those of bA. Syllable types are indicated as follows: O, open syllable; O′, open syllable under main stress; C, closed syllable; C′, closed syllable under main stress. The letter 'f' following one of these signs (e.g. C′f) indicates that the syllable is word final.[2]

[2] 'Word' here refers to a word or 'word group' as defined by stress-pattern. That is, forms such as על, normally followed by *maqqef* in bA, are not classed as 'word final' syllables.

The script of the mss studied is of great interest, as in some cases it is similar in most or all of the mss in a class. Similarities can also be seen in the characteristic scripts of classes which use the vowel signs in similar ways. The scripts of the mss of each class have, therefore, been described briefly, and general dates given for their production. These dates are not based on training or wide experience in the field of palaeography, but on such information as I could acquire from the publications of others. They cannot, therefore, be taken as expert opinion. Their main significance for the argument of the book is that they show that the various classes of pointing do not represent stages in a unilinear development (see v.18). It is my belief that this conclusion is imposed on one by the similarity of the writing of some mss of different classes. The dates given are only a convenient method of stating this. The absolute dates of the mss are of little significance, save perhaps for the study of the external relationships of the Palestinian pointing.

CLASS 1

A TS H2:1 (recto only) TS H6:40 (?) TS NS 249:2 (II.1)
TS H6:38 TS H16:10[3]

Members of this class use the vowel signs ⟨u⟩, ⟨o⟩, ⟨a⟩, ⟨a′⟩, ⟨e⟩, ⟨e′⟩, and ⟨i⟩ in the following way:

B ≑ *shureq*

⟨u⟩ *passim. Waw* conjunctive is never pointed in a situation where bA would use *shureq*.

⟨o⟩ H6:38 r10 syllable O.

C ≑ *ḥolem*

⟨o⟩ *passim.*

⟨u⟩ H2:1 r9 syllable O.

D ≑ *qameṣ*

⟨a⟩ *passim.*

[3] Published in Edelmann, 1934, as MS D. The numbers in parentheses following the references to this ms refer to the page and line of Edelmann's edition. Note that, regardless of the usage of any editor, references to all mss are made to r(ecto) and v(erso).

⟨a′⟩ only H16:10 r14 (15:7) syllable O′f.

⟨e⟩ H2:1 לגרגרות r29.

E ≑ *qameṣ ḥaṭuf*[4]

⟨a⟩ H6:38 r17, NS 249:2 r12.

⟨o⟩ H16:10 r16 (15:9).

G ≑ *pataḥ*

⟨a′⟩ *passim.*

⟨a⟩ H6:38 r25, H16:10 v13 (16:8), both before a doubled consonant. NS 249:2 2 cases, one before a doubled consonant, one before a laryngeal (see II.1.D).

H ≑ *ḥaṭef pataḥ*

⟨a′⟩ *passim.*

⟨a⟩ H16:10 v3 (15:24).

I ≑ *segol*

⟨e⟩ *passim.*

⟨e′⟩ H6:38 r23,[5] v14,[6] both questionable.

⟨a′⟩ H6:38 r23.[7]

J ≑ *ḥaṭef segol*

⟨e⟩ (Only in H6:38.)

K ≑ *ṣere*

⟨e′⟩ *passim.*

⟨e⟩ H16:10. Stressed syllable, closed, final, v5, 7 (15:26, 16:2); open, non-final, r2 (14:20). Unstressed, open, r26 (15:19).

[4] The form לחוננם in H6:38 v22 is derived from Ps. 102:14.

[5] רחם bA has רֶחֶם or רַחַם. The use of ⟨e′⟩ in the second syllable of 'segolate' forms is typical in many biblical mss. See Revell, 1970, I, nos, 10, 11.

[6] מימנו suggesting מִמֵּנּוּ the 'Oriental' spelling. (See, for example, Ginsburg, 1897, p. 200. Cf. also the form מנו in this ms, e.g. v7.)

[7] See note 5.

⟨a′⟩ H16:10 בירך v6 (16:1), also r23 (15:16).[8]

⟨i⟩ H6:38 קריבה r18.

L ≑ *ḥireq*

⟨i⟩ *passim.*

⟨e′⟩ H16:10 איתון r4 (14:22).

⟨e⟩ H16:10 שתהא v16 (16:11).

⟨a′⟩ H16:10 ומקח v22 (16:16).[9]

M ≑ *shewa*

⟨e⟩ *passim.*

⟨e′⟩ H2:1 ליקרביים r30 misplaced (?), נקדש r34 (?). H16:10 יאמירו v13 (16:8).

⟨a′⟩ NS 249:2 כאיין v11 (possibly under the influence of the following *ʾalef* with 'a' vowel).[10]

⟨i⟩ Before *yod* H2:1 בעינניהם r14 (misplaced?). H16:10 r7, 10 (14:25, 15:3), also r6.[11] NS 249:2 v22.

N The diacritical signs are used as follows:

_<_ *dagesh forte* H2:1r, H6:38, NS 249:2.
dagesh lene H16:10.
Marking *he* as closing a syllable H2:1 וכהמות r2. (See IV.1.N, _<_ (iii).)
Marks *ʾalef* as consonantal. H6:38 r14; *yod*, H16:10, r24.

_ᴖ_ *rafe* NS 249:2 r17.
Marks *ʾalef* as quiescent H6:38 r24, H16:10 r25, 26 (15:18, 19), also באת v28 (?).[12]

ש marks ⟨ś⟩.

[8] A *nitpaʾel* form. Forms from this stem are taken as equivalent to the biblical *hitpaʿel*, even though they are normally written as *nitpaʿal* in Palestinian mss.

[9] מקח The same form occurs in H2:1 r11, where it is best considered as a masculine form of מַקָּחָה 'merchandise,' and not מֶקַח 'buying.' For such masculine forms, cf. VII.4 and note 3 there.

[10] On the tendency of some Palestinian mss to write '*shewa* vowels' before a laryngeal with the sign for the vowel following the laryngeal, see III.2.M. This feature occurs in a new ms of class 1, TS H3:4, e.g. באפל v1, כמלואו v7, בערמה r15 (?,) יעוות r3, שאיר v13, לאידו v18 (!), but inconsistently, e.g. מילאו v15, מואם v16. Cf. also IV.1.

[11] בימין where Edelmann reads ⟨e⟩ (14:24).

[12] Questionable, but Edelmann's reading באפ]יו (16:23) is, I think, certainly wrong. However, the sign _ᴖ_ is used on intervocalic *ʾalef*; see IV.1 under _ᴖ_ ≑ *rafe.*

Occasionally in mss of this sort a dot appears within a graph representing a laryngeal consonant. This would be interpreted as the '*dagesh*' sign borrowed from the Tiberians, used to indicate that the graph represents a consonantal sound (as, for example, bA *mappiq*). There are possible cases in H2:1 r20, 20, 27. However, it is difficult to determine whether or not these are intentional pen marks. (Cf. the similar dot in final *mem* r25.) Dots are used in this way in biblical mss of this class, but I am not certain that they were ever used by the original pointing hand of any non-biblical ms.

o In this class, then, the use of vowel signs is very similar to that of bA. The use of ⟨a⟩, ⟨a′⟩, ⟨e⟩, and ⟨e′⟩ corresponds almost exactly to the bA use of *qameṣ*, *pataḥ*, *segol*, and *ṣere*, save that ⟨e⟩ is used where bA uses not only *segol*, but also *shewa*. This can hardly be ascribed to the influence of the bA tradition, since classes 2, 4, and 6, which obviously do not attempt to copy bA in any other respect, show the same use of ⟨a⟩ and ⟨a′⟩. Furthermore, in class 1 there are sufficient typically Palestinian features to make it difficult to argue that these mss deliberately set out to copy bA. Examples are the sign for ⟨ś⟩, the Palestinian *dagesh* and *rafe*, and the lack of a special sign used only for '*shewa* vowels.' The use of ⟨o⟩ where bA has *qameṣ ḥaṭuf* could also be included here. ⟨o⟩ is, however, less common in this position than is ⟨a⟩. It seems to me that the use of ⟨a⟩ in this position may well be due to bA influence (see V.22, 24), but this seems the only likely mark of such influence in this class.

As regards the script, TS H6:38, TS H16:10, and TS NS 249:2 form the core of the group. The script, a Syrian type of the ninth century, is similar in all three. The script of TS H6:40 is probably somewhat later. The script of TS H2:1r also differs from that of the first three texts and is probably earlier. It is a typical 'free Syrian square' hand, as used in class 7, to which the pointing of the verso belongs. Apparently the recto and verso of this leaf were written by the same hand, but, for some reason, pointed by different ones. The vocalization of mss in this class is normally sparse.

CLASS 2

A TS 12:191
TS 16:93[13]
TS E1:107[14]
TS H2:45 + H2:58
TS H16:6[15]
TS H16:7 + Leningrad Ant. 369[16]
TS NS 118:38 (11.2)
Bod. Heb. d55, f. 12v–14v[17]
Bod. Heb. d63, f. 98[18] + f. 97
+ TS 10H5:7

Members of this class use the vowel signs ⟨u⟩, ⟨o⟩, ⟨a⟩, ⟨a′⟩, ⟨e⟩, ⟨e′⟩, and ⟨i⟩ in the following way:

B ≑ *shureq*

⟨u⟩ *passim*, including situations where bA would point conjunctive *waw* as *shureq* in E1:107, H16:6, H16:7+ (cf. the note on signs ≑ *shewa*).

⟨o⟩ E1:107 1v12. H2:45+ v12. Heb. d55 13r10, 17, 19, 14r4, 23, 14v18. H16:7+ 15:6, 16:1, 19:8, 16, 16.

C ≑ *ḥolem*

⟨o⟩ *passim*.

⟨u⟩ H16:7+ 12:18, 22:18. Heb. d55 14v30. Heb. d63 f. 98v15.

⟨a⟩ H16:6 בקודש 1r9 (1:9).

⟨a′⟩ H16:7+ לקרב 20:19, לרכב 20:19.

D ≑ *qameṣ*

⟨a⟩ *passim*.

⟨a′⟩ sporadically in all mss: O′f 24 cases, O 26 cases, C′f 29 cases.

⟨e⟩ Heb. d55 13v23, 14v2 (both O).

⟨e′⟩ H16:6 possibly 2v9 (4:15),[19] also O. Heb. d55 13r27, 14r28 (both O).

[13] Published in Allony and Díez-Macho, 1959a.
[14] Published in Allony, 1963.
[15] Published in Edelmann, 1934, as MS A.
[16] Published in Kober, 1929. All references to this text are to page and line of this edition, which I have checked against photographs where possible.
[17] Published in Murtonen, 1958, as part of MS a.
[18] Folio 98 verso was published in Murtonen, 1958 as MS b.
[19] בני (so Edelmann) but probably to be taken as בני corrected to בני, as the ⟨e′⟩ sign is above the *nun*.

E ≑ *qameṣ ḥaṭuf*

	⟨o⟩	⟨a⟩	⟨a′⟩
TS H16:6	—	9	—
TS H16:7+	7	1	—
Bod. Heb. d55 f. 12v–14v	6	4	3[20]

F ≑ *ḥaṭef qameṣ*

⟨a⟩ H2:45+ v4. Heb. d55 13r20, 14v8.

⟨a′⟩ Heb. d55 13r3, 13v30.

G ≑ *pataḥ*

⟨a′⟩ *passim*, including '*pataḥ* furtive' H16:7+, 18:11.[21]

⟨a⟩ sporadically in all mss: O, 13 cases; C′f, 17; C, 25, of which 8 occur before a doubled consonant.

⟨e⟩ Heb. d55 13v20, 14v26, before a medial laryngeal. H16:7+ 17:8, 18, before a medial laryngeal; 18:11 before a final laryngeal (unstressed syllable), also 19:18 (?).

⟨e′⟩ Heb. d63 חי 98v18.[22]

H ≑ *ḥaṭef pataḥ*

⟨a′⟩ *passim.*

⟨a⟩ Heb. d55 f. 12v–14v, 6 cases; H16:7+ 4 cases.

⟨e⟩ Heb. d55 13r14, 14v26, both following '*ayin.*

⟨e′⟩ Heb. d55 12v5, 13v7, 18 (אשר); 14v3, 18, following '*ayin.*

I, K 'e' vowels

	≑ *segol*		≑ *ṣere*	
	⟨e⟩	⟨e′⟩	⟨e⟩	⟨e′⟩
TS 12:191	—	3	2	2
TS 16:93	11	8	3	10
TS E1:107	8	1[23]	8	1
TS H2:45+	—	1	—	1
TS H16:6	14	36	9	50

[20] Heb. d55 13r20, 34, 14r25.

[21] Also in a new ms, TS H15:69, שבוע, r29. Cf. also II.8.D.

[22] Possibly חי ≑ חי was intended; cf. the use of ⟨e′⟩ to mark consonantal *yod* in TS 12:191 in place of the commoner ⟨i⟩ (see 2.N below).

[23] שדין 2r19. Allony שדין. The sign is peculiar, but much closer to ⟨e′⟩ than to the '*dagesh*' sign of 1r12.

TS H16:7+	70	9	55	44
TS NS 118:38	—	1	3	—
Bod. Heb. d55[24]	(76)	(—) 1	(51)	(6) 22
Bod. Heb. d63 f. 98+	26	6	14	20

I ≑ *segol*

⟨a⟩ Heb. d55 13r9, 14r23 (the latter was corrected to ⟨e⟩).

⟨a′⟩ E1:107 1r20; H16:6 2r20; Heb. d55 14v20.

⟨i⟩ H16:7+ 16:4, 22:1.[25]

J ≑ *ḥaṭef segol*

⟨e⟩ *passim.*

K ≑ *sere*

⟨a′⟩ C′f only: H16:6 2v18 (5:9). Heb. d55 12v13, 21, 25, 13v28, 14r7, 18. H16:7+ 18:14, 17.

⟨a⟩ H16:6 2r15 (3:9) (?).[26] Also in C′f syllables, Heb. d55 14r2, 17, 14v25.

⟨i⟩ E1:107 2r7; Heb. d55 14r21, 14v9, 19; H16:7+ 16:14.

⟨o⟩ Heb. d55 הפיץ 14v22, probably due to a correction of ⟨e⟩ to ⟨e′⟩ or vice versa.

L ≑ *ḥireq*

⟨i⟩ *passim.*

⟨e⟩ E1:107 1r12; H16:6 1v1 (2:4); H16:7+ 12:3, 5, 17:4, 21:3; Heb. d55 13r22, 13v28, 14r11, 14, 27, 28; in syllables of all types.

⟨e′⟩ H16:6 1v16 (2:19), 2r18 (4:1), 2v19 (5:10); H16:7+ 23:3 all in stressed syllables. In Heb. d63 f. 98+, ⟨e′⟩ is used where bA would have *ḥireq* some 55 times – much more commonly than ⟨i⟩ is used in this position. There is no clear distinction between the signs in use, but ⟨i⟩ appears more common in closed unstressed syllables.

⟨a⟩ H16:7+ 13:15, 22:22, both before *yod* followed by bA *qameṣ*,

[24] The figures within the parentheses are from fols. 12v and 13r, which were taken as a sample. The other figures give the total uses of ⟨e′⟩ in these positions in fols. 12v–14v.

[25] Edelmann's קשה H16:6 (5:7) is a misprint for קשה 2v16.

[26] The photograph seems to show the sign in question as a diagonal stroke אליך.

a situation which occurs sporadically elsewhere (see 5.L below and note 48).

M ≑ *shewa*

	⟨e⟩	⟨a′⟩	⟨a⟩	⟨e′⟩	⟨i⟩	⟨o⟩	ˊ
TS 12:191	—	—	—	—	—	—	—
TS 16:93	3	—	1	—	—	—	—
TS E1:107	2[27]	—	—	1[28]	—	—	—
TS H2:45+	1	—	—	—	—	—	—
TS H16:6	1	1	—	2	—	—	—
TS H16:7+	—	1	11	4	1	—	—
TS NS 118:38	—	1	—	—	—	—	—
Bod. Heb. d55	208	49	22	16[29]	14	3	42
Bod. Heb. d63	—	3	—	—	1	—	—

In Heb. d63 and H16:7+ ⟨i⟩ ≑ *shewa* is used before *yod.*

In Heb. d55 f. 12v–14v it is used in this position, after *yod,* and before *ʾalef* followed by an 'i' vowel. In this ms also ⟨o⟩, and to a lesser extent ⟨e′⟩, is restricted in use to situations in which bA would have *shewa* before *ʾalef* or *he* followed by *ḥolem* or *ṣere* respectively. ⟨a⟩ and ⟨a′⟩ are used before any laryngeal followed by an 'a' vowel.[30]

In Heb. d55 f. 12v–14v ⟨e⟩ and ⟨a′⟩ are both used, presumably to indicate '*shewa* vowels,' on conjunctive *waw* where bA would point with *shureq*; e.g. 12v25, 13r11.

N Diacritical signs are used as follows:

⟨ś⟩ is rarely marked. The following signs are used: שׂ H2:45+, שׂ NS 118:38, Heb. d55 f. 12v–14v. The latter ms also uses שׂ, and a combination of the two signs שׂ.

_<_ ≑ *dagesh forte* in all mss but E1:107, H16:6, and NS 118:38.
≑ *dagesh lene* in TS 16:93, Heb. d55 f. 12v–14v, Heb. d63

[27] למקום 1v11, שונת 2v7.

[28] 2r10. In my opinion, Allony's reading ונותנין (2v11) is to be read נותנין (with a damaged ⟨o⟩ sign).

[29] Including the two forms שאת 12v4, 17 (see Murtonen, 1958, p. 33), on which see _∩_ ≑ *rafe* and note 32.

[30] The signs used ≑ bA *shewa* in this ms are fully described in Revell, 1970, II, no. 11.

f. 98. Peculiar uses, perhaps also corresponding to *dagesh lene*, are found in TS 16:93 כבשים 2r10, and in Heb. d63 f. 98+ on *ṭet* 98v18, 20, 24, on *nun* TS 10H5:7, 2r2, on *qof* Heb. d63 98v25, TS 10H5:7, 2r15, 15, and on *taw* Heb. d63 98v27.

≑ *dagesh forte* 'conjunctive' Heb. d63 98v23, 29, H16:7+ 20:1.

≑ *mappiq* H16:7+, 14:16; Heb. d55 13v9.

This sign marks a graph other than word final *he* as indicating a consonant in TS 12:191 r16, E1:107 1r12 (both *'alef*), Heb. d55 13r23 *(waw)*, 13r24 *(waw* and *yod?)*,[31] and Heb. d63 98v27 *(ḥet)*.

_ⁿ_ ≑ *rafe* in Heb. d55 f. 12v–14v, Heb. d63 f. 98+. In the latter text it is also used on *qof* where *rafe* seems meaningless (v23). Presumably this corresponds to the unexpected uses of _‹_ in this ms.

The same sign marks graphs as indicating a consonant in TS 16:93 4r3 *('ayin)*, Heb. d55 12v4, 17 *('alef)*,[32] and Heb. d63 98v12, 12, 13, 17, 18, 25, 25 *(waw)*, 97r28 *(yod)*. Cf. IV.3.N, and note 8 to chapter IV.

⟨i⟩ and ⟨e′⟩ mark consonantal *yod* in TS 12:191 בניי r28, צוויי v7. ⟨e′⟩ may also be used in Heb. d63 f. 98+ (see note 22).

O This class, then, uses all seven vowel signs, but is distinguished from class 1 by the fact that the use of ⟨e⟩ and ⟨e′⟩ does not correspond to the bA use of *segol* and *ṣere*. It is also characteristic of this class that ⟨a⟩ and ⟨a′⟩ are used almost exactly as bA uses *qameṣ* and *pataḥ*, with the exception of *qameṣ ḥaṭuf*. ⟨a′⟩ can correspond to *qameṣ ḥaṭuf* in this class, as well as ⟨o⟩ and ⟨a⟩, a usage not found in class 1.

The majority of the mss in this class make no attempt at consistent representation of '*shewa* vowels.' It is, in fact, rare to

[31] My photograph does not appear to support Murtonen's reading וילדה, but it is not very clear at this point.

[32] Murtonen, 1958, p. 33 considers that the sign _ⁿ_ here marks the *'alef* as quiescent. My own view is defended in Revell, 1970, II, no. 11 and notes there. The '*rafe*' sign can be taken as indicating an unusual type of consonantal value (see IV.1.N), or possibly as equivalent to masoretic *rafe* ≑ *ḥaṭef* (see 5.N below and note 51). The suggestion that this form was bisyllabic in this dialect need cause no difficulty. Cf. bA שְׂאֵת. Cf. also צאת Bod. Heb. d55 f. 4r8.

find a vowel sign used where bA would use *shewa*. Heb. d55 f. 12v–14v is an obvious exception to this rule. It seems certain that the present vocalization of the ms does not derive from a single hand, but the extent to which addition has been made is not clear.[33] My own opinion is that the pointing was originally of class 2, and that the later additions were by a scribe or scribes of the same class who produced a more developed form of the pointing of this class. The representation of '*shewa* vowels,' then, I would ascribe to the most developed form of class 2.[34]

The use of diacritics varies considerably among the mss of this class. This is not surprising, as the use of these signs is only rarely homogeneous in the other classes. However, it seems that the marking of ⟨ś⟩ is atypical in this class. Again Heb. d55 f. 12v–14v is an exception. '*Dagesh*' is shown fairly frequently, but Heb. d63 f. 98+ is unique in its wide use of this sign and of '*rafe*.'

Finally it should be noted that mss of this class seem, possibly under the influence of bA, to show a care for the minute details of pointing which extends, in some cases, to hypercorrection. For example, in TS H16:6 ⟨a⟩ is used not only where bA has *qameṣ ḥaṭuf*, but also in קוׄדש 1r9 (1:9), and in כׄל 1v7, 2r18 (2:10, 4:1), where its use is almost equally unexpected. The use of ⟨a′⟩ where bA would use *qameṣ* before a laryngeal is probably an example of the same phenomenon. *Pataḥ* normally occurs in such a position, and so ⟨a′⟩ is used, e.g., in TS H16:7+, 18:12, 19:8, 13. The pointing of '*shewa* vowels' in Heb. d55 f. 12v–14v should probably

33 In Murtonen, 1958, p. 30, it is stated that four hands were involved in the production of his MS a. One of these, the hand that produced the original pointing of fols. 4r–7v, 9r–12r, is presumably not involved in the pointing of fols. 12v–14v. The signs which are not to be ascribed to the original hand of these folios are, however, only noted in certain cases, and no attempt is made to ascertain the general character of the additions. I myself have only seen this ms briefly, and no criteria by which the separate hands might be distinguished are visible in the photograph.

34 It seems to me that the following arguments might be raised against this view. There is a correction (probably) of ⟨e⟩ to ⟨e′⟩, which suggests class 1, ש is used to mark ⟨ś⟩, as in class 1, and detailed representation of the quality of '*shewa* vowels' is also found in class 1 (biblical, see IV.1). This could, therefore, be a ms corrected by a hand of class 1. However, if all cases of ⟨e′⟩ ≑ *ṣere* are taken as corrections, then the original pointing must have been of class 4, where ש ≑ ⟨ś⟩ is not used (see 4 below). ש ≑ ⟨ś⟩ is used in another ms of class 2. A similar marking of the quality of '*shewa* vowels' is found in TS 12:195+ of class 3 (biblical, see IV.3), a ms which also shows the use of _ᐢ_ to indicate that certain graphs have a consonantal value. There is therefore no reason why any feature of the pointing of Heb. d55 f. 12v–14v should not be assigned to class 2.

also be taken as an example of the attention to minor detail typical of this class.

The scripts used in the mss of this class show considerable variety, but can be grouped in three main types. The first group, including TS H16:6 and TS E1:107, shows similarities to the typical 'free Syrian' script of classes 5 and 7 *(q.v.)*. The second group includes TS 16:93 and TS 12:191. These two mss show further possible connection in that they are both palimpsests, although the lower writing of the one is Greek, and of the other Syriac. The third group is typified by TS NS 118:38 and TS H2:45+, which show writing of a more formal square type than do the mss of the other groups. TS E1:107 and TS 16:93 have both been dated to the eighth or ninth century by Allony (for references to these and the other dates noted see chapter VI under the ms number). Mandelbaum dates TS 16:93 to the tenth or eleventh century, and TS 12:191 to the ninth or tenth century. My own opinion would be that the mss in this class were written over a long period, ranging from the seventh (TS H16:6) to the ninth or tenth (TS H16:7) centuries. The pointing of the texts ranges from scant (TS 12:191) to thoroughgoing (Bod. Heb. d55 f. 12v–14v).

CLASS 3

A TS 20:182 TS H5:222 TS NS 119:42+ (II.3)
TS H2:44 TS H7:15 + NS 272:2 Leningrad Ant. 959[35]

Members of this class use the vowel signs ⟨u⟩, ⟨o⟩, ⟨a⟩, ⟨a′⟩, ⟨e⟩, ⟨e′⟩, and ⟨i⟩, in the following way:

B ≑ *shureq*

⟨u⟩ *passim.*

C ≑ *ḥolem*

⟨o⟩ *passim.*

⟨u⟩ TS 20:182 r25; Ant. 959 20:8.

[35] Published in Edelmann, 1934, as MS E. The references are to the page and line of that edition.

D, G 'a' vowels

	≑ *qameṣ*		≑ *pataḥ*	
	⟨a⟩	⟨a′⟩	⟨a⟩	⟨a′⟩
TS 20:182	1	—	2	—
TS H2:44	3	1	2	2
TS H5:222	—	4	1	11
TS H7:15+	1	—	—	2
TS NS 119:42+	3	—	5 (?)	5
Leningrad Ant. 959	3	2	1	2

E ≑ *qameṣ ḥaṭuf*

⟨o⟩ H2:44 v7.

I, K 'e' vowels

	≑ *segol*		≑ *ṣere*	
	⟨e⟩	⟨e′⟩	⟨e⟩	⟨e′⟩
TS 20:182	—	1	4	4
TS H2:44	1	1	—	1
TS H5:222	8	2	2	7
TS H7:15+	—	3	—	3
TS NS 119:42+	6	3 (?)	11 (?)	2
Leningrad Ant. 959	—	—	—	5

I ≑ *segol*

⟨a′⟩ H7:15+, שֿבּֿע v17.

J ≑ *ḥaṭef segol*

⟨e⟩ Ant. 959.

L ≑ *ḥireq*

⟨i⟩ *passim.*

M ≑ *shewa*

⟨e⟩ TS 20:182 r47; H5:222 v41 (Aram.).

⟨a′⟩ H5:222 v38, 41.

⟨i⟩ Before *yod*, H7:15+, v7 (?); elsewhere H5:222 v17, 19 (?).

N The following diacritical signs are used:

ש̊ marks ⟨ś⟩ H2:44; H7:15+; Ant. 959.

ש̇ marks ⟨ś⟩ NS 119:42+; H7:15+. The latter contains some other Tiberian points.

שׁ̊ marks ⟨š⟩ H2:44, H7:15+.

◌̱ ≑ *dagesh forte* NS 119:42+; Ant. 959.
Marks initial *'alef* as consonantal, H2:555 r7 (?).

◌̱ ≑ *rafe* NS 119:42+; Ant. 959.

O It is difficult to evaluate the characteristics of this group from the very sparse vocalization of the fragments assigned to it. Its major characteristic is its use of all four 'a' and 'e' signs with no relation to the use of the corresponding signs in bA. Apart from this there appears to be no feature which characterizes the pointing of the whole group except its sparseness. The mss in this class show a diversity of scripts, probably written in the eighth and ninth centuries, with TS NS 119:42+ and TS 20:182 showing the extremes. The latter ms is written in a hand similar to that of TS 12:191 (see 2.O above), and is written over a western Syriac text, as is TS 12:191. Schechter dated it to the tenth or eleventh century,[36] but on the basis of more recent knowledge, it seems that this date should be reduced. The pointing is sparse in all mss of this class.

CLASS 4

A TS H2:72 — TS NS 117:6+ (II.4a)
TS H16:4[37] — H.U.C. MS 1001+ (II.4)
TS 13H2:10[38]

Members of this class use the vowel signs ⟨u⟩, ⟨o⟩, ⟨a⟩, ⟨a'⟩, ⟨e⟩, ⟨e'⟩, and ⟨i⟩ as follows:

B ≑ *shureq*

⟨u⟩ *passim*, including conjunctive *waw* in situations in which bA would point it as *shureq*, in TS H16:4, H.U.C. MS 1001+. No other sign is used in this position.

⟨o⟩ H16:4 v20; 13H2:10 1r9, 1v6 (?); NS 117:6+ 1r18, 2r3; and 2 cases in H.U.C. 1001+ (see ⟨o⟩ in II.4.D).

C ≑ *ḥolem*

⟨o⟩ *passim*.

[36] In Lewis and Gibson, 1900, under nos. I and VIII.
[37] Published in Murtonen, 1958, as MS e.
[38] Published in Murtonen, 1958, as MS d.

⟨u⟩ H2:72 v19 (?); 13H2:10 1v5 (possibly also in H.U.C. 1001+, see II.4.D).

⟨a⟩ 13H2:10 קרא 1r2.

D ≑ *qameṣ*

⟨a⟩ *passim.*

⟨a′⟩ sporadically in all mss except NS 117:6+, in syllables of the following types: O′f, 4; C′f, 22; O, 14, of which 6 occur before a laryngeal, and 7 in 13H2:10 in the form היתה (e.g. 2r10).

⟨e′⟩ H16:4 r10; and 1 case in H.U.C. 1001+ (see II.4.D).

E ≑ *qameṣ ḥaṭuf*

(⟨u⟩ NS 117:6+ 1v10 [see II.4[a].D].)

⟨o⟩ H2:72 r10, 12, v11; H16:4 r10, v11, 14; 13H2:10 1r15, 18, 2r11, 16, 23, 2v2, 14, 20; H.U.C. 1001+, 19 cases (see II.4.D).

⟨a⟩ H2:72 v8.[39]

F ≑ *ḥaṭef qameṣ*

⟨a⟩ 3 cases in H.U.C. 1001+ (see II.4.D).

⟨o⟩ H2:72 v8.[39]

G ≑ *pataḥ*

⟨a′⟩ *passim.*

⟨a⟩ sporadically in all mss, in syllables of the following types: C′f, 46 (9 of which precede a laryngeal); O, 14 (12 of which precede a laryngeal, the other two *yod* followed by ‘i’); C, 11 (2 of which precede a laryngeal, and 5 a doubled consonant).

H ≑ *ḥaṭef pataḥ*

⟨a′⟩ 8 cases in all.

⟨a⟩ 5 cases in all.

⟨e′⟩ H.U.C. 1001+ 4 cases (see II.4.D).

[39] כאני The pointing with ⟨o⟩ is normal for קְלָי forms (see 11.F below and IV.2.F, 7.K). This pointing probably represents a ‘*shewa* vowel’ followed by a ‘full vowel’ (i.e. {kŏʾòníy} not {kòʾŏníy} as in bA) since in this class, and indeed in all Palestinian mss, the normal usage is ⟨o⟩ ≑ *qameṣ ḥaṭuf* and ⟨a⟩ ≑ *ḥaṭef qameṣ* (see V.4, 6). For a similar pointing of a ‘*shewa* vowel,’ see IV.1.M.

I ≑ *segol*

⟨e⟩ *passim.*

⟨e′⟩ possibly 13H2:10 נֿעשקה 2v23, a similar form in 2v24, and one in H.U.C. 1001+. The ⟨e′⟩ sign could ≑ *segol* (contextual form), *ḥaṭef segol* ('pausal' form), or even *shewa*, as it is farther to the left than would be normal if the vowel indicated followed the *ʿayin*. See also IV.3.J.

J ≑ *ḥaṭef segol*

⟨e⟩ *passim.*

K ≑ *ṣere*

⟨e⟩ *passim.*

⟨a⟩ 13H2:10 1r25; NS 117:6+ 1r15; H.U.C. 1001+ 6 cases (see II.4.D), all but one in C′f syllables.

⟨a′⟩ 13H2:10 1r26; H.U.C. 1001+ 2 cases (see II.4.D), all in C′f syllables.

⟨i⟩ H.U.C. 1001+ 1 case (see II.4.D).

L ≑ *ḥireq*

⟨i⟩ *passim.*

⟨a′⟩ H16:4 יישך r18.[40]

⟨e⟩ H2:72 r25; 13H2:10 1r9, 1v6, 2r15, 2v2, 20; H.U.C. 1001+ 11 cases (see II.4.D). This occurs in the following types of syllables: O′, 1; O, 11, of which 8 precede laryngeals; C, 5, of which 4 precede a doubled consonant.

M ≑ *shewa*

	⟨e′⟩	⟨a′⟩	⟨a⟩	⟨e⟩	⟨i⟩
TS H2:72	3	—	1	—	4
TS H16:4	14	1	—	—	4
TS 13H2:10	18	7	2	1	4
TS NS 117:6+	5	—	4	1	—
H.U.C. 1001+	40	15	10	—	8

The examples of ⟨i⟩ ≑ *shewa* listed all occur before *yod.* H.U.C. 1001+ apparently contains 2 further examples in other positions (see II.4.D).

40 Imperative for perfect *piʿel?* See Zulay, 1938, p. 171 and note there.

N The following diacritical signs are used:

ש̥ marks ⟨ś⟩ in H2:72, 13H2:10,[41] NS 117:6+.

ש̣ marks ⟨ś⟩ in H16:4, H.U.C. 1001+.

ש̊ marks ⟨ś⟩ in H.U.C. 1001+ (one page only, see II.4.E).

ש֯ marks ⟨š⟩ in H.U.C. 1001+ (one page only, see II.4.E).

_<_ ÷ *dagesh forte* in all mss. Misplaced יויקך 13H2:10 1r26 (?).

÷ *dagesh forte* 'conjunctive' 13H2:10 2r12, H.U.C. 1001+ (see II.4.E).

÷ *mappiq* in all mss but NS 117:6.

Marks a laryngeal as closing a syllable H2:72 דעתה r4, and in 7 cases in H.U.C. 1001+ (see II.4.E). The example in H2:72, and some of the others, correspond also to bA *dagesh lene*, which also marks the preceding syllable as closed.

Marks *'alef* and *waw* as having consonantal pronunciation in H.U.C. 1001+ (see II.4.E).

_^_ ÷ *rafe* in all mss.

O The mss of this group, then, also use all seven vowel signs. They are distinguished from members of the preceding classes, however, by the fact that the use of ⟨e'⟩ is almost completely restricted to situations in which bA would use *shewa*, while ⟨e⟩ is used where bA would use both *segol* and *ṣere*. ⟨e'⟩ is never the only sign used where bA uses *shewa*, but in the mss described it is always the most common sign used in that position. There does not seem to be any distinction made in the use of the various signs used where bA has *shewa*, save that ⟨i⟩ is consistently used in this position before *yod*.

It is a further characteristic of the vocalization of this class that ⟨a⟩ and ⟨a'⟩ are used almost exactly as bA uses *qameṣ* and *pataḥ*, except in the case of *qameṣ ḥaṭuf*, where members of this class regularly use ⟨o⟩. ⟨a⟩ is, however, used where bA would have *ḥaṭef qameṣ*. This usage is typical for members of 'Group A' (see V.22, 24) to which this class belongs. Both vowel signs of the form כאני (H2:72 v8) are exceptions, but see note 39.

The usage of the diacritical signs also seems to be typical of this group, although the characteristics are perhaps rather vague

41 E.g. 1r26, 1v7, 2v18, apparently overlooked by Murtonen.

and negative. Some sign other than ש˂ is used to mark ⟨ś⟩. ⟨ś⟩ is marked relatively rarely compared to the use of the '*dagesh*' sign ˂.[42]

The scripts used in the five mss are very similar, suggesting origin in the same area and period; probably southern Palestine in the eight century with TS NS 117:6 as the earliest and TS H16:4 as the latest of the group. This homogeneity of script is all the more striking when it is remembered that the content also is homogeneous. All of these mss contain poems by Yannai. The pointing of all these mss is quite thoroughgoing, but in many syllables no vowel is marked. H.U.C. 1001+ is typical in this respect.

CLASS 5

A TS H16:8[43]

TS H16:9 + Bod. Heb. d55 f. 4–12r[44]

Jewish Theological Seminary MS E.N.A. 2020 f. 23 (II.5)

Leningrad Ant. 912[45]

Members of this class use the vowel signs ⟨u⟩, ⟨o⟩, ⟨a⟩, ⟨a'⟩, ⟨e⟩, ⟨e'⟩, and ⟨i⟩ in the following way:

B ÷ *shureq*

⟨u⟩ *passim.*

⟨o⟩ sporadically in all mss except E.N.A. 2020 f. 23, in syllables of the following types: Of, 11 (mostly stressed); O, 1; C'f, 12, 2 of which precede laryngeals; C, 7, of which 1 precedes a laryngeal and 6 precede doubled consonants.

(On signs used where bA points conjunctive *waw* as *shureq*, see under *shewa*.)

[42] E.g. in H.U.C. MS 1001+, ⟨ś⟩ is marked 28 times, while ˂ ÷ *dagesh, mappiq,* etc. is used some 107 times. Both these totals exclude the Levias fragment. Levias' copy was obviously a careful one, but he may have missed the subscript dot marking ⟨ś⟩. This is easy to do, and Levias had further reason for ignoring such dots as his text did use another method (due to a second hand?) of marking ⟨ś⟩ and ⟨š⟩.

[43] Published in Edelmann, 1934, as MS B.

[44] H16:9 was published in Edelmann, 1934, as MS C. Bodleian MS Heb. d55 f. 4r–7v, 9r–12r, part of the same ms, was published in Murtonen, 1958, as the first part of MS a.

[45] Published in Ormann, 1934. References are to page and line of that edition.

C ≑ *ḥolem*

⟨o⟩ *passim.*

⟨u⟩ H16:9+, 4 cases.

D, G 'a' vowels

	≑ *qameṣ*		≑ *pataḥ*	
	⟨a⟩	⟨a′⟩	⟨a⟩	⟨a′⟩
TS H16:8	133	59	73	75
TS H16:9+[46]	316	97	103	112
J.T.S. MS E.N.A. 2020 f. 23	64	23	32	23
Leningrad Ant. 912	234	111	87	189

D ≑ *qameṣ*

⟨e⟩ H16:8, 2v13 (10:10) (2 cases, probably a variant); H16:9+, Heb. d55 4r1 (2ms suffix; cf. חילך NS 249:14 r31, see II.9.D), 6r19, 7r15, 12r20, 21;[47] Ant. 912, 33:12.

⟨e′⟩ H16:8, 2v23 (11:1); H16:9+; Heb. d55 4r7; Ant. 912, 26:2.

E ≑ *qameṣ ḥaṭuf*

⟨o⟩ in all mss, 35 cases in all.

⟨a⟩ H16:8, 3 cases; H16:9+, 8 cases.

⟨a′⟩ H16:8, 2 cases, e.g. מתניה 2r11 (8:22); H16:9+, 7 cases; Ant. 912, 1 case.

F ≑ *ḥaṭef qameṣ*

⟨a⟩ H16:8, 1 case; H16:9+, 5 cases.

⟨a′⟩ H16:9+; בטהרה Heb. d55 10r28.

G ≑ *pataḥ*

⟨e⟩ H16:9+, 16 cases, 10 of which occur before laryngeals and 6 after laryngeals and before doubled consonants.

⟨e′⟩ H16:9+; אמיץ Heb. d55 9v10.

H ≑ *ḥaṭef pataḥ*

⟨a′⟩ in all mss, 50 cases in all.

⟨a⟩ H16:8, 4 cases; H16:9+, 15 cases; Ant. 912, 5 cases.

[46] These numbers refer only to Heb. d55 f. 4–5, which was taken as a sample.

[47] In the last two cases, לזה is possibly intended as לזה. Cf. ⟨e⟩ ≑ *shewa* in II.8.D.

⟨e⟩ H16:8 1v23 (8:1); H16:9+; Heb. d55 10r27.

⟨e′⟩ H16:9+, 13 cases, Ant. 912, 1 case, all following initial laryngeals.

I ≑ *segol*

⟨e⟩ *passim.*

⟨a′⟩ H16:8 1r17 (6:6); H16:9+; Heb. d55 4r17, 10r21, 10v23, 11v17 (?); Ant. 912, 26:17.

⟨a⟩ H16:9+; H16:9 r10 (11:22); Heb. d55 10r5 (cf. 7.I below), 12r9, 26.

⟨e′⟩ H16:9+; H16:9 r10 (11:22); Heb. d55 7v6.

⟨i⟩ H16:9+; Heb. d55 10r5, 11r7 (?); Ant. 912, 26:1, 10.

J ≑ *ḥaṭef segol*

⟨e⟩ *passim.*

K ≑ *ṣere*

⟨e⟩ *passim.*

⟨a′⟩ H16:8 1 case, C′f; H16:9+, 3 cases, C′f.

⟨a⟩ H16:9+; Heb. d55 4v5; E.N.A. 2020 23v14; Ant. 912, 27:10, 11, all *piʿel* or *n/hitpaʿel*, all but one C′f.

⟨i⟩ H16:9+; Heb. d55 4v29, 5r24, 5v4 (?), 10r13; Ant. 912, 28:2.

L ≑ *ḥireq*

⟨i⟩ *passim.*

⟨e′⟩ H16:8 לשגבכם 2v21 (10:18).

⟨e⟩ in all mss except H16:8, 20 cases in all, in the following types of syllable: O, 5; C′f, 5; C, 10, of which 4 precede a doubled consonant.

⟨a′⟩ H16:9+; over nominal prefix *mem*. Heb. d55 9v21, 10r23, 10v12; elsewhere, Heb. d55 5r15, 11v17.

⟨a⟩ H16:9+; in ירמיהו Heb. d55 4v4, 5, 7, 24, 5r18, 5v32.[48]

M ≑ *shewa*

	⟨e′⟩	⟨a′⟩	⟨e⟩	⟨a⟩	⟨o⟩	⟨i⟩
TS H16:8	9	2	1	3	—	—

[48] There are a number of other cases in which an ‘a’ vowel is used where bA would use *ḥireq* before *yod* followed by an ‘a’ vowel. See 2.L above, 7.L below, and also the similar cases where ⟨a⟩ or ⟨a′⟩ ≑ bA *shewa* before *yod* IV.2.M, 3.M.

TS H16:9+	75	241[49]	—	17	1	13
J.T.S. MS E.N.A. 2020 f. 23	2	10	1	—	—	—
Leningrad Ant. 912	7	24	2	9	—	—

The single case of ⟨o⟩ ≑ *shewa* is תזכוריהו Heb. d55 9r31 (cf. IV.3.M).

The uses of ⟨i⟩ ≑ *shewa* occur before *yod*, and also in other positions, e.g. ברית Heb. d55 9v9 (also three other cases). Signs other than ⟨i⟩ also occur where bA has *shewa* before *yod*, e.g. לישר (E.N.A. 2020 f. 23 r17). ⟨a′⟩ and ⟨e′⟩ are used in H16:9+ to point conjunctive *waw* where bA would point it as *shureq*, e.g. Heb. d55 4r13, 4v17. No other ms in this group marks vowels in this position.

N The following diacritical signs are used:

שׂ marks ⟨ś⟩ in all four mss.

ש marks ⟨ś⟩ in H16:9+, but is rare there.

שׁ may possibly mark ⟨š⟩ in three cases in H16:9+.[50]

_ ≑ *dagesh forte* H16:9+, Ant. 912. Misplaced in הצמים Heb. d55, 11v13 (?).

≑ *dagesh lene* H16:8 2v7 (10:4); H16:9+; Heb. d55 9r18, 12r32.

≑ *mappiq* H16:9+, Heb. d55 7r6.

The meaning is obscure in H16:9+, Heb. d55 12r24, Ant. 912, 31:15. In these cases the sign appears virtually equivalent to a '*shewa* vowel' sign. The case in H16:8 2v7 listed above could be included here, but the sign there could also indicate the presence of the definite article (see II.11.E).

_ *rafe* H16:9+; כעבדים Heb. d55 6r4, probably as '*rafe* ≑ *ḥaṭef pataḥ*.'[51]

_ This sign, identical with ⟨a′⟩, appears to be used in H16:9+ as a diacritic, e.g. over consonantal *waw*, Heb. d55 9v12,

[49] Some 30 of these examples are used where the *shewa* would be 'silent' in bA, but see note 52.

[50] See Murtonen, 1958, p. 33, but the same sign appears in other positions (*ibid.*, p. 34). The same sign may mark ⟨š⟩ in H2:55, v25 (see 6.N below).

[51] See Ginsburg, 1897, p. 123.

12r16, 26, and possibly also elsewhere with the meaning of Tiberian *rafe* as used in some mss divergent from bA.[52]

o Manuscripts in this class also use seven vowel signs, as have those in the classes previously described. As in class 4, ⟨e′⟩ is in this class virtually restricted to positions in which bA would use '*shewa* vowels.' ⟨e⟩ is used where bA would use both *ṣere* and *segol*. Class 5 is distinguished from class 4 by the fact that ⟨a⟩ and ⟨a′⟩ are not used as bA would use *qameṣ* and *pataḥ*. Besides ⟨e′⟩, other signs are used where bA uses *shewa*. In contrast to class 4, ⟨a′⟩ is, in most mss, more frequent than ⟨e′⟩ in this position. There does not appear to be any distinction in the use of these two signs. ⟨i⟩ is used relatively rarely where bA would have *shewa* before *yod*. Its use ≑ *shewa* is not confined to this position, nor is it exclusive there.

The use of the diacritics is characteristic in this class. שׁ is the typical mark of ⟨ś⟩. The rare use of ש in H16:9+ is probably not due to the original class 5 hand.[53] Class 5 further contrasts with class 4 in the fact that in class 5 ⟨ś⟩ is marked relatively commonly, and *dagesh*, etc. relatively rarely.[54]

All these fragments use a similar script, the typical free Syrian square style of *ca.* 800. Vocalization is typically thoroughgoing in this class. The form of ⟨a′⟩ is remarkable in that in mss of this class it characteristically appears as a dot only slightly elongated horizontally.[55] The form of the _ʟ_ sign marking ⟨ś⟩ and

[52] See, for example, Bét-Aryé, 1965, p. 44. The sign _⁄_ also appears over final *mem* in H16:9 (so the notes in Murtonen, 1958, p. 60 (Hebrew)). If this sign is considered as equivalent to bA *rafe* in these cases (cf. the use of _ⁿ_ to mark consonantal *waw* in 2.N above and IV.3.N), it is possible that some apparent cases of ⟨a′⟩ ≑ 'silent' *shewa* are really uses of *rafe* (e.g. מיתלבנים Heb. d55 12r23). However, only a few such cases could be explained in this way. In other cases, the use of a vowel sign where bA has 'silent' *shewa* is perhaps to be explained as a characteristic morphological difference between bA and the Palestinian dialect, e.g. 2ms. perfect forms such as עזבתה (Heb. d55 5v19, but forms corresponding to the normal bA type are also found; see Revell, 1970, II, no. 17). However, most cases of these uses of ⟨a′⟩ ≑ 'silent' *shewa* do not appear to belong to either category, and must be taken as showing that, in some cases, a vowel sound was pronounced where bA had none, but that this probably depended on the phonological context, not the grammatical form (e.g. והיסעיר Heb. d55 4v15, וינעם *ibid.* 5v18).

[53] See Murtonen, 1958, p. 33 and (Hebrew) 60.

[54] For example, in H16:9+, _ʟ_ ≑ *dagesh*, *mappiq*, etc., appears 14 times, שׁ ≑ ⟨ś⟩, 29 times. (In six other cases the sign could have either value.)

'*dagesh*' is also characteristic, in that the sign is normally formed by a vertical and a horizontal stroke meeting at right angles.

CLASS 6

A	TS E2:76	TS H16:12 + Bod. Heb. c. 20, f. 5–6	TS 13H2:11 + 12
	TS H2:30 (II.6)	TS 10H7:1	TS NS 119:43
	TS H2:55		TS NS 249:11

Members of this class use the vowel signs ⟨u⟩, ⟨o⟩, ⟨a⟩, ⟨a'⟩, ⟨e⟩, and ⟨i⟩ as follows:

B ÷ *shureq*

⟨u⟩ *passim*, including situations in which bA would point conjunctive *waw* as *shureq* in E2:76, H2:30, 10H7:1, and 13H2:11+. The latter is not consistent in this respect (see signs ÷ *shewa* below).

⟨o⟩ H2:55, r20, v24; H16:12+; Heb. c20 6r12.

C ÷ *ḥolem*

⟨o⟩ *passim*.

⟨u⟩ H2:55, two doubtful cases in r24.

D ÷ *qameṣ*

⟨a⟩ *passim*.

⟨a'⟩ E2:76, 1 case; H2:55, 3; H16:12+, 1; 13H2:11+, 1; in syllables of the following types: O'f, 1; O, 2; C'f, 3.

⟨e⟩ H2:30, 2v1.

E ÷ *qameṣ ḥaṭuf*

⟨o⟩ in H2:30, H2:55, H16:12+, and 13H2:11+, 12 cases in all. In H16:12+ עׄרפו Heb. c20 5r8, the two lower dots are accidentally joined.

F ÷ *ḥaṭef qameṣ*

⟨a⟩ 13H2:11+; אׄהׄלי 13H2:12, 2r22.

G ÷ *pataḥ*

⟨a'⟩ *passim*.

[55] TS H16:8 seems to be exceptional, but does use this form many times.

⟨a⟩ in all mss except NS 119:43 and NS 249:11. 9 cases in all, in syllables of the following types: O, 1; C′f, 2; C, 6, of which 4 precede a doubled consonant.

⟨e⟩ H2:55 v3, 3 (?); 13H2:11+; 13H2:12 1v4, 2r25.

H ≑ *ḥaṭef pataḥ*

⟨a′⟩ H2:55 r20 (?), 24.

⟨a⟩ H2:55, H16:12+, 10H7:1, 13H2:11+, one case each.

⟨e⟩ 13H2:11+, 13H2:11 1v30, also נעשׂו 2v26; assuming that the sign is badly placed, 13H2:12 2v25.

I ≑ *segol*

⟨e⟩ *passim*.

(⟨a⟩ and ⟨a′⟩ in 13H2:11+, אחת and אחת in 'pausal' position 13H2:12 1v5, 5.)

J ≑ *ḥaṭef segol*

⟨e⟩ 13H2:11+.

K ≑ *ṣere*

⟨e⟩ *passim*.

⟨a′⟩ H2:30, 2v9; H2:55, v18; both in C′f syllables.

L ≑ *ḥireq*

⟨i⟩ *passim*.

⟨e⟩ H2:30, H2:55, 10H7:1, and 13H2:11+, 7 cases, all in open syllables, three before laryngeals (see II.6.D).

M ≑ *shewa*

	⟨e⟩	⟨a′⟩	⟨a⟩	⟨i⟩
TS E2:76	—	—	—	2
TS H2:55	2	3	—	2
TS H16:12+	1	—	1	1
TS 10H7:1	2	—	—	3
TS 13H2:11+	1	2	5	4

All the cases of ⟨i⟩ ≑ *shewa* occur before *yod*, save ייפלל (H2:55 v3) *(pi'el)* which follows it. The case in H16:12+, מצביון (H16:12 2v5) corresponds to bA 'silent' *shewa* (cf. I.M above). It could, from its position, be considered a marker of consonantal *yod*, but the use of ⟨i⟩ for this purpose on medial *yod* would be unique.

In 13H2:11+ ⟨a⟩ is used to point conjunctive *waw* where bA would point it as *shureq* (וצדקה 13H2:11, 1v16).

N The following diacritical signs are used:

ש̥ marks ⟨ś⟩ in H16:12+.

ש̣ marks ⟨ś⟩ in 13H2:11+.

ש̊ marks ⟨ś⟩ in NS 249:11.

ש̓ appears to mark ⟨š⟩ in H2:55 v25, but the text is obscure. Cf. 5.N above.

‿ᶜ ≑ *dagesh forte* in all mss except NS 119:43 and NS 249:11.
≑ *dagesh lene* H2:30 and H2:55. Also (wrongly) הילויתיך E2:76, 2r20, and הפליגו Heb. c20 5r19 (?).
≑ *mappiq* 13H2:11+.

The same sign marks consonantal value in אשר H2:55 r9, and 13H2:12 2r17, and in על H2:55 v16. In לחלות H 2:55 r16 it presumably marks the preceding syllable as closed by the *ḥet* (see note to II.4.E). The Tiberian pointing is apparently contradictory, but for similar forms see Morag, 1959, p. 224. The sign corresponds to *dagesh forte* 'conjunctive' in H2:30 (see II.6.E), H2:55 r26, also זה לזה H2:55 v19,[56] and perhaps ימינך שלח 13H2:11 2r11.[57]

‿ᵔ ≑ *rafe* in H2:30, 10H7:1, 13H2:11+, and NS 119:43; 8 cases in all, including NS 119:43 2r2 where it marks final *he* as 'quiescent.'

O Mss of this class differ from those previously described in that they do not use ⟨e′⟩, and therefore have only six vowel signs. ⟨e⟩ is used where bA would use both *segol* and *ṣere*. ⟨a⟩ and ⟨a′⟩ are used almost exactly as bA would use *qameṣ* and *pataḥ*. The sign used where bA has *qameṣ ḥaṭuf* is ⟨o⟩, and ⟨a⟩ is used where bA would have *ḥaṭef qameṣ*. Signs are rarely used where bA would

[56] The placing of the sign between the two words is unusual. Cf. IV.3.N, and Bergsträsser, 1962, no. 10p (p. 65).

[57] This interpretation on the '*dagesh*' sign requires the pronunciation *–ka* for the preceding suffix. This form occurs elsewhere in Palestinian texts only if it is preceded by a 'full vowel' or if it forms part of a biblical quotation, but I cannot explain the use of the '*dagesh*' sign otherwise.

have *shewa*. It is probable that H2:30, which has none, is more typical in this respect than H2:55, which has seven in a short text. H2:55 shows a number of other unusual features. Also in 13H2:11+, the only other text in the class which has any number of signs in this position, four of the uses of ⟨a⟩ ≑ *shewa* occur in inflected forms, in a position in which an 'a' vowel is used in the base form. These may well represent full vowels, not '*shewa* vowels,' since ⟨a⟩ is not often used ≑ *shewa* in Palestinian Hebrew. They would then indicate a stress pattern different from that of bA. The four uses of ⟨i⟩ ≑ *shewa* in this text can also be considered 'special cases.' If this interpretation is acceptable, it can be said that the marking of vowels where bA would have *shewa* is atypical in this class.

Among the diacritics, it is characteristic of this class that signs other than שׂ are used to mark ⟨ś⟩. The form of the *dagesh* sign is typically ᶜ, although it can vary from ᵛ to ᶜ. These forms contrast with the ᴸ form typical in classes 5 and 7. A final characteristical of the use of the diacritics in this class is the fact that the marking of *dagesh*, etc. is relatively more common than the marking of ⟨ś⟩.[58]

As regards script, the mss of this class do not form a homogeneous group. TS H2:30 shows definite Egyptian characteristics, as does TS NS 119:43. They are probably to be dated *ca.* 900. The other mss show a formal type of square script similar to that typical in class 4. In TS 13H2:11+ and TS NS 249:11 the upper stroke of *lamed* is prolonged into the upper margin as it is in H.U.C. MS 1001+. These mss are probably to be dated *ca.* 800, with TS H16:12+ and TS 10H7:1 intermediate between the mss of this group and TS H2:30. Vocalization is typically sparse in mss of this class. TS H2:30 and TS H2:55 are rather exceptional in this respect.

CLASS 7

A	TS D1:12[59]	TS NS 249:12+
	TS H2:1, verso only	Bod. Heb. d63 f. 82–9+

[58] For example, in TS 13H2:11+, שׂ is used in 4 cases, ᶜ in 12 cases.

[59] Published in Weil, 1962.

TS H2:75
TS H6:39
TS H6:97
TS H16:1+[60] (II.7)
TS H16:3+
TS H2:2+
TS H16:2+
Mosseri P171/2[61]
TS H16:5[62]
Bod. Heb. d41 f. 11–15[63]
John Rylands Gaster
Geniza frags. 18, 21
Leningrad Ant. 222[64]

Members of this class use the vowel signs ⟨u⟩, ⟨o⟩, ⟨a⟩, ⟨a′⟩, ⟨e⟩, and ⟨i⟩ as follows:

B ÷ *shureq*

⟨u⟩ *passim.*

⟨o⟩ H2:75; H6:97; H16:1+; H16:3+; H16:5; Heb. d41 f. 11–15; 24 cases in all, in syllables of the following types: O′f, 5; O, 7; C′f, 2; C, 10, all before doubled consonants.

(On signs used where bA points conjunctive *waw* as *shureq*, see under *shewa*.)

C ÷ *ḥolem*

⟨o⟩ *passim.*

⟨u⟩ H2:75; H16:3+; Heb. d41 f. 11–15; 35 cases in all, in syllables of the following types: O′f, 10; O, 18; C′f, 7.

D, G ‘a’ vowels

	÷ *qameṣ*		÷ *pataḥ*	
	⟨a⟩	⟨a′⟩	⟨a⟩	⟨a′⟩
TS D1:12	3	1	1	8
TS H2:1v	48	14	15	40
TS H2:75	31	5	14	19
TS H6:39	5	8	3	4

[60] TS H16:1 was published in Edelmann, 1934, as MS F (see II.7).

[61] TS H16:3, H16:2, and Bod. Heb. d63 f. 82–9 were published in Kahle, 1927. TS H2:2 and Mosseri P171/2 were published in Zulay, 1939, pp. 113–18. Numbers in parentheses following references to these texts refer to the page and line of that edition. TS NS 249:12 (discovered by Dr. Dietrich) is not yet published.

[62] Published by Edelmann, 1934, as MS G. Numbers in parentheses after the references to this ms refer to the page and line of this edition.

[63] Folio 15v and 15r1–15 were published in Bar, 1936. The pointing of the remainder of this ms is unpublished. Numbers in parentheses after the references to this ms refer to the line numbering in Bar's edition.

[64] Published in Murtonen, 1958, as MS f.

TS H6:97	63	15	19	23
TS H16:1+	88	37	21	53
TS H16:3+[65]	183	51	62	70
TS H16:5	44	27	12	25
Bod. Heb. d41 f. 11–15	681	309	251	342
J.R.G.G. fr. 18	7	1	4	1
J.R.G.G. fr. 21	5	2	4	3
Leningrad Ant. 222	17	8	3	22

D *qameṣ*

⟨o⟩ Heb. d41 צוֹעקוּ, קמוּ (?) 14v25.

⟨e⟩ D1:12 r1:3, 12; Heb. d41 14r15, 15r33; Ant. 222 2v8.

E ≑ *qameṣ ḥaṭuf*

⟨o⟩ in all mss except D1:12, H2:1v, H6:39, J.R.G.G. fr. 18, Ant. 222. 68 cases in all.

⟨a⟩ H6:97, H16:3+, Heb. d41 f. 11–15, 13 cases in all.

⟨a′⟩ H2:1v, H16:1+, H16:3+, Heb. d41 f. 11–15, 12 cases in all (e.g. משכיני H2:1v5).

F ≑ *ḥaṭef qameṣ*

⟨a⟩ H2:1 קדשים v9, H16:3+, באניה Bod. Heb. d63 88r16 (Jonah 1:5).

⟨a′⟩ Heb. d41 בטהרה 15v24 (30).

G ≑ *pataḥ*

⟨e⟩ H6:39, 1r24; H16:3+; Heb. d63 82r4, 28, 84v24, 87v13, 88v15, 15, 16, 16; H16:5, 2r8 (31:21); Heb. d41 15r24, 12r29, 31, 14r18; Ant. 222 1r7, 2r4. Most of these cases occur before laryngeals.

H ≑ *ḥaṭef pataḥ*

⟨a′⟩ in all mss except D1:12, J.R.G.G. frags. 18, 21, 55 cases in all.

⟨a⟩ H2:1v, H2:75, H16:3+, H16:5, Heb. d41 f. 11–15, 65 cases in all.

⟨e⟩ H2:75, 1 case; H16:3+, 2 cases, all following initial laryngeals.

⟨e′⟩ H16:1+ 1 case (see II.7.D), H16:3+, Heb. d63 87r8 (see Kahle, 1927, p. 38*, note 1, but cf. ⟨e′⟩ ≑ *ṣere* below).

[65] These numbers refer only to TS H16:3, which was taken as a sample.

I ÷ *segol*

⟨e⟩ *passim.*

⟨a⟩ H16:3+, Heb. d63 83r15, Heb. d41 14r6, also כארלי, a correction at 15v25 (33) (probably a variant form; cf. the same pointing Bod. Heb. d55 10r5).

⟨a′⟩ Heb. d41 11r9, 13r27 (?).

⟨i⟩ H16:3+, Mosseri (p. 116, Ḥapiṣeṣ 5), Heb. d41 15v2 (3), 12r3, 14r31, all in נע/חטל forms, elsewhere *ibid.* 15r27.

J ÷ *ḥaṭef segol*

⟨e⟩ *passim.*

K ÷ *ṣere*

⟨e⟩ *passim.*

⟨a′⟩ H16:3+; הושיעני Heb. d63 82v13; Heb. d41 f. 11–15, 7 cases, all in C′f syllables, e.g. ריכב 15v33 (43).

⟨a⟩ H16:3+, Mosseri (p. 116, Ḥapiṣeṣ, 5), Heb. d41 11v29, 12v24 (?) (all in C′f), also יצא 15r25 (perf. for imperf.) and Ant. 222 1r15 (in C′f).

⟨i⟩ H16:3+; Heb. d41 f. 11–15; Ant. 222; 18 cases in syllables of the following types: O′f, 2; O, 12; C′f, 4. In addition there are in H16:3+ 3 cases of ירושלם (Heb. d63 82v10–12) which, according to Kahle (1927, Heb. p. 5, note 1) ÷ ־לֵם, but which could equally well ÷ ־לַם.

⟨e′⟩ Heb. d41 11r2 (?), 11v18. In H16:3+, H2:2 Zulay gives רווני (113:2) and מיניקותייך (114:8). In the former the dots are not made by pen (r2). In the latter I read ־מי (r14).

L ÷ *ḥireq*

⟨i⟩ *passim.*

⟨e⟩ in all mss except D1:12, H16:5, J.R.G.G. frags. 18, 21. 36 cases in syllables of the following types: O′, 2; O, 8, 6 of which precede laryngeals; C′f, 3; C, 23, 9 of which precede a doubled consonant and 3 of which occur in the 'diphthong' ־ַי (cf. IV.7.L).

⟨a⟩ Heb. d41 תחיית 15r20, 14r30,[66] and 3 other cases.

[66] See 5.L above and note 48, for related forms.

⟨a′⟩ Heb. d41 מֲנהגייך 15v5 (7), בתֲחיית 13r29,[67] פֲיו 15v15 (21) (÷ פְיו) (a mechanical pointing dependent on the customary pointing of the pronominal suffix form ־ָיו – with ⟨a′⟩, see Revell, 1970, I, no. 9).

M ÷ *shewa*

	⟨e⟩	⟨a′⟩	⟨a⟩	⟨e′⟩	⟨i⟩
TS D1:12	3	—	—	—	—
TS H2:1v	3	6	1	1 (?)	—
TS H2:75	2	—	—	—	—
TS H6:39	1	—	1	—	—
TS H6:97	—	—	1	—	—
TS H16:1+	6	7	1	—	—
TS H16:3+	7	many	27[68]	—	17
TS H16:5	—	2	2	—	—
Bod. Heb. d41 f. 11–15	7	95	54	1	2
J.R.G.G. fr. 18	—	1	—	—	—
J.R.G.G. fr. 21	2	—	—	—	—
Leningrad Ant. 222	4	3	1	—	1

The cases of ⟨i⟩ ÷ *shewa* occur before *yod* (16), or after it (4). However, in Heb. d41 f. 11–15, and Ant. 222, ⟨e⟩ is used where bA would have *shewa* before *yod*. A number of the cases of ⟨a⟩ and ⟨a′⟩ ÷ *shewa* in H16:3+ and Heb. d41 f. 11–15, and of ⟨a′⟩ in Ant. 222, correspond to bA 'silent' *shewa*. Where bA would point conjunctive *waw* as *shureq* ⟨e⟩ is used in Heb. d41 13v11, and ⟨a′⟩ in H16:3+ (e.g. H16:3 r12).

N The following diacritical signs are used:

- ש marks ⟨ś⟩ in H2:1v, H2:75, H16:1+, H16:3+, H16:5, and Heb. d41 f. 11–15.
- שׂ is also used to mark ⟨ś⟩ in H2:1v, H16:5, and Heb. d41 f. 11–15. The dot within the graph is presumably an addition later than the original pointing.[69]
- ש marks ⟨ś⟩, שׁ marks ⟨š⟩ in H6:39.

[67] See note 66.

[68] Eleven of these occur in the Mosseri fragment. Most of them could be due to the misplacing of a sign by the printer in Zulay's edition (I have not seen either the text itself or a photograph), but four (still a disproportionate number for this small fragment) could not be explained in this way.

[69] See Edelmann, 1934, p. 59.

ש̊ marks ⟨ś⟩, ש̬ marks ⟨š⟩ in Ant. 222.

ᴸ ≑ *dagesh forte* in H6:39, H6:97, H16:3+, H16:5, Heb. d41 f. 11–15, and Ant. 222.

≑ *dagesh lene* in H16:5,[70] Ant. 222 (including נעמתו 3r23 ?).

≑ *mappiq* in H2:1v, H16:3, and Heb. d41 f. 11–15.[71]

Marks *ʿayin* as closing a syllable, possibly רעננה H6:39, 1r18 (for the double writing, cf. II.6.E, and 9.N below).

Marks a graph as consonantal, as follows: *ʾalef*, Ant. 222, 3r8; *he*, H2:1, v26, H16:3+, H16:2 v18, Heb. d41 11r21; *ḥet* H16:1+, r22 (29:17, but see II.7.E); *waw* H16:3+ ועונתך H2:2 v6 (Zulay 115:8 reads ⟨a⟩).

ᴖ ≑ *rafe* H6:97 r8, Ant. 222 3r2, possibly הביאה H16:5 1v11 (cf. 31:9).

O Members of class 7 use only six vowel signs. ⟨a⟩ and ⟨a′⟩ are used for 'a' vowels, but their use bears no resemblance to the bA use of *qameṣ* and *pataḥ*. ⟨e⟩ is used where bA would use both *ṣere* and *segol*. ⟨e′⟩ does appear in several of the mss assigned to this class, but so rarely that it cannot be considered characteristic of the pointing system. In these cases it is very likely the work of a hand later than that of the original pointing. This is almost certainly the case (e.g., in Heb. d41 f. 11–15) where other additions can be traced (see note 71). It should be pointed out, however, that, save for the use of ⟨e′⟩, mss of class 7 are very similar to those of class 5. The use of ⟨e′⟩ is not common in some of the latter, so indecision about the classification of small texts is to be expected.

Members of class 7 usually use ⟨o⟩ where bA has *qameṣ ḥaṭuf*, but the use of ⟨a⟩ and ⟨a′⟩ is not uncommon. ⟨a⟩ and ⟨a′⟩ are also used where bA has *ḥaṭef qameṣ*, but ⟨o⟩ is not. Some members of this class do not normally use any vowel sign where bA has *shewa*, but in about half the mss a sign is frequently used, ⟨a′⟩ being the most common in this position. The use of ⟨i⟩ where

[70] משפטים 1v15, against Edelmann (31:11).

[71] This ms also occasionally marks *mappiq* in the Tiberian manner (e.g. f. 13r17). This is no doubt due to a second hand, probably that which inserted the few cases of ⟨e′⟩ ≑ *ṣere* and ש ≑ ⟨ś⟩ (see above). In תחישנה (Heb. d63 86r24) the sign is presumably an error caused by the *mappiq*s in forms nearby.

bA has *shewa* before *yod* is relatively uncommon in this class, and other signs are also used in that position.

The diacritics are of considerable interest in this group. ⟨ś⟩ is normally marked by שׂ. In only two mss is a circle above the graph used for this purpose. H6:97 is the only ms of any length which does not mark ⟨ś⟩. ⟨ś⟩ is marked relatively much more commonly than is *dagesh*, etc.[72] It is also noteworthy that a very high proportion of uses of ˪ indicate consonantal value in a graph which might otherwise be read as quiescent or as syllable final. I only have 18 cases listed for the whole class in which ˪ corresponds to *dagesh forte* or *lene*. The same sign is used with other values in 99 cases.

As regards the script and pointing, these mss form a remarkably homogeneous group with characteristics strongly similar to those of class 5. Nearly all of them use the neat, free Syrian square script of which H16:3+ is a typical example. They are mostly to be dated in the ninth century. H6:39 and Ant. 222 are divergent. In these texts the letters are larger, and not so freely written, or so neat. The individual forms also differ somewhat. They may, perhaps, represent an earlier type of the same script, to be dated *ca.* 800. TS D1:12 is perhaps intermediate between the two groups.[73]

The pointing in mss of this class is characteristically thoroughgoing. TS D1:12, TS H6:39, and Ant. 222 are exceptions here also. The form of ⟨a′⟩ in this class is typically a dot, only slightly elongated horizontally. The same three mss are again exceptions. The form of the '*dagesh*' sign ˪ is also characteristic, being a horizontal and a vertical stroke meeting at right angles. TS H6:39 and Ant. 222 are exceptions here too. TS D1:12 contains no examples.

CLASS 8

The pointing system of TS NS 249:14+ is, as far as I know, not found in any other ms.[74] Consequently it must be set up in a separate

[72] In H16:3+, ˪ ÷ *dagesh* is used so rarely that Kahle, having few mss for comparison, did not appear to recognize the significance of the sign in some cases. See Kahle, 1927, p. 11*, n. 6, and also Kahle, 1956, p. 41.

[73] This text is dated *ca.* 700 in Weil, 1962, p. 69. In my opinion it is somewhat later.

[74] Pointing of this type is now to be found in TS NS 301:63, a text closely similar

class of which it is the only member. Its most important feature is the use of ⟨a′⟩ almost solely where bA would use *shewa*. Otherwise ⟨a⟩ is used for 'a' vowels, and ⟨e⟩ for 'e' vowels.

The following characteristics would appear to be significant for comparison with other classes. ⟨o⟩ is most commonly used where bA would have *qameṣ ḥaṭuf*, but ⟨a⟩ is also used once in this position. ⟨i⟩ is used quite commonly where bA would have *shewa* before *yod*, and no other sign is used in this position. ⟨ś⟩ is marked by שׂ and ⟨š⟩ by שׁ. However, since this only occurs on the recto of TS NS 249:14, this could possibly be considered an addition, and not characteristic of the original pointing. The sign ◌ corresponds to bA *dagesh forte* in all its uses, if the two abnormal uses on *ṣade* are included. This sign is more common than the ⟨ś⟩ sign, being used 17 times, while ⟨ś⟩ is marked only 7 times. The script of this ms is similar to that of H.U.C. MS 1001+ (class 4) and TS 13H2:11+ (class 6). It is probably to be dated in the early ninth century.

CLASS 9

A TS H5:25[75] TS H7:44 TS NS 117:13
TS H7:1 TS 10H10:7 TS NS 249:14ᵃ+ (II.9)

Members of this class use the vowel signs ⟨u⟩, ⟨o⟩, ⟨a⟩, ⟨e⟩, and ⟨i⟩ in the following way:

B ≑ *shureq*

⟨u⟩ *passim.*

C ≑ *ḥolem*

⟨o⟩ *passim.*

D ≑ *qameṣ*

⟨a⟩ *passim.*

(⟨e⟩ NS 249:14ᵃ+; see II.9.D.)

---

in all respects to NS 249:14+. E.g. ⟨a′⟩ ≑ *shewa* in 5 cases, ≑ *pataḥ* only in על (v8). שׂ marks ⟨ś⟩ (v7). The only difference is the use of ⟨e⟩ where bA would have *pataḥ* in פסח (r5, 6), נעשה (v7), but this can be considered complementary to the use of ⟨a′⟩ where bA would have *segol* in NS 249:14+. The scripts of the two mss are similar, and TS NS 301:63 is also palimpsest over western Syriac.

[75] Published in Edelmann, 1934, as MS D_1. The assignment to class 9 is provisional as the pointing is so sparse (see chapter VI under TS H5:25).

E ≑ *qameṣ ḥaṭuf*

⟨o⟩ *passim.*

F ≑ *ḥaṭef qameṣ*

⟨a⟩ *passim.*

G ≑ *pataḥ*

⟨a⟩ *passim.*

H ≑ *ḥaṭef pataḥ*

⟨a⟩ NS 117:13, NS 249:14^{a}+.

(Also Tiberian *shewa*, NS 249:14^{a}+, see II.9.D.)

I ≑ *segol*

⟨e⟩ *passim.*

J ≑ *ḥaṭef segol*

⟨e⟩ 10H10:7.

K ≑ *ṣere*

⟨e⟩ *passim.*

⟨a⟩ NS 249:14^{a}+, NS 249:14 v33. C'f syllable.

L ≑ *ḥireq*

⟨i⟩ *passim.*

M ≑ *shewa*

⟨e⟩ 10H10:7.

⟨a⟩ 10H10:7, NS 249:14 r32.

(Also Tiberian *shewa* NS 249:14^{a}+, see II.9.D.)

N The following diacritical signs are used:

שׁ̊ marks ⟨ś⟩ in H7:1, H7:44.

שׂ marks ⟨ś⟩ in NS 249:14a+, where other Tiberian signs are used.

˂ ≑ *dagesh forte* in H5:25, H7:44, 10H10:7, and NS 249:14^{a}+. Note the double writing in גדייתי H7:44 r16. Cf. II.6.E and 7.N above.

Marks the consonantal value of *ḥet* in 10H10:7, לחבל 1v8. In לדורות NS 249:14 v32, the '*dagesh*' probably marks the presence of the definite article (see II.11.N).

O Members of this class use only five vowel signs. ⟨a⟩ represents all 'a' vowels, and ⟨e⟩ all 'e' vowels. ⟨o⟩ is used where bA would have *qameṣ ḥaṭuf*, ⟨a⟩ where bA would have *ḥaṭef qameṣ*. ⟨ś⟩, where it is marked, is indicated by signs other than שׂ. The '*dagesh*' sign ‹ is used relatively more commonly than is the marker of ⟨ś⟩. It is used mostly where bA would use *dagesh forte*.

The peculiar pointing of TS NS 249:14[a]+ fits this class, if the use of the Tiberian *śin* and *shewa* signs is ignored. This text has, in fact, been given as the 'type' example of this class, despite these irregularities. One reason for this is the fact that the only other ms with much pointing, TS 10H10:7, is largely written in Aramaic, and is therefore unsuitable, as this study is basically concerned with Hebrew grammar. Apart from this, however, and from the inherent interest of the pointing, this text is used here to show that some types of Tiberian pointing will fit these Palestinian classes, or classes very similar to them, a fact which should be of interest in the further study of the so-called ben Naftali mss and related types.

Most mss of this class show a rather formal type of script, often with Egyptian characteristics. TS NS 249:14[a]+ is a more cursive type and is much less neatly and carefully written than the other mss in this class, no doubt in part reflecting the awkwardness of writing in the lower margin of a book. Its script seems, however, to be of the same type as the others. The group is probably to be placed in the eighth and ninth centuries, with TS NS 117:13 as the earliest example and TS NS 249:14[a] as the latest. The pointing of most mss in this class is sparse. TS 10H10:7 and NS 249:14[a]+ have rather more pointing than most.

CLASS 10

A TS H6:29 TS NS 116:15b TS NS 117:7+ (II.10)

Members of this class use the vowel signs ⟨u⟩, ⟨o⟩, ⟨a⟩, ⟨e′⟩, and ⟨i⟩ in the following way:

B ≑ *shureq*

⟨u⟩ *passim*.

C ≑ *ḥolem*

⟨o⟩ *passim*.

D ÷ *qameṣ*

⟨a⟩ *passim.*

G ÷ *pataḥ*

⟨a⟩ *passim.*

I ÷ *segol*

⟨e′⟩ NS 117:7+.

K ÷ *ṣere*

⟨e′⟩ *passim.*

⟨a⟩ H6:29 r25 C′f syllable.

L ÷ *ḥireq*

⟨i⟩ *passim.*

M ÷ *shewa*

⟨a⟩ NS 117:7+, v64.

⟨e′⟩ NS 117:7+, v57 (and two other possible examples, see II.10.D).

N The following diacritical signs are used:

שׂ marks ⟨ś⟩ in NS 116:15b and NS 117:7+. Both mss also contain other Tiberian signs.

◌ֿ ÷ *rafe* NS 116:15b IV9.

O The main characteristic of this group is, then, the use of ⟨a⟩ for all 'a' vowels and ⟨e′⟩ for all 'e' vowels. None of the three mss assigned to this class provides a very good example of this usage, since their pointing is so sparse. For the same reason no other characteristic usage of this class can be distinguished. However, the fact that ⟨a′⟩ and ⟨e⟩ do not seem to be used seems sufficient reason for classing these mss together. The script of the mss supports this grouping. TS NS 116:15b and TS NS 117:7+ have the same type of formal square script. These two mss are probably to be assigned to the end of the ninth century. The script of H6:29 is somewhat similar, but closer to that of classes 5 and 7, and is therefore probably earlier. As has been noted, pointing is sparse in all three texts.

CLASS 11

A TS H2:29 (II.11) TS H2:61

Members of this class use the vowel signs ⟨u⟩, ⟨o⟩, ⟨a′⟩, ⟨e⟩, and ⟨i⟩ in the following way:

B ≑ *shureq*
⟨u⟩ *passim.*
⟨o⟩ H2:29 2r18.

C ≑ *ḥolem*
⟨o⟩ *passim.*
⟨u⟩ H2:61 3r22.

D ≑ *qameṣ*
⟨a′⟩ *passim.*
⟨e⟩ H2:61 הלבנה 3r21 (Isa. 24:23). The sign is possibly misplaced.

E ≑ *qameṣ ḥaṭuf*
⟨o⟩ H2:29 2v21.

F ≑ *ḥaṭef qameṣ*
⟨o⟩ H2:29 2r6.[76]

G ≑ *pataḥ*
⟨a′⟩ *passim.*

H ≑ *ḥaṭef pataḥ*
⟨a′⟩ H2:29.

I ≑ *segol*
⟨e⟩ *passim.*

J ≑ *ḥaṭef segol*
⟨e⟩ H2:29.

K ≑ *ṣere*
⟨e⟩ *passim.*

[76] The ⟨o⟩ here may not actually represent a '*shewa* vowel.' See note 39.

L ≑ *ḥireq*

⟨i⟩ *passim.*

⟨e⟩ H2:29 1r20, 2r28, 2v1.

M ≑ *shewa*

⟨e⟩ H2:61, 2 cases.

⟨a′⟩ H2:29, 13 cases.

⟨i⟩ H2:29, 5 cases before *yod*, 1 elsewhere (2r2).

N The following diacritical signs are used:

שׂ marks ⟨ś⟩ in H2:29.

שׂ marks ⟨ś⟩ in H2:61 (3r1).

Also

שׂ marks ⟨ś⟩ and שׁ marks ⟨š⟩ in H2:61. This ms has other Tiberian signs.

_<_ ≑ *dagesh* in H2:29, with some unusual uses (see II.11.E). Also *dagesh forte* in H2:61 3r19.

_>_ ≑ *rafe* in H2:29 (see II.11.E).

O The main characteristic of this class is the fact that all 'a' vowels are represented by ⟨a′⟩ and all 'e' vowels by ⟨e⟩. Apart from the fact that they share this characteristic, the two mss are dissimilar. H2:61 uses very few vowel points at all, whereas in H2:29, although the vocalization is not thoroughgoing, many more vowel signs are used. Consequently, while H2:29 can be taken as showing a complete vocalization system, there is some doubt as to whether H2:61 does show a complete system and should be assigned to this class.

Apart from the use of ⟨a′⟩ and ⟨e⟩, the following features of the pointing of H2:29 are noteworthy. ⟨o⟩ is the only sign used where bA would use *qameṣ ḥaṭuf*. The same sign is used where bA would have *ḥaṭef qameṣ* (but see note 76). Vowel signs are often used where bA would have *shewa*. ⟨a′⟩ is usually used in this position, but ⟨e⟩ also occurs. Some sign other than שׂ is used to mark ⟨ś⟩. The '*dagesh*' sign _<_ is used relatively much more frequently than is the sign marking ⟨ś⟩. The form of the '*rafe*' sign, _>_, is unique in this ms, as is frequent use of '*dagesh*' and '*rafe*' to indicate the presence or absence of the definite article (see II.11.E).

The two mss differ considerably in script. H2:29 is a freely written ms, although neat. It is remarkable among the carefully written Palestinian mss for its lack of line rulings, and consequent irregularity of its lines. It is probably to be dated to the late ninth century.[77] H2:61, on the other hand, is written in a stiff formal hand, somewhat similar to that of TS NS 117:7+. The script is characterized by ornamental prolongation of the upper stroke of *lamed* into the upper margin, and by the occasional horizontal prolongation of letters to fill a line (e.g. *kaf* 1r2–5, *taw* 5r5, *lamed* 3v11). It is perhaps a tenth century ms.

CLASS 12 (mixed classes)

The work of hands subsequent to that which produced the original vocalization has been noted in a number of the mss described above. In most cases where it can be discerned, such secondary vocalization seems to be designed to complement the original, not to change or correct it. This may be the case even where Tiberian signs are added to a Palestinian text, such as in H2:30 (see II.6.c). In many cases, for this reason, it is extremely difficult to distinguish completely between the original vocalization and the subsequent additions. Where such a difficulty exists, there does not appear to be any purpose in attempting such a distinction. The reading of the ms as it is can be said to give what is only a developed example of the class to which the first hand belonged. (Cf. the note on Heb. d55 12v–14v in IV.2.0 above.)

In some cases vocalization by a second hand includes changes in the pointing of the original hand. Where this is confined to a few signs, and is not sufficient to change the general character of the original vocalization, the classification of the ms presents no problem.[78] In a few cases, however, enough signs are added to confuse the

[77] This was my opinion from comparison with the other mss. However, a title (1r1), apparently in the same hand as the text, ascribes the poems to Yehuda Zebida, who may have lived a century or more later (see Schirmann, 1965, pp. 87f.). (Whether Yehuda Zebida actually wrote the poems or not is, of course, immaterial to the present point.) This text should, then, perhaps be dated *ca.* 1100, in which case the dates of many of the other texts must be correspondingly revised.

[78] For example, Heb. d41 f. 11–15. This is probably a class 7 ms to which a scribe of class 1 made a few additions (see note 71). These additions were, however, so few that they could not raise doubts as to the correct classification of the ms.

analysis of vowel usage. Such vocalization can be said to be 'mixed.' It sometimes can be definitely assigned to two classes.

TS H7:7 is an example of such a ms. The original hand was of class 5. This is shown by the frequent use of both ⟨a⟩ and ⟨a'⟩ where bA would have either *qameṣ* or *pataḥ*, the use of these two signs as well as ⟨o⟩ where bA would have *qameṣ ḥaṭuf*, the use of ש to mark ⟨ś⟩, and of _ to mark '*dagesh*,' the relative frequency of the marking of ⟨ś⟩, against the rarity of '*dagesh*,' the typical 'free Syrian' style of script, and the form of ⟨a'⟩, which is normally dotlike. All these features are characteristic of both class 5 and class 7, but the use of ⟨e'⟩ ≑ *shewa* in v24 suggests that the original hand of H7:7 was of class 5.

To this pointing of class 5, a second hand added a number of cases of ⟨e'⟩ ≑ *ṣere*. This was only done where the first hand had already used ⟨e⟩, and so produced a sign _. This second hand also marked ⟨ś⟩ as שׂ in several cases. This was done in some cases where the first hand had used its own diacritic ש, and in some cases where it had not. This second hand also made other additions and corrections, but only these two features can be assigned to a particular class. They suggest a hand of class 1, since the marking of ⟨ś⟩ and the use of ⟨e'⟩ only where bA would have *ṣere* are typical of that class. It is, however, somewhat difficult to explain why only a few cases of the first hand's ⟨e⟩ ≑ *ṣere* were corrected. It can be suggested that the correcting hand was not interested in making a thoroughgoing correction, but only in marking his preferred reading in a few places. This I believe to be the correct explanation.[79] If it does not seem acceptable, the correcting hand must be assigned to class 2, where its characteristic features are possible, but unusual.

[79] There are so many cases of the sporadic use of pointing in a few lines or pages of a text that the likelihood of this need not be argued.

IV

The Classification of Biblical Texts

The classification described in chapter III was derived solely from non-biblical mss. It can also, however, be applied to the pointing of biblical texts. These are treated separately here, because Palestinian biblical texts show certain characteristic differences in the use of vowel signs from non-biblical texts. Consequently the minor characteristics of the biblical texts in each class may differ slightly from those of the non-biblical. The characteristics on which the classification is based are, however, the same for both.

The classification in this chapter comprehends all biblical texts with Palestinian vocalization known to me. Most of the material has been published before. In many of the original descriptions of these texts, however, the analysis of the vocalization system is not sufficiently detailed for the present purpose. Consequently I have given for each class a schematic description of the use of vowel signs as compared to that of bA, as was done for the non-biblical texts in chapter III.

CLASS 1

A *TS 2nd 1:44[1] (Num. 32:41 to Deut. 1:22)
    Bod. Heb. e30 f. 48–9+[2]
        Bod. Heb. e30 f. 48–9 (Isa. 5:8–9:8, 44:4–48:11)

[1] Published in Dietrich, 1960, as MS Cb 4.

[2] Bod. Heb. e30 f. 48–9, and TS A43:1 were published in Kahle, 1901, and as MS M in Kahle, 1930 (see p. 88, where a detailed list is given). The other Taylor-Schechter fragments were published in Dietrich, 1960, as MS Cb 1, save TS NS 301:29, which is not published.

TS A43:1 (Exod. 28:29–29:39, Isa. 10:9–13:20, 53:4–59:8, 59:10–64:4, Jer. 23:23–29:31)
TS K25:108 (Lev. 13:25–14:27)
TS NS 249:5 (Ezek. 31:4–36:7)
TS NS 249:9 (Isa. 42:8–12, 43:4–9)
TS NS 301:29 (Isa. 41:10–19, 43:22–44:3)
J.T.S. MS 504 f. 2+[3] (Jer. 48:44–49:30)

Members of this class use the vowel signs ⟨u⟩, ⟨o⟩, ⟨a⟩, ⟨a′⟩, ⟨e⟩, ⟨e′⟩, and ⟨i⟩ in the following way:

B ≑ *shureq*

⟨u⟩ *passim*, including a situation in which bA points conjunctive *waw* as *shureq*, Heb. e30 f. 48–9+, Ezek. 35:7 (a second hand).

⟨o⟩ Heb. e30 f. 48–9+, Ezek. 34:5.

C ≑ *ḥolem*

⟨o⟩ *passim*.

⟨a⟩ Heb. e30 f. 48–9+, Ezek. 34:18, 36:25.

(⟨a′⟩ J.T.S. MS 504 f. 2+, a variant, see under ⟨a′⟩ ≑ *ṣere*.)

D ≑ *qameṣ*

⟨a⟩ *passim*.

⟨a′⟩ Heb. e30 f. 48–9+, Isa. 6:6, 10:14, 59:15, Jer. 25:24, Ezek. 32:13, 35:10.

(⟨e⟩ *ibid*., (ה)נחלמ(י) Jer. 29:24, 31, variant.)

E ≑ *qameṣ ḥaṭuf*

⟨a⟩ *passim* (101 cases).

⟨o⟩ Heb. e30 f. 48–9+, (מ)ב(צרה) Isa. 63:1.

F ≑ *ḥaṭef qameṣ*

⟨a⟩ *passim* (7 cases, cf. also ⟨a⟩ ≑ *shewa*).

G ≑ *pataḥ*

⟨a′⟩ *passim*.

⟨a⟩ Heb. e30 f. 48–9+, Isa. 10:9, 44:4, 63:18.

⟨e⟩ *ibid*. ((מ(ר)חק(י Isa. 8:9 2nd hand), (ת)בק(ע) Isa. 59:5.

[3] Folio 2 of this ms was published, and fols. 7 and 8 described, in Díez-Macho, 1954, pp. 253–60. Information on other parts of the same ms is given in Yeivin, 1963, pp. 124–7.

H ∸ *ḥaṭef pataḥ*

⟨a′⟩ *passim.*

⟨e⟩ Heb. e30 f. 48–9+, א(חיש)נ(ה) Isa. 60:22, י(ר)דפ(ך) Ezek. 35:6.[4]

I ∸ *segol*

⟨e⟩ *passim.*

⟨e′⟩ Heb. e30 f. 48–9+, Isa. 8:5, 14, 43:24, 25, 45:24, 56:7, 7, (57:1 2nd hand), 58:9, Ezek. 34:14, 36:11.

⟨i⟩ *ibid.* ת(הגה) Isa. 59:3.

⟨a′⟩ *ibid.* (וכ)פ(ר) Lev. 14:20, J.T.S. MS 504 f. 2+, ונדחתם (?) Jer. 49:5.

J ∸ *ḥaṭef segol*

⟨e⟩ *passim.*

(Also ⟨a⟩ in a variant form; see under ⟨e⟩ ∸ *qameṣ*.)

K ∸ *ṣere*

⟨e′⟩ *passim.*

⟨e⟩ Heb. e30 f. 48–9+, Isa. 60:16, Jer. 29:14.

⟨a′⟩ *ibid.* מפר Isa. 44:25. Also J.T.S. MS 504 f. 2+, ויפרש Jer. 49:22, which must be a *pi‘el* form for bA *qal*.[5]

L ∸ *ḥireq*

⟨i⟩ *passim.*

⟨e⟩ Heb. e30 f. 48–9+, כלי(ון) Isa. 10:22, ת(תה)ל(ל) Isa. 41:16.

⟨e′⟩ *ibid.* ל(י) Ezek. 35:10.

(⟨a⟩ *ibid.* Isa. 57:8, presumably *qal* for bA *pi‘el*.)

M ∸ *shewa*

⟨e⟩ *passim.*

⟨a′⟩ Heb. e30 f. 48–9+, before bA *’alef* or *‘ayin* followed by *pataḥ* Isa. 5:11, 48:3, 57:18, 59:18, 63:5, Ezek. 33:13 (against Dietrich, 1968, p. 40, n. 3). Also in probable variant forms, Jer. 24:6 (with article), 29:31 (*pi‘el* for *qal*).

[4] In the first of these instances, the colour of the vowel may be affected by the 'i' vowel following the laryngeal (see Revell, 1970, II, nos. 11, 12). In the second, ⟨e⟩ no doubt represents a simple *shewa* sound (see *ibid.*, I, no. 36).

[5] According to Díez-Macho, 1954, p. 260, the form intended was perfect *qal*, but there is no indication that the *yod* was to be omitted.

⟨a⟩ *ibid.*, before bA *ʿayin* or *ḥet* followed by *qameṣ ḥaṭuf*, Jer. 25:6, 11. (Also in a variant form in J.T.S. MS 504 f. 2+; see under ⟨a′⟩ ∻ *ṣere*.)

⟨o⟩ Heb. e30 f. 48–9+, before bA *ʾalef* followed by *ḥolem*, Isa. 10:13.

⟨e′⟩ *ibid.*, (ו)ד֗(ברי) Isa. 59:21.

⟨i⟩ Before *yod*, *passim*.

After *yod*, Heb. e30 f. 48–9+, (ו)י֗(מה)ר(ו) Isa. 59:7, also, in the same situation, Isa. 60:20.[6] *Shewa* is used in this position in the Worms *Maḥzor*, which has pointing of the so-called ben Naftali type (see Bét-Aryé, 1965, p. 40). Presumably the use of ⟨i⟩ here indicates a pronunciation {wiyĭmahărū} for bA {wīmahărū}. Consequently the *shewa* used in the Worms *Maḥzor* is to be taken as a vowel sign (as in that position it would represent a short 'i' vowel) and not merely a peculiarity of the writing system, as Bét-Aryé suggests it might be. Cf. the use of ⟨e⟩ in this position in TS 16:96 (see 3.M below). Forms which could be interpreted in this way occur in many mss, but the intention of the vocalizer is usually not clear, since -וי֗ could represent {wiyĭ-} or {wī-}. In the above cases, however, it is certain that the vowel must follow the *yod*. Other examples of ⟨i⟩ ∻ *shewa* after *yod* are noted in III.2.M, 6.M, 7.M and in 3.M and 7.M below.

N The following diacritical signs are used:

שׁ marks ⟨ś⟩ in Heb. e30 f. 48–9+. According to Kahle, 1930, p. 32*, שׁ is used to mark ⟨š⟩ in the same ms, but it seems more probable to me that in all cases the dot in question is an accent sign *(tifḥa)*.

_ᶜ_ ∻ *dagesh forte* and *dagesh lene* in Heb. e30 f. 48–9+.

The same sign is also used in the following situations:

(i) Where one word ends, and the next begins, with *lamed* (Isa. 57:11) or *mem* (Isa. 46:12, Ezek. 32:10) on the second of the two consonants (see Ginsburg, 1897, pp. 116f.).

[6] יסת Isa. 54:11 presumably indicates *piʿel* for bA *qal* (cf. BH^3).

(ii) Equivalent to *dagesh forte* 'conjunctive': Isa. 44:24, 47:9, 54:12, 58:3, Ezek. 33:5 (?), 34:14, 20. All as BH³ save Ezek. 33:5, 34:20.

(iii) On a consonant following *he* (?), *ḥet*, or *'ayin* which closes a syllable; 10 cases in all. E.g. (נח)שׁ(בו) Isa. 5:28, (ה(ע)מ(ק Isa. 7:11. *He* only נֶהֱמֶה Isa. 59:11. The second ⟨e⟩ could indicate a dual reading, but cf. Morag, 1959, p. 224 (e). This ms is unique in that it uses the sign in this way on a consonant following word-final *'ayin* in (ז(רע) ק(דש Isa. 6:13, and (ו)מ(ש)ק(ע)־מ(ים) Ezek. 34:18.

(iv) On *'alef*, *he*, and *'ayin*, to indicate consonantal value; 13 cases. E.g. Isa. 6:11, Jer. 25:19, Ezek. 34:21.

_ᐢ_ ÷ *rafe* in Heb. e30 f. 48–9+, marking the absence of *dagesh forte* and *dagesh lene*.[7]

The same sign is also used in the following situations:

(i) On consonantal *yod*, (והאל)י(ה) Exod. 29:22, (מ(מע)י(נ)(י Isa. 12:3.[8]

(ii) On a consonant following *ḥet* or *'ayin* which does not close a syllable (cf. *dagesh* (iii)). E.g. פעמן Exod. 28:34, (א(ח)ש(ה Isa. 62:1. Also Isa. 44:12, 57:16, 62:6.

(iii) On non-consonantal *'alef* and *he* (cf. *dagesh* (iv)). E.g. (ול)אמ(ר) Isa. 44:28, and on final *he* Isa. 5:19. This is the traditional explanation of this usage. The uses on intervocalic *'alef* in (ו)בא(ו) (Isa. 45:20) and (ו)בא(ו)י (Jer. 27:22) suggest, however, that א and א may mark something other than the normally accepted glottal stop and zero. The sign _ᐢ_ marks consonantal *yod* in this ms (see above), and other graphs which must have consonantal value in some mss of class 2 (non-biblical, see III.2.N) and class 3 (biblical, see 3.N below). These mss do not otherwise deviate widely from normal Palestinian con-

[7] I cannot explain the use of this sign in (ח) מִשְׁל Isa. 11:14.

[8] In a number of other possible instances, the sign could be interpreted as marking the absence of *dagesh forte*. *Rafe* is used to mark consonantal *waw* and *yod* in some mss of the 'Tibero-Palestinian' (so-called ben Naftali) type. See, for example, Morag, 1959, pp. 219f. and Bét-Aryé, 1965, p. 44. Cf. also David Qimḥi's statement that, whereas other consonants may be 'soft' *(qal)* or 'hard' *(ḥazaq)* according to their position in the word, *yod* is always 'soft,' except where it has *dagesh (forte)* (*Miklol*, Lyk ed., p. 140).

ventions. It seems possible, then, that אᶜ and אᶰ indicate different types of consonantal value (perhaps glottal stop and some postvocalic glide) rather than consonantal value and lack of it.

The Tiberian form of *mappiq* is used consistently in Heb. e30 f. 48–9+ to show that final *he* has consonantal value.

⟨o⟩ is used to indicate that *waw* has consonantal value in J.T.S. MS 504 f. 2+, Jer. 49:16.[9]

O The mss of this group resemble the non-biblical mss of class 1 in that the four 'a' and 'e' signs are used almost exactly as are those of bA, with the exception that ⟨e⟩ is used where bA uses both *segol* and *shewa*. As in those mss, both ⟨a⟩ and ⟨o⟩ are used where bA has *qameṣ ḥaṭuf*, but the proportion of uses of ⟨a⟩ to ⟨o⟩ is much greater among biblical than among non-biblical mss. Nearly all our information on biblical mss of this class, however, comes from Heb. e30 f. 48–9+. It is possible that the preponderant use of ⟨a⟩ in this position is characteristic of this ms, but not the class as a whole, but this cannot be decided without further information.[10]

A feature of particular interest in Heb. e30 f. 48–9+ is the use of vowel signs before laryngeals where bA has *shewa*. The vowel sign used in this position is the same as would be expected after the laryngeal, i.e. this ms demonstrates the situation described by the early grammarians, that a '*shewa* vowel' before a laryngeal had the colour of the vowel following the laryngeal.[11] Among the non-biblical mss, only Heb. d55 f. 12v–14v indicates the pronunciation of '*shewa* vowels' in similar detail (see III.2.M). Similar usage is found in biblical mss in class 3 (see 3.M below). Again it is impossible to tell whether such detail was normally shown in biblical members of class 1, or whether it is peculiar to this ms.

[9] It is possible that the Palestinian scribe intended, by adding a dot above the Babylonian _̈_ sign, to create an 'e' sign (cf. Díez-Macho, 1954, p. 260). However. the use of ⟨o⟩ to indicate consonantal *waw* is well attested in Palestinian biblical mss. See classes 2, 3, and 7.

[10] One can now study TS NS 246:22, a ms of this class with full text and much pointing, published in Díez-Macho, 1967. In this text only ⟨a⟩ is used where bA has *qameṣ ḥaṭuf* (II Chron. 14:14, 15:4). The pointing of the text is in other respects characteristic of the class: slight interchange of ⟨a⟩ and ⟨a′⟩, and of ⟨e⟩ and ⟨e′⟩, ⟨e⟩ ≑ *shewa*, _ᶰ_ marks medial *'alef* as not closing a syllable (II Chron. 13:18; cf. _ᶰ_ (ii) in I.N above).

[11] See Revell, 1970, II, nos. 11, 12. This usage is not, however, consistent.

It should be noted for the biblical texts of class 1, as it was for the non-biblical, that their vocalization is in no sense a copy of bA. The influence of that system is a possible source for a number of features, but other features far outweigh these. The vowel signs are typically Palestinian, so are the diacritics (except for *mappiq*),[12] and also the accent signs. The use of a single sign to mark most '*shewa* vowels' might seem to suggest bA or other Tiberian influence, but the fact that the sign used, ⟨e⟩, also marks a particular vowel quality is a typical Palestinian characteristic. A few other features, such as the pointing of '*shewa* vowels' before laryngeals, are not typical of Palestinian mss, but were certainly not derived from bA. Non-biblical mss of classes 2, 4, and 6 show that the use of ⟨a⟩ and ⟨a'⟩ as bA uses *qameṣ* and *pataḥ* is characteristic of some groups of typically Palestinian mss. I see no reason to suppose that the use of ⟨e⟩ and ⟨e'⟩ as bA uses *segol* and *ṣere* might not be equally characteristic of the Palestinian dialect. Consequently I feel that the use of ⟨a⟩ where bA has *qameṣ ḥaṭuf* is the only feature characteristic of class 1 which is really likely to derive from the influence of bA.

CLASS 2

A TS NS 249:6+[13]
  TS NS 249:6 (I Chron. 2:25–3:5, 5:23–6:33)
  TS NS 172:11 (I Chron. 3:16–5:22)
Bod. Heb. d44 f. 1–4+[14]
  Heb. d44 f. 1–4 (I Kings 16:31 to II Kings 8:5)
  Heb. d37 f. 38–9 (Isa. 32:14–37:24, 54:10–58:7)
  TS K26:8 (II Kings 8:5–10:1)
J.T.S. MS 594, box b, env. 12[15]

Members of this class use the vowel signs ⟨u⟩, ⟨o⟩, ⟨a⟩, ⟨a'⟩, ⟨e⟩, ⟨e'⟩, and ⟨i⟩ as follows:

[12] But note that the Tiberian form is probably confined to biblical mss. Cf. III.1.N.
[13] TS NS 249:6 is published in Dietrich, 1960, as MS Cb 9. I hope to publish NS 172:11 shortly.
[14] Published in Dietrich, 1960, as MS Ob 2/Cb 3.
[15] Published in Kahle, 1959, pp. 338–44 and plates 5–6.

B ≑ *shureq*

⟨u⟩ *passim*, including situations in which bA would point conjunctive *waw* as *shureq* in NS 249:6+.

⟨o⟩ J.T.S. 594, Eccles. 12:3.

C ≑ *ḥolem*

⟨o⟩ *passim*.

D ≑ *qameṣ*

⟨a⟩ *passim*.

⟨a′⟩ NS 249:6+, I Chron. 2:30, 37, 4:22, 5:21, 30; J.T.S. 594 *(pataḥ)*, Eccles. 11:6.

E ≑ *qameṣ ḥaṭuf*

⟨a⟩ in all mss.

F ≑ *ḥaṭef qameṣ*

⟨o⟩ Heb. d44 f. 1–4+, מחלי II Kings 8:8.[16]

G ≑ *pataḥ*

⟨a′⟩ *passim*.

⟨a⟩ Heb. d44 f. 1–4+, II Kings 6:26,[17] 8:16, 9:29, Isa. 33:20; NS 249:6+, I Chron. 4:19, 21, 5:20; J.T.S. 594, Lam. 1:11, 12.

H ≑ *ḥaṭef pataḥ*

⟨a′⟩ NS 249:6+; J.T.S. 594 *(pataḥ)*.

⟨a⟩ Heb. d44 f. 1–4, I Kings 21:29.

I, K 'e' vowels

	≑ *segol*		≑ *ṣere*	
	⟨e⟩	⟨e′⟩	⟨e⟩	⟨e′⟩
TS NS 249:6+	28	1	10	20
Bod. Heb. d44 f. 1–4+	4	4	—	16
J.T.S. MS 594	24	2	6	12

J ≑ *ḥaṭef segol*

⟨e⟩ NS 249:6+, I Chron. 5:24 (against Dietrich); J.T.S. 594, Lam. 1:4.

[16] The ⟨o⟩ here probably does not represent a '*shewa* vowel'; see note 39 to III.4.F.
[17] So Dietrich, 1968, p. 31.

K ≑ *ṣere*

⟨i⟩ NS 249:6+, ו(יבי)אׄ(ם) I Chron. 5:26.

L ≑ *ḥireq*

⟨i⟩ *passim.*

M ≑ *shewa*

	⟨e⟩	⟨a⟩	⟨a′⟩	⟨e′⟩	⟨i⟩
TS NS 249:6+	6	2	1	1	12
Bod. Heb. d44 f. 1–4+	2	—	—	—	2
J.T.S. MS 594	3	—	—	—	6

Of the cases of ⟨a⟩ ≑ *shewa*, one is used on conjunctive *waw* (I Chron. 4:34) and one before bA *yod* followed by *qameṣ* (I Chron. 2:28).[18] The case of ⟨e′⟩ ≑ *shewa* occurs at I Chron. 6:16, ⟨a′⟩ at I Chron. 5:17 (see below). All cases of ⟨i⟩ ≑ *shewa* occur before *yod*. In NS 249:6+, an example at I Chron. 5:24 precedes bA *yod* followed by *pataḥ*, thus contrasting with the use of ⟨a′⟩ noted above.

N The following diacritical signs are used:

שׁ̊ and שׂ mark ⟨ś⟩ in NS 249:6+ (I Chron. 4:36, 6:25).

_<_ ≑ *dagesh forte* in all mss.

≑ *dagesh lene* in Heb. d44 f. 1–4+, NS 249:6+.

≑ *dagesh forte* 'conjunctive' J.T.S. MS 594, Lam. 1:4.

Marks *ḥet* as consonantal, J.T.S. MS 594, Lam. 1:2; *'ayin* NS 249:6+, I Chron. 2:35.

The use on הבכור NS 249:6+, I Chron. 3:1 seems inexplicable, unless it marks the same feature as bA *legarmeh* (cf. 3.N below). In J.T.S. MS 594 לנדה (Lam. 1:8) is a variant (cf. BH³).

In NS 249:6+, I Chron. 5:17, חשׁו for הִתְיַחְשׂוּ, ⟨a′⟩ is probably equivalent to bA *ḥaṭef pataḥ*, and _<_ marks the *ḥet* as closing a syllable, thus showing an alternative reading.

_^_ ≑ *rafe* in NS 249:6+.

Marks *'alef* as 'quiescent' in NS 249:6+, I Chron. 5:20, 25; Heb. d44 f. 1–4, II Kings 2:21.

[18] See 3.M below, under ⟨a⟩, also III.5.L, and note 48 there, for related forms. ⟨a⟩ on conjunctive *waw* marked by Dietrich at I Chron. 2:28 is an ⟨i⟩ sign, as is probable for the case at I Chron. 4:34 also.

Indicates that *yod* has a consonantal value NS 249:6+, I Chron. 4:16.

⟨o⟩ is used to indicate that *waw* has a consonantal value in Heb. d44 f. 1–4+, וישתחוו II Kings 2:15.[19]

o In this group of mss then, ⟨a⟩ and ⟨a′⟩ are used almost exactly as are bA *qameṣ* and *pataḥ*, while the use of ⟨e⟩ and ⟨e′⟩ bears no resemblance to the bA use of *segol* and *ṣere*. Indication of '*shewa* vowels' is rare. ⟨ś⟩ is marked only rarely. One method of its marking is typical of class 1, so even this case may be secondary. _˂_ '*dagesh*' and _ˆ_ '*rafe*' are quite widely used, the use of '*dagesh*' being relatively much more common than the marking of ⟨ś⟩. All these features are typical of the non-biblical mss of class 2. The use of ⟨o⟩ ≑ *ḥaṭef qameṣ* is unusual in this or any other class. Palestinian mss normally use ⟨a⟩ in this position. I take the use of ⟨o⟩ here to indicate that a '*shewa* vowel' was not used in this situation. (See note 16.)

J.T.S. MS 594 is atypical in a number of ways, chiefly in its use of 'a' signs. ⟨a⟩ is used almost exclusively where bA has *qameṣ*. Where bA has *pataḥ*, this ms also appears to use the *pataḥ* sign, but the use of this sign is relatively rare. Several possible examples of the use of the ⟨a′⟩ sign for an 'a' vowel do occur, but these probably all represent the accent *rebiaʿ*, not a vowel. In my opinion this is certainly the case in בשוליה Lam. 1:9, despite Murtonen's note in Kahle, 1959, p. 338, and also with עוד in Eccles. 12:9 (cf. Díez-Macho, 1957, p. 28). The _-_ sign in ותשב Lam. 1:8, which Díez-Macho also lists there as a vowel sign, is considered by Kahle and Murtonen to be a Tiberian *rafe* sign (Kahle, 1959, pp. 338, 343). It is unlikely to be a vowel sign in view of the use of ⟨a⟩ over the *śin*.

CLASS 3

A TS 12:195+[20]

TS 12:195 (Pss. 51:21–53:6, 54:9–55:18)

[19] Dietrich, 1968, p. 31 understands this as ⟨o⟩ ≑ *shureq*. There is, however, no other example of ⟨o⟩ ≑ *shureq* in an open, stressed, final syllable in a biblical text, although examples do occur in non-biblical texts. Similar examples of ⟨o⟩ indicating that *waw* has consonantal value are to be found in classes 1, 3, and 7.

[20] TS 12:195 and 12:196 were published in Kahle, 1930, as MS L. TS NS 249:3 was published in Dietrich, 1960, as MS Cb 8.

TS 12:196 (Pss. 69:21–71:3, 71:5–72:4)
TS NS 249:3 (Pss. 74:11–77:21)

TS 16:96+[21]

TS 16:96 (Dan. 9:24–12:13)
TS NS 208:23
TS NS 301:75 (Dan. 7:4–6, 10–14, 20–25, 8:3–6)

TS 20:53+[22]

TS 20:53 (Pss. 26:11–33:1)
TS 20:52 (Pss. 52:5–62:4)
TS 20:54 (Pss. 35:17–40:13)
TS 20:58 (Pss. 41:5–46:11)

TS 20:59+[23]

TS 20:59 (Ezek. 13:11–16:31)
*TS 2nd 1:125 (Ezek. 1:3–2:6)

TS NS 249:8+[24]

*TS NS 249:8 (Judg. 6:2–8:24)
TS NS 281:2 (Judg. 8:30–9:48)

Members of this class use the vowel signs ⟨u⟩, ⟨o⟩, ⟨a⟩, ⟨a′⟩, ⟨e⟩, ⟨e′⟩, and ⟨i⟩ in the following way:

B ≑ *shureq*

⟨u⟩ *passim*, except in TS 20:53+. Note also that TS 12:195+ uses an allograph ֻּ, not the normal sign ֻ. Conjunctive *waw* is vocalized with ⟨u⟩ in situations where bA would use *shureq* in TS 16:96+, and TS NS 249:8+. For the signs used in the other mss in these situations, see under *shewa*.

⟨o⟩ TS 20:53+ uses ⟨o⟩ in all cases in which bA uses *shureq*. TS 16:96+, TS 20:59+, and TS NS 249:8+ use ⟨o⟩ ≑ *shureq* in a total of 11 cases in syllables of the following types: C′f, 4

[21] TS 16:96 was published in Kahle, 1930, as MS J. TS NS 208:23 and 301:75 are not yet published. The Aramaic parts are not considered here.

[22] The four fragments of TS 20:53+ were published as parts of a single ms (MS c) in Murtonen, 1958. They were independently published as parts of two mss in Allony and Díez-Macho, 1958a and 1958b. They are here treated as parts of the same ms for reasons stated under TS 20:53+ in chapter VI.

[23] TS 20:59 was published in Kahle, 1930, as MS H. *TS 2nd 1:125 was published in Dietrich, 1960, as MS Cb 5.

[24] TS NS 249:8 was published in Dietrich, 1960, as MS Cb 10. TS NS 281:2 was published in Díez-Macho, 1963a.

(all זבֻּל); C, 3, all before a doubled consonant; O, 4, of which 2 precede a laryngeal.

⟨i⟩ TS 20:59+, Ezek. 16:4.

C ≑ *ḥolem*

⟨o⟩ *passim.*

⟨a⟩ TS 20:53+, Ps. 39:12, a variant (pl.); TS 20:59+, Ezek. 13:20.

⟨e⟩ TS 20:53+, Ps. 58:8, probably a miswritten ⟨o⟩ sign.

D, G 'a' vowels

	≑ *qameṣ*		≑ *pataḥ*	
	⟨a⟩	⟨a′⟩	⟨a⟩	⟨a′⟩
TS 12:195+	216	21	90	77
TS 16:96+	140	13	89	26
TS 20:53+	66	147	7	114
TS 20:59+	many	1	many	3
TS NS 249:8+	9	1	3	2

D ≑ *qameṣ*

⟨e⟩ TS 12:195+, Ps. 69:28; TS 20:53+, Ps. 39:14; TS 20:59+, Ezek. 16:16; all in O syllables. In addition in TS 16:96+, there are 5 cases of ֶה ≑ ָה as the final syllable of a noun, and also לך for לְךָ Dan. 10:19. All are presumably variant forms.

⟨e′⟩ TS 20:59+, Ezek. 14:6, in O syllable.

E ≑ *qameṣ ḥaṭuf*

⟨o⟩ TS 12:195+, TS 20:53+, and TS 20:59+, 19 cases in all.

⟨a⟩ TS 12:195+, TS 16:96+, and TS 249:8+, 10 cases in all.

⟨a′⟩ TS 12:195+, וצהרים Ps. 55:18; TS 16:96+, אהלי Dan. 11:45.

F ≑ *ḥaṭef qameṣ*

⟨a′⟩ TS 16:96+, אהלי Dan. 11:45.

G ≑ *pataḥ*

⟨e⟩ TS 12:195+, Ps. 71:10, TS 20:59+, Ezek. 16:13; both before laryngeals.

⟨i⟩ TS 12:195+, 2 cases; TS 20:53+, 1 case; TS 20:59+, 6 cases; mostly unique forms probably produced by deterioration of an original ⟨a⟩ sign, or misplacing of signs. However, in TS 20:59, מׄלבושך Ezek. 16:13, and תׄרבי Ezek. 16:25, 26, 29, may have some significance.

H ≑ *ḥaṭef pataḥ*

⟨a′⟩ 24 cases in all mss except TS NS 249:8+.

⟨a⟩ 16 cases in all mss except TS NS 249:8+ and TS 20:53+.

⟨e⟩ TS 12:195+, 7 cases; TS 16:96+, 1 case; all over initial laryngeals.

⟨u⟩ TS 16:96+ יתבררו Dan. 12:10 might be a case of a '*shewa* vowel' harmonizing with the quality of the following vowel but is more probably a sign misplaced and corrected.

I, K 'e' vowels

	≑ *segol*		≑ *ṣere*	
	⟨e⟩	⟨e′⟩	⟨e⟩	⟨e′⟩
TS 12:195+	78	32	80	21
TS 16:96+	all	—	many	3
TS 20:53+	42	28	40	31
TS 20:59+	18	18	13	53
TS NS 249:8+	7	1	2	5

I ≑ *segol*

⟨a′⟩ TS 16:96+, Dan. 10:8; TS 20:53+, Pss. 38:2, 39:6, 12, 12.

⟨a⟩ TS 12:195+, אוֹן Ps. 55:4, 11; TS 16:96+, הדר Dan. 11:20; עמך Dan. 12:1; all probably variants.

⟨i⟩ TS 20:53+, Ps. 39:6; TS 20:59+, Ezek. 13:20.

⟨o⟩ TS 20:53+, העלית Ps. 30:4, presumably ⟨e⟩ corrected to ⟨e′⟩ (or vice versa).

⟨u⟩ TS 12:195+, לפניהם Ps. 69:23, presumably also a corrected 'e' sign.

J ≑ *ḥaṭef segol*

⟨e⟩ *passim.*

⟨e′⟩ TS 12:195+, ואהמיה Ps. 77:4. Cf. the use of ⟨e′⟩ ≑ *segol* noted in III.4.I, and the reference there.

K ≑ *ṣere*

⟨a′⟩ TS 20:53+, Ps. 39:11, in a C′f syllable.

⟨a⟩ TS 16:96+, Dan. 11:36, 12:7; TS 20:53+, Ps. 39:5; TS 20:59+, Ezek. 14:3; 3 in C′f syllables, one in O.

⟨o⟩ TS 20:53+, קדש Ps. 29:8; either a corrected 'e' sign (cf. ⟨o⟩ ≑ *segol*) or a variant.

L ≑ *ḥireq*

⟨i⟩ *passim.*

⟨e⟩ 8 cases in all mss except TS NS 249:8+ in the following types of syllables: O′, 1; C′f, 1; C, 6.

⟨e′⟩ TS 20:53+, Pss. 30:8 (variant), 10, 39:4, 7; TS 20:59+, Ezek. 16:11.

⟨a′⟩ TS 20:53+, Pss. 32:4 (variant), 37:23, 38:3 (variant?), 61:4; 2 of these cases vocalize the *mem* prefix of a noun form.

⟨a⟩ TS 16:96+, בשבי, Dan. 11:33, a variant using the article; cf. the following ובביזה.

M ≑ *shewa*

The following vowel signs are used (the question mark indicates that one case, or more, is uncertain):

	⟨e⟩	⟨e′⟩	⟨a⟩	⟨a′⟩	⟨i⟩	⟨o⟩	⟨u⟩
TS 12:195+	80	2	5	2	11?	2	2?
TS 16:96+	45	11	10	4	3	1	—
TS 20:53+	44	10	1	6	4?	—	—
TS 20:59+	16	—	2	1	1	—	—
TS NS 249:8+	—	—	—	—	—	—	—

The following uses should be noted:

⟨u⟩ TS 12:195+, יסבבה Ps. 55:11 is probably a misplaced sign. וישתו Ps. 75:9 may be a corrected 'e' sign (cf. ⟨u⟩ ≑ *segol*).

⟨o⟩ TS 12:195+, before bA *'alef* and *ḥet* followed by *ḥolem*, Pss. 55:12, 69:37.

TS 16:96+, יעמדו Dan. 11:14 (cf. III.5.M).

⟨a⟩ TS 12:195+, before *'alef*, *he*, and *ḥet* followed by 'a' vowels, Pss. 55:11, 15, 69:28, 77:18. Before *yod* followed by 'a' vowel, Ps. 70:3. (See 2 above under *shewa* and note 18.)

TS 16:96+, ≑ bA 'silent' *shewa* preceding *ḥet* followed by 'a' vowel, Dan. 11:11. Following *ḥet*, *yod*, or *resh* preceded by 'a' vowel, Dan. 9:24, 12:5, 10. On conjunction preceding *yod* followed by ⟨a⟩, Dan. 11:15, 16, 16, 17; by ⟨e⟩, Dan. 11:5. Variant, Dan. 11:33 (cf. ⟨a⟩ ≑ *ḥireq*).

TS 20:53+, ויפלטם Ps. 37:40, sign misplaced?

TS 20:59+, before *he* followed by 'a' vowel, Ezek. 16:17. ילדת Ezek. 16:20 is probably an error.

⟨a'⟩ TS 12:195+, before bA *'alef* or *he* followed by *pataḥ*, Pss. 52:9, 55:14.

TS 16:96+, before bA *'alef* or *ḥet* followed by *pataḥ*, Dan. 11:13, 20, on conjunction preceding *yod* followed by *ḥireq*, Dan. 11:11, 15.

⟨e⟩ TS 12:195; this sign is used ≑ bA *shewa* before *yod* followed by *ḥireq*, e.g. Ps. 52:7, ≑ bA 'silent' *shewa* Ps. 71:18, and where bA points conjunctive *waw* as *shureq*, e.g. Ps. 55:4.

TS 16:96+; used where bA has 'silent' *shewa*, Dan. 9:26. Also in וישרים Dan. 11:17. Cf. the use of ⟨i⟩ in this position in class 1 (1.M above). The use of ⟨e⟩ here is presumably exactly parallel to the use of *shewa* in this position in the Worms *Maḥzor* (see Bét-Aryé, 1965, p. 40).

⟨i⟩ TS 12:195+, before bA *he* followed by *ḥireq*, Pss. 53:2, 71:6, 8, before bA *yod* followed by *ḥireq* or *ṣere* Pss. 52:8, 8, 69:36, 70:3, 5, after *yod*, Ps. 55:11 (elsewhere Pss. 69:21, 72:3, probably accent signs).

TS 16:96+, before *yod* followed by various vowels, Dan. 11:10, 22, 12:10.

TS 20:53+, Ps. 37:22, 22,[25] and, on conjunctive *waw* where bA would use *shureq*, Ps. 39:3.

TS 20:59+, Ezek. 13:20 (see also Kahle, 1930, p. 18*).

N The following diacritical signs are used:

	⟨ś⟩	⟨š⟩	
TS 12:195+	ש̊	ש with ש above	
TS 16:96+	ש̮	ש̑	(only Dan. 11:14)
TS 20:53+	ש̑	—	
TS 20:59+	ש̑	—	

[25] Perhaps also בקצפך Ps. 38:2. So Allony and Díez-Macho (1958a), but Murtonen reads the sign as ⟨e'⟩. It is an unusual form either for ⟨i⟩ or ⟨e'⟩.

_<_ ≑ *dagesh forte* in TS 12:195+, TS NS 249:8+.

≑ *dagesh lene* in TS 12:195+. (Wrongly וצדקתך Ps. 71:19.)

≑ *dagesh forte* 'conjunctive' TS 12:195+, Pss. 55:7, 69:26, 76:9, 77:17, 17.

In TS 12:195+, ע[ליך נסמכתי (Ps. 71:6) the sign possibly marks the same feature as bA *legarmeh.*[26] In ת[ורך (Ps. 74:19) and ואצעקה (Ps. 77:2) the sign could possibly relate to the consonantal value of *resh* and *'alef*. Otherwise its presence seems inexplicable.

_ᴖ_ ≑ *rafe* in TS 12:195+. In יחדו (Ps. 55:15) the sign over the *dalet* presumably indicates that the *ḥet* is followed by a vowel (cf. 1.N above, _ᴖ_ (ii)), not (as suggested by Kahle, 1930, p. 29*) that it is quiescent.

This sign marks a graph as having consonantal value in TS 12:195+, as follows: *waw* Pss. 53:2, 55:12 (≑ bA *dagesh forte*!) and nine other cases;[27] *yod* Pss. 52:8, 74:19 (≑ bA *dagesh forte*!); *he* Pss. 55:15, 77:4, 17 (?); *ḥet* Ps. 53:4; *'ayin* Ps 55:2 (?). For similar usage see III.2.N, also 1.N above and note 8 there.[28]

⟨o⟩ is used frequently in TS 20:53+ to indicate that *waw* has consonantal value.[29]

⟨i⟩ indicates that *yod* has consonantal value in TS 20:53+, Ps. 38:3 (probably also Ps. 42:7, where only one dot of the two now remains) in TS 16:96+, Dan. 12:7 (!), and in TS 20:59+, Ezek. 14:21.

[26] Cf. 2.N above. The placing of the sign in Kahle's edition is wrong.

[27] Also יהוה Ps. 75:9 (?), but my photograph is not clear here.

[28] In TS 20:53+, Ps. 55:13, the sign on לא could possibly be intended for _ᴖ_ ≑ *rafe* marking the *'alef* as quiescent, but, since it is very clumsily made, and quite unnecessary, it probably is not. This value is denied in Murtonen, 1958, p. 34, but ascribed to it in Murtonen, 1964, p. 20. Allony and Díez-Macho evidently do not consider the sign as a product of the pointing hand.

[29] At least 9 cases, possibly more. E.g. שועתי Ps. 30:3, ושועתי Pss. 39:13, 40:2, קוה Ps. 40:2. The sign is written above *lamed*, but refers to the following *waw*, in בשלוי Ps. 30:7. (So Murtonen, but not Allony and Díez-Macho. The sign appears faintly in my photograph.) It is misplaced by Murtonen in אולתי Ps. 38:6. Allony and Díez-Macho, 1958a, p. 264, say that פיו Ps. 36:3 can be connected with 'ben Naftali' forms. Otherwise they treat this use of ⟨o⟩ as the mark of an 'o' vowel 'interchanging' with other vowels (see *ibid.*, p. 263). Other instances of this use of ⟨o⟩ occur in classes 1, 2, and 7 *(q.v.)*.

o The mss assigned to this group characteristically use all four 'a' and 'e' signs in a way that bears no resemblance to the bA use of *qameṣ*, *pataḥ*, *segol*, and *ṣere*. This is the major characteristic of class 3. Apart from this, these mss do not appear to form a homogeneous group. They are not, however, as diverse in some of the minor details as it might seem at first.

The representation of 'u' vowels is unique in TS 20:53+, which has no ⟨u⟩ sign, but uses ⟨o⟩ in all cases, and in TS 16:96+, which uses ∵, an allograph of the normal Palestinian ⟨u⟩ (‥). The use of this allograph, an inverted ⟨o⟩ sign, might suggest some connection with the consistent use of ⟨o⟩ ÷ *shureq* in TS 20:53+. This seems unlikely, however, in view of other differences between these mss, such as in their use of the 'a' signs. The use of ⟨u⟩ in this class is further noteworthy in that some mss do, and some do not, use it where bA points conjunctive *waw* as *shureq*.

The use of the 'a' vowels in TS 20:53+ is unique in that ⟨a⟩ is used almost solely in open final syllables. Most mss of classes 3, 5, and 7 use ⟨a'⟩ more frequently in this position, and ⟨a⟩ most commonly in open, unstressed, medial syllables. TS 20:59+ is unique in its very sparse use of ⟨a'⟩.

Where bA uses *qameṣ ḥaṭuf*, most of these mss use either ⟨a⟩ or ⟨o⟩. Only TS 12:195+ uses both. Even in this ms, however, the apparent tendency to specialize can be seen, since ⟨a⟩ and ⟨o⟩ appear to be used in different sets of forms. This may, however, be due to the accident of preservation.

TS 16:96+ is unique in its very sparse use of ⟨e'⟩.

The vowel signs in TS 12:195 where bA has *shewa* are very interesting, as they appear to reflect faithfully the rules for the pronunciation of '*shewa* vowels' before laryngeals given in the early grammars. The same usage is found in mss of classes 1 (see 1.O above) and 2 (non-biblical), and possibly to some extent in other mss of this class. It is particularly interesting to see that the same rule appears to be followed in the use of signs before *yod* where bA has *shewa* in TS 12:195+ and TS 16:96+. This is most common where an 'a' vowel follows the *yod* but neither ms is consistent. The harmonization of a vowel preceding *yod* with an 'a' vowel following it has been noted above (see 2.M and note 18). Presumably this usage is related. The other mss of this group do not show this peculiar usage of signs where bA has *shewa* before *yod*, but the group can be said to be homogeneous in that, in contrast to some classes, its members do not consistently use ⟨i⟩ in this position.

The use of diacritical signs is very varied, as it is in most classes. TS 12:195+ is atypical in its very extensive use of them. All mss but TS NS 249:8+ (from which there is very little material) mark ⟨ś⟩, but besides TS 12:195+, only TS NS 249:8+ uses ◌̭ '*dagesh*,' and only TS 20:53+ uses ◌̮ '*rafe*.' The use of this sign in TS 20:53+ to mark 'quiescent' *'alef* (in any case questionable, see note 28) seems to be in direct contrast to that of TS 12:195+, where it shows that a graph has consonantal value. However, it may be that, as suggested in the description of class 1 (biblical), the use of *rafe* on laryngeals, as on other graphs, indicates a particular type of consonantal value and not lack of consonantal value. If this is the case, the use of it in these two mss is not necessarily contradictory. The extensive marking of graphs as having consonantal value is only found in TS 12:195+, but other mss in the class are concerned to indicate consonantal value in *waw* and *yod*.

Apart from the other differences noted, TS 20:53+ is unique among Palestinian biblical mss for the small number (2) of accent signs which it uses. Perhaps this ms, with all its unique features, should have been set up in a separate class. However, it has been retained in this one, since no other ms of its type is known, and because other mss in this class also show distinctly individual features. The biblical mss of class 3, in fact, form a varied group. It is possible that further knowledge would show that some division should be made other than that proposed here. The non-biblical mss of this class also form a heterogeneous group. They contain too little information to show any parallels or contrasts with the biblical group other than in the use of the 'a' and 'e' signs. However, at the present state of our knowledge, the usage of these signs seems sufficient reason for assigning these mss, diverse though they be, to this class and not to any other.

CLASS 7

A TS B17:25 (?)[30] (Isa. 53:3, 56:3–5, Hos. 10:6–9, Isa. 11:8–11, 63:7–9, Mic. 7:17–18)

[30] Published in Yeivin, 1963, pp. 121–4.

TS K26:1[31] (Ezra 3:1–4:2)
*TS 2nd 1:130[32] (Hos. 10:2–6)
Bod. Heb. d29 f. 17–20[33] (Josh. 14:3–21:31)

The mss use the vowel signs ⟨u⟩, ⟨o⟩, ⟨a⟩, ⟨a′⟩, ⟨e⟩, and ⟨i⟩ in the following way:

B ≑ *shureq*

⟨u⟩ *passim.* This sign does not appear in TS B17:25 or *TS 2nd 1:130, from which there is very little material. The other two mss use ⟨u⟩ where bA points conjunctive *waw* as *shureq*.

⟨i⟩ TS K26:1 יִסד Ezra 3:6 (variant, *nif'al* for *pu'al*).

C ≑ *ḥolem*

⟨o⟩ *passim.*

⟨u⟩ Heb. d29 f. 17–20, Jos. 16:9, 19:14.

D, G 'a' vowels

	≑ *qameṣ*		≑ *pataḥ*	
	⟨a⟩	⟨a′⟩	⟨a⟩	⟨a′⟩
TS B17:25	1	2	—	—
TS K26:1	7	4	11	2
*TS 2nd 1:130	1?[34]	4	1	—
Bod. Heb. d29 f. 17–20	114	19	20	40

D ≑ *qameṣ*

⟨e⟩ TS K26:1, Ezra 3:3; Heb. d29 f. 17–20, Josh. 15:29, 19:3; all pausal forms of 'segolate' nouns.

E ≑ *qameṣ ḥaṭuf*

⟨o⟩ TS K26:1 and Heb. d29 f. 17–20, 1 case each.

H ≑ *ḥaṭef pataḥ*

⟨a′⟩ Heb. d29 f. 17–20.

[31] Published in Dietrich, 1960, as MS Cb 2.

[32] Published in Dietrich, 1960, as MS Cb 6.

[33] Published in Dietrich, 1960, as MS Ob. 1. Since the two hands distinguished by Dietrich make identical use of the vowel signs (cf. e.g. ועצם hand A Josh. 15:29, B/C Josh. 19:3; נפתוח hand A Josh. 15:9, B/C Josh. 18:15), they are not distinguished here.

[34] The possible case is לך (bA לָךְ), Obadaiah 15.

I ≑ *segol*

⟨e⟩ *passim.*

⟨a⟩ Heb. d29 f. 17–20, Josh. 15:30, 19:4, probably variants.

⟨a′⟩ *ibid.*, Josh. 19:28, also לֹהם Josh. 21:21, but the sign might represent an accent.

⟨i⟩ *ibid.*, Josh. 15:9, 18:15.

K ≑ *ṣere*

⟨e⟩ *passim.*

⟨a′⟩ TS K26:1, Ezra 3:6, in a closed, stressed, non-final syllable.

⟨o⟩ Heb. d29 f. 17–20, חרֹם Josh. 19:38. bA חֳרֵם. The ⟨o⟩ sign was possibly intended for the first syllable (cf. note 39 to III.4).

L ≑ *hireq*

⟨i⟩ *passim.*

⟨e⟩ Heb. d29 f. 17–20. Always where bA has *ḥireq* after *yod* preceded by *pataḥ*. Also perhaps elsewhere, but cf. Dietrich, 1968, p. 23 n. 2, p. 24. Cf. III.7.L.

⟨a′⟩ *ibid.*, Josh. 17:10, יִפגעון (variant, *hif'il* for *qal*?).

⟨a⟩ *ibid.*, Josh. 18:24, 19:12 (?).

M ≑ *shewa*

	⟨e⟩	⟨a′⟩	⟨i⟩
TS B17:25	—	—	—
TS K26:1	7	—	—
*TS 2nd 1:130	—	1	—
Bod. Heb. d29 f. 17–20	3	22	25

24 of the uses of ⟨i⟩ ≑ *shewa* occur before *yod*, the 25th after *yod* (Josh. 17:2).

N The following diacritical signs are used:

ש marks ⟨ś⟩ in TS K26:1, Ezra 3:9.

ש marks ⟨ś⟩ in Heb. d29 f. 17–20, Josh. 19:27.

ש marks ⟨š⟩ in *ibid.*, Josh. 19:6.

< occurs only in ולגבעות TS B17:25, Hos. 10:8, a clear case of the sign indicating the presence of the definite article (see II.11.E and note there).

^ occurs only in ויהי Heb. d29 f. 17–20, Josh. 17:13, perhaps marking the *he* as consonantal (see 3.N above).

⟨o⟩ is used to mark consonantal *waw* in TS B17:25, Mic. 7:18.[35]

O The members of this group use only six vowel signs. ⟨a⟩ and ⟨a′⟩ represent 'a' vowels, but their use bears no resemblance to the bA use of *qameṣ* and *pataḥ*. ⟨e⟩ is used for 'e' vowels. ⟨e′⟩ is not used. ⟨o⟩ is used where bA has *qameṣ ḥaṭuf*. No other sign is used in this position, but since there are so few examples, this is hardly significant. Either ⟨e⟩ or ⟨a′⟩ is normally used where bA has *shewa*. These characteristics are those of the non-biblical mss of class 7. The use of ⟨e⟩ ≑ *ḥireq* in ִי in both non-biblical and biblical members of this class is interesting, but possibly coincidental. The common and consistent usage of ⟨i⟩ where bA has *shewa* before *yod* in Heb. d29 f. 17–20 is paralleled by the usage in TS H16:3 among the non-biblical mss, although most of them do not use ⟨i⟩ in this position. The use of diacritics is rare in these biblical mss, and the signs used are not those typical of the non-biblical texts of this class. The script of these biblical mss is not that characteristic of the non-biblical class, nor is the 'dot' form of ⟨a′⟩ sign used in them. However, a difference in script between biblical and non-biblical mss is not surprising, and there were exceptions in these matters in the non-biblical class.

CLASS 12 (mixed classes)

A As was noted for the non-biblical mss, additions by hands subsequent to that of the original vocalization are often noticeable in biblical texts. These additions are usually so few that they do not change the character of the original vocalization. Occasionally, however, extensive alterations are made, so that the resultant vocalization can be assigned to two different classes. An example of a biblical text with pointing of this sort is TS 12:197.[36] The vowel signs in this ms are used as follows:

B ≑ *shureq*

⟨u⟩ *passim*.

[35] Examples of this usage have already been noted in classes 1, 2, and 3. In the present instance ⟨o⟩ could be considered a vowel sign. Similar instances occur in several other mss, which, because of the ambiguity, I have not bothered to note. Yeivin (1963, p. 123) appears to believe (following the note in Kahle, 1930, p. 18*, to which he refers) that the ⟨o⟩ here indicates that the *waw* over which it stands has no consonantal value, an assumption which seems to me unnecessary, and indeed indefensible.

[36] Published in Kahle, 1930, as MS K. Contains Jer. 1:1–2:29.

C ÷ *ḥolem*

⟨o⟩ *passim.*

D ÷ *qameṣ*

⟨a⟩ *passim.*

⟨a′⟩ יאשמו Jer. 2:3, ותבאו Jer. 2:7. (Note that in this ms the '*dagesh*' sign ˂ is normally placed to the left of a vowel sign when both are placed over the same consonant.)

E ÷ *qameṣ ḥaṭuf*

⟨o⟩ Jer. 2:2, 21.

⟨a⟩ Jer. 1:5, 15, 17, 2:16, 19, 24.

G ÷ *pataḥ*

⟨a′⟩ *passim.*

⟨a⟩ Jer. 1:5, 10, 2:17. All in closed, unstressed syllables before doubled consonants.

⟨e⟩ תחפנס bA תחפנחס Jer. 2:16. (Cf. Kahle's note *ad loc.*)

⟨i⟩ ויגע Jer. 1:9.

H ÷ *ḥaṭef pataḥ*

⟨a′⟩ 4 cases.

⟨e⟩ Jer. 1:7, over initial ʾ*alef.*

I ÷ *segol*

⟨e⟩ *passim.*

K ÷ *ṣere*

⟨e′⟩ 19 cases.

∵ (i.e., ⟨e⟩ corrected to ⟨e′⟩) 14 cases.

⟨e⟩ 14 cases. These cases, which were not corrected to ⟨e′⟩ by the second hand, are of considerable interest. 11 are in C′f syllables, suggesting a possible connection with the use of ⟨a′⟩ in syllables of this type where bA has *ṣere.*[37] 10 of these 11 cases are the 2fs. pronominal suffix, bA ךְ. The remaining 3 cases are in open syllables (Jer. 1:4, 15, 2:18). The

[37] There are 10 cases of ⟨e′⟩ and ∵ in C′f syllables: Jer. 1:6, 7, 11, 11, 2:2, 10, 16 (see Kahle's note *ad loc.*), 21, 21, 25.

correction was not, however, fully consistent. Cf. the 2fs. pronoun in לכתך Jer. 2:2, and מי with מי in Jer. 2:18.

L ÷ *ḥireq*

⟨i⟩ *passim.*

⟨e⟩ עשית Jer. 2:23.

⟨e′⟩ סיר Jer. 1:13.

M ÷ *shewa*

⟨e⟩ 9 cases, including נהפכת Jer. 2:21.

⟨a′⟩ 4 cases.

N The following diacritical signs are used:

‹ ÷ *dagesh forte*. I cannot explain the usage in יאשמו Jer. 2:3.
Marks ʾ*alef* as closing a syllable in Jer. 1:17, 2:3 (cf. '*dagesh* ÷ *shewa*'), Jer. 2:17 (*dagesh forte* ÷ *dagesh forte* 'conjunctive' Jer. 2:5, 17, 18).
Marks ʾ*alef* as having 'consonantal value' Jer. 2:25.
Mappiq is marked in the Tiberian manner in Jer. 2:7, 7, 24, 24, probably by the correcting hand.

O The most noticeable characteristic of this ms is its use of three signs for the 'e' vowels. It seems obvious that it originally used only ⟨e⟩ for all 'e' vowels, but that ⟨e′⟩ was later added, both where no sign had been used before, and where ⟨e⟩ had been used. In the latter case the sign ∵ was produced. The original pointing, then, used ⟨e⟩ for all 'e' vowels, and used ⟨a⟩ and ⟨a′⟩ much as bA uses *qameṣ* and *pataḥ*. It is therefore to be ascribed to class 6. The correcting hand, since it used ⟨e′⟩ exclusively where bA used *ṣere*, is to be ascribed to class 1.

It is difficult to know what other characteristics are to be ascribed to class 6, since this is the only available example of a biblical ms of this class. If the characteristics of the non-biblical mss of class 6 are taken as an example, the five uses of ⟨a⟩ where bA uses *qameṣ ḥaṭuf* are also to be ascribed to the correcting hand of class 1, since class 6 mss do not use ⟨a⟩ in this way. Most, or all, of the uses of ⟨e⟩ ÷ *shewa* will also be attributed to the class 1 hand, since class 6 mss rarely represent '*shewa* vowels.' The frequency of the '*dagesh*' sign, ‹, and its variety of uses would fit class 6 well enough. The Tiberian form of *mappiq* is, however, probably also to be ascribed to the class 1 hand (cf. 1 above).

APPENDIX

The Accent Signs in Biblical Manuscripts

The division of the biblical texts into classes based on their use of the vowel signs does, then, produce the same classes as the classification of the non-biblical mss. Certain differences from non-biblical texts can be seen, such as the wider use of וֹ ≑ ו conjunctive, and of ⟨a⟩ ≑ *qameṣ ḥaṭuf*, and the special pointings noted in Revell, 1970, 1, nos. 8, 10. The classes do have the same general characteristics, however, as are found in the non-biblical classes, although these are not so clear, and the division not so obvious, in the biblical texts. The biblical texts, however, offer a further criterion for class division, the various forms in which the accent signs appear.

These accent signs vary in a peculiar way, so that it would seem impossible to build a useful classification of mss based on this criterion alone. For example, J.T.S. MS 504 f. 2+ (class 1) uses a Tiberian form of *zaqef*, but a form of *rebiaʿ* typical of classes 7 and 3, the farthest from the bA system as far as the use of vowel signs goes. In most cases, however, an accent sign appears in only two or three different forms among the different mss. The way in which these different forms are used seems to me to support the division into classes already suggested on the basis of the use of vowel signs. As a rule classes 7 and 3 use one form of sign, and classes 2 and 1 the other. Even if classes 2 and 1 show mixed usage, classes 1 and 7 are usually clearly different.

The forms of the accent signs have been used by Dr. Dietrich as a criterion for his classification of Palestinian biblical mss.[38] I would maintain, however, that this criterion shows that the classification suggested here is a better reflection of the usage of the mss than that suggested by Dr. Dietrich, since the groupings formed are less scattered. That is, mss widely separated on Dr. Dietrich's list may use the same form of accent, while the intermediate ones use a different form. A comparable situation is rarer with the classification suggested here.

The information on the forms of the accent signs used here is taken

[38] In Dietrich, 1968. See particularly the final tabulation, p. 88*.

from Dr. Dietrich's work referred to above. The various forms in which the accent signs appear are shown there. The only new material comes from TS B17:25, described in Yeivin, 1963 (pp. 121ff.).[39] When considering the following descriptions, it should be remembered that the pointing referred to as 'class 12' is mixed. The forms it shows are to be ascribed either to class 6 or class 1.

The accent signs (given the names of the bA accents to which they correspond in use) occur as follows:

Silluq Only used in class 7, and in one ms of class 3.

Atnaḥ The typical form, a subscript dot, is used in all classes. J.T.S. MS 594 (class 2) and Bod. Heb. e30 f. 48–9+ (class 1) use the Tiberian form. TS 20:59+ (class 3) uses a supralinear dot.

Tifḥa The typical form, a subscript dot, is used in all classes. *TS 2nd 1:130 and in some cases TS B17:25 (both class 7) use a subscript line. Bod. Heb. e30 f. 48–9+ (class 1) uses an internal dot.

Zaqef J.T.S. MS 504 f. 2+ (class 1) uses a Tiberian form. Other mss in classes 1, 2, and 12 use a supralinear dot, as does TS 20:69+ of class 3. Other mss of classes 3 and 7 use a vertical line (supralinear).

Pashṭa The typical form, two dots, one beside the other (supralinear), is used in all mss.

Tebir The typical form, two dots, one beside the other (sublinear), is used in all mss but Bod. Heb. e30 f. 48–9 (class 1), which uses a single subscript dot.

Rebia' The most common form, a horizontal line (supralinear), is used in classes 12, 7, 3, and also in J.T.S. MS 594 of class 2 and J.T.S. MS 504 f. 2+ of class 1. In the other mss of classes 1 and 2, a supralinear dot is used. This also appears in TS 20:59+ of class 3, but it is there prepositive, in contrast to its position in classes 1 and 2.

Geresh In classes 7 and 3 a slanting line is used, supralinear, and usually prepositive. TS B17:25 of class 7, however, uses two horizontal lines, one above the other (also supralinear and pre-

[39] Now also TS NS 246:22, the accents of which are typical for class 1, save *rebia'*, which is marked by a horizontal line (as in J.T.S. MS 504 f. 2+). See Díez-Macho, 1967, p. 19.

positive). In classes 12, 2, and 1, a supralinear dot is used, also usually prepositive.

Legarmeh In classes 12, 7, and 3, a slanting line is used, usually below the line. In TS 16:96, it is used between the words. Various different forms are used in classes 2 and 1.

Segolta In classes 12, 7, and 3, a subscript dot is used, except in TS 20:59+ of class 3, where a supralinear postpositive dot is used. This form is also used in classes 2 and 1, save in J.T.S. MS 504 f. 2+ of class 1, where the subscript dot again appears.

Zarqa Classes 7 and 3 usually use a slanting line in various positions. This is used also in Bod. Heb. e30 f. 48–9 of class 1. Classes 1 and 2 usually use a dot in various positions. This form also occurs in TS 20:59+ of class 3.

Telisha The most common form, two dots one above the other (supralinear), occurs in one ms of each class. The next most common form occurs once in class 7 and once in class 3.

Pazer Various forms are used, none twice in the same class, or more than twice in all.

It is interesting to note that most mss which diverge from the norm of their class diverge in more than one case. Thus in class 1 Bod. Heb. e30 f. 48–9+ has four divergent usages, J.T.S. MS 504 has three. In class 2, J.T.S. MS 594 has two; in class 3 TS 20:59 has four; and in class 7, TS B17:25 has two. The only other mss which can be said to have forms divergent from the norm of their class are *TS 2nd 1:130, and perhaps TS 16:96. TS 20:53+ is divergent in that it uses only *tifḥa* and *tebir*. Of these divergent mss, those in classes 2 and 3 also show uses of vowel signs atypical in their class. This question can hardly be established for classes 1 and 7 because of the paucity of information. It would seem, therefore, that the evidence from the forms of the accent signs agrees with that from the use of the vowel signs, and supports the classification based on it.

V

The Dialects of Palestinian Hebrew

THE VOWELS OF PALESTINIAN HEBREW

1 The descriptions in chapters III and IV show that, for the most part, Palestinian vowel signs correspond to the Tiberian as follows: ⟨u⟩ ÷ *shureq*, ⟨o⟩ ÷ *ḥolem*, ⟨a⟩ ÷ *qameṣ*, ⟨a′⟩ ÷ *pataḥ*, ⟨e⟩ ÷ *segol*, ⟨e′⟩ ÷ *ṣere*, ⟨i⟩ ÷ *ḥireq*. The Palestinian use of ⟨u⟩, ⟨o⟩, and ⟨i⟩ is very similar to the bA use of *shureq*, *ḥolem*, and *ḥireq*. There are, admittedly, many cases divergent from bA usage. However, these have been catalogued and counted in the preceding pages, and it is quite obvious that their number is infinitesimal compared to the number of cases that do correspond to bA usage. Consequently it is logical to conclude that the Palestinian signs represented much the same sounds as did those of bA. The same argument can be used for the 'e' signs in class 1 and the 'a' signs in classes 1, 2, 4, and 6. Their use is so similar to that of the corresponding bA signs that it is impossible not to assume that they represented closely similar sounds.[1] The situation in those classes in which the two 'a' signs or the two 'e' signs are confused is more difficult to assess. However, the preponderant use of ⟨a⟩ and ⟨e⟩ in such mss, and among mss that use only one 'a' or 'e' sign, would suggest that, where only one 'a' or 'e' vowel was used, the sounds were closer to those represented by *qameṣ* and *segol* than to those indicated by *pataḥ* and *ṣere*. This suggestion is borne out by the observation that, in general, there is more confusion in the representation of vowels where bA uses *pataḥ* and *ṣere* than where *qameṣ* and *segol* occur. The following paragraphs summarize the main uses of the Palestinian vowel signs.

[1] Cf. the use of *pataḥ* instead of ⟨a′⟩ in J.T.S. MS 594 (see IV.2).

2 ⟨u⟩ and ⟨o⟩. These two signs are consistently distinguished in use in all mss but one, and so presumably represent different sounds. In many mss they interchange to a slight extent in a few positions, presumably indicating that the sounds they represented were also interchanged in these positions. Many of these interchanges result from developments which took place after the Hebrew language had reached the stage recorded in bA. An example is the replacement of ⟨u⟩ by ⟨o⟩ before originally doubled *ḥet* or *ʿayin*, as in *puʿal* forms. This sound change has already occurred before *ʾalef* and *resh* in the stage of Hebrew recorded in bA.[2] Some cases of interchange appear to result simply from confusion, but their number is far too small to be taken as an indication that general confusion and loss of distinction between the vowels represented by ⟨u⟩ and ⟨o⟩ were either in existence or incipient. TS 20:53+, however, presumably does represent a dialect in which no distinction was made between 'u' and 'o' vowels, since this ms uses ⟨o⟩ where other Palestinian texts use either ⟨u⟩ or ⟨o⟩. This ms is, however, not in the main Palestinian tradition, as it differs from typical mss in several other ways also (see IV.3). Its use of ⟨o⟩ may possibly connect it with the Samaritan pronunciation of Hebrew.

3 ⟨u⟩ is used in a good many mss where bA would point conjunctive *waw* as *shureq*. This usage is more common in biblical than in non-biblical mss, and more common in mss which use the 'a' and 'e' signs as does bA. It does not occur in non-biblical mss of classes 3, 5, and 7. Its use in Palestinian mss shows that it derives from the more conservative strata of the Palestinian community. The use of a 'u' vowel in this position is probably earlier in the Hebrew language in general than is the alternative use of ⟨w⟩ + '*shewa* vowel.'[3]

4 ⟨o⟩ is the sign most commonly employed where bA has *qameṣ ḥaṭuf*. In mss of classes 4 and 6, which otherwise use their 'a' signs as does bA, it is virtually the only sign used in this position. There is no reason to suppose that the sound represented by ⟨o⟩ in this position differed much from the sound it represented in any other position. The use of an 'o' vowel where bA has *qameṣ ḥaṭuf* reflects development of the language subsequent to the stage recorded by bA.[4]

[2] See Revell, 1970, I, no. 17.
[3] On these points see Revell, 1970, I, no. 35.
[4] See Revell, 1970, I, no. 32.

The use of ⟨o⟩ where bA has *ḥaṭef qameṣ* is rare, and confined to a single noun type. It is therefore reasonable to suppose that the vowel pattern of this particular type differs from that used in bA. Presumably, then, ⟨o⟩ in this position represents a vowel of the same quantity and quality as it does when used where bA has *qameṣ ḥaṭuf*.[5]

5 ⟨a⟩ and ⟨a′⟩. In classes 1, 2, 4, and 6, these signs are used distinctly, much as are *qameṣ* and *pataḥ* in bA. There is no reason to suppose that this spelling did not reflect pronunciation, since classes 4 and 6 at any rate could not be imitations of bA pointing. Consequently mss using the signs in this way are considered to reflect a pronunciation with two 'a' phonemes. In classes 3, 5, and 7, the two signs are used to a large extent indiscriminately. There are, however, a number of morphs in which either one sign or the other is normally used. This phenomenon can be interpreted as reflecting the vestigial traces of a distinction which is still maintained in classes 1, 2, etc., and in bA.[6] It is questionable whether this partial distinction was reflected in speech, but it would seem most likely that it was. The Palestinian scribal conventions obviously permitted the use of only one 'a' sign (as in classes 8–11). The use of two signs cannot, therefore, be ascribed to the force of tradition, but must have had a purpose. Mss of classes 3, 5, and 7 do not show any evidence of bA influence unless the number of 'full vowel' signs used be taken so. Considering the fact that many mss were written with Tiberian signs, but also use two 'a' signs indiscriminately, or only one 'a' sign, and show other typically 'Palestinian' features,[7] it seems unlikely that the use of two 'a' signs is itself a mark of bA (or Tiberian) influence. Hence it is a reasonable assumption that two 'a' signs were used in mss of classes 3, 5, and 7 in order to indicate those few morphs in which two qualities of 'a' vowel were still distinguished. There does not appear to be any reasonable basis for suggesting that this distinction was phonemic. Thus mss of classes 3, 5, and 7 are to be taken as representing a pronunciation using one 'a' phoneme which had two allophones which were used distinctly in only a few morphs for historical reasons. Mss using only one 'a' sign presumably represent a pronunciation in which only one 'a' phoneme was used and which did not make any written distinction between allophones.

[5] See note 39 to III.4.
[6] See Revell, 1970, I, nos. 8, 9, 33.
[7] See Díez-Macho, 1963b, especially pp. 20ff., and Morag, 1965, section 3.

6 ⟨a⟩ is normally used where bA has *ḥaṭef qameṣ* (cf. 4 above). ⟨a⟩ is also used where bA has *qameṣ ḥaṭuf*. In mss of class 1 this is common, and probably due to bA influence (see III.1, IV.1). In mss of classes 4 and 6, which otherwise use the 'a' signs as does class 1, this usage is very rare and probably secondary. In mss of classes 3, 5, and 7, which use the 'a' signs for the most part indiscriminately, and in mss of class 2, ⟨a⟩ is characteristically a free variant of ⟨o⟩ where bA has *qameṣ ḥaṭuf* (see 19–21 below for the significance of these groupings). In mss of these classes ⟨a′⟩ is also used where bA has *qameṣ ḥaṭuf* or *ḥaṭef qameṣ*, a further indication that in classes 3, 5, and 7 ⟨a⟩ and ⟨a′⟩ did not normally represent distinct sounds. The existence of this usage in class 2 is taken as indicating that it belonged to the same dialect group as classes 3, 5, and 7 (see 21 below). The usage in these mss presumably shows that the sounds used where bA has *qameṣ ḥaṭuf* and *ḥaṭef qameṣ* were, at least in some cases, closer to the allophones of the 'a' phoneme than to those of the 'o' phoneme, but the phonetic and historical interpretation of this is uncertain.

7 Both ⟨a⟩ and ⟨a′⟩ interchange to some extent with ⟨e⟩, ⟨e′⟩, and ⟨i⟩ in many mss. Such interchanges appear to reflect developments which took place in the language subsequent to the stage recorded by bA, or confusion resulting from the breakdown of the older vowel system. Since these texts reproduce language used for literary purposes rather than colloquial speech, the latter factor may be expected to have been significant. Perhaps the most interesting examples of such interchange are the use of ⟨e⟩ where bA has *pataḥ* before a laryngeal, and the use of ⟨a′⟩ (and ⟨a⟩) where bA has *ṣere* in a closed final stressed syllable. The former case undoubtedly represents the beginning of a process of quality change ('compensatory lengthening') due to the fact that laryngeals can, in some positions, no longer close syllables.[8] The use of an 'a' sign where bA uses *ṣere* in a closed final stressed syllable represents an extension of the change known as 'Philippi's Law' into final syllables. This extension has already begun in the stage of the language recorded by bA.[9]

8 ⟨e⟩ and ⟨e′⟩. In mss of class 1, these signs are used distinctly, much as are *segol* and *ṣere* in bA. They may, therefore, be presumed

[8] Cf. bA use of *segol* to represent the first stage in the change of /a/ *(pataḥ)* to /ɔ/ *(qameṣ)*. See Revell, 1970, 1, no. 19.

[9] See Revell, 1970, 1, no. 29. The same extension was well advanced in Babylonian Hebrew (*ibid.*, note 60). For other changes, see *ibid.*, 1, nos. 23, 27.

to represent two phonemes.[10] In mss of classes 2 and 3, ⟨e⟩ and ⟨e′⟩ are used to a large extent indiscriminately. As was argued for ⟨a⟩ and ⟨a′⟩, the use of two signs where one was perfectly acceptable must have had a purpose. This argument is much more compelling in the case of the 'e' signs than in that of the 'a' signs, as the majority of Palestinian mss use only one 'e' sign. Mss of classes 2 and 3 do not show any evidence of an attempt to use the 'e' (or any other) signs in imitation of bA. It must therefore be concluded that their pointing had as its purpose the distinction of those few morphs in which the signs are used distinctly.[11] They are therefore taken as representing a pronunciation using only one 'e' phoneme, but distinguishing two of its allophones in certain morphs for historical reasons. Classes 4–11 presumably represent dialects in which only one 'e' phoneme was used. No allophones are distinguished in writing.

9 Both ⟨e⟩ and ⟨e′⟩ interchange to some extent with the 'a' signs (see 7 above) and with ⟨i⟩. As with the other interchanges, the replacement of ⟨i⟩ by an 'e' sign often reflects development of the language subsequent to the stage recorded in bA. An example is the common use of 'e' signs before originally doubled *ḥet* or *'ayin*. The same change has already occurred in bA before the 'weaker' laryngeals.[12]

10 ⟨i⟩. Save for the relatively few cases of interchange with 'a' or 'e' signs mentioned above, ⟨i⟩ is consistently distinguished in use in all mss but Bod. Heb. d63 f. 98. In this ms ⟨e′⟩ is very frequently written where ⟨i⟩ is expected. The significance of this is debatable, but it is here ascribed to scribal carelessness rather than phonological confusion. The ⟨i⟩ sign deviates from the vertical to one side or the other in many mss,[13] although never so consistently as in this one. The ms in question does not seem to be outside the main stream of Palestinian tradition, although it does have other unusual features (see III.2).

[10] There is some question whether *segol* and *ṣere* do represent two phonemes in bA. While such a question can probably never be settled for a written language, it would seem likely that two 'e' phonemes were used. Pairs of written words of different meaning contrasting only in their use of *segol* or *ṣere* can be drawn up (e.g. *'ɛl* 'to,' *'el* 'God'). There can be no doubt that the two signs represent phonetically different sounds (see Revell, 1970, I, no. 40). Consequently it is logical to assume that they were phonemically distinct.

[11] See Revell, 1970, I, nos. 10–12.

[12] See Revell, 1970, I, no. 20.

[13] For example, Bod. Heb. d29 f. 17–20; see Dietrich, 1968, p. 23, note 2.

11 Where bA uses *shewa*, all seven vowel signs are used, but only ⟨a′⟩, ⟨e⟩, and ⟨e′⟩ are common in this position. ⟨u⟩ is so rare as to be negligible. ⟨o⟩ is used in a few specific phonologically conditioned positions in a few mss. ⟨a⟩ is used a few times in many mss, but mostly in a few interrelated positions, where its use may be the result of a stress pattern differing from that of bA, in which case it would not represent a '*shewa* vowel' at all. ⟨i⟩ also appears where bA has *shewa* a few times in most mss. The majority of its uses are phonologically conditioned. The value of the signs used where bA has *shewa* has been discussed at length in " '*Shewa* Vowels' in Palestinian Hebrew."[14] The conclusion reached there is that '*shewa* vowels' were used and pronounced in Palestinian Hebrew very much as they were in that of bA. Definite differences did exist (such as that suggested by the use of ⟨a⟩) but they were certainly few. The reason that a variety of signs is used in Palestinian mss and not in bA is that in the Tiberian system a special sign, which did not indicate any particular vowel quality, was used to indicate all '*shewa* vowels' (except '*ḥaṭef*' vowels), even though such vowels were pronounced with different qualities in different circumstances. Palestinian Hebrew never developed a sign with a comparable function, although moves in this direction were made. Consequently only a sign indicating a particular quality could be used to indicate a '*shewa* vowel,' and so the signs used varied according to the vowel quality required in a given position. In accordance with that study it is assumed here that the various different forms of Palestinian pronunciation all used much the same system of '*shewa* vowels,' although the different classes of mss indicate these vowels in different ways. This system was similar to that used in bA pronunciation. The number of phonemes involved is uncertain.[15]

THE RELATION OF THE PALESTINIAN DIALECT TO THAT OF bA

12 The majority of scholars hold that Palestinian Hebrew represents a stage of the language earlier than that recorded in bA. The view taken here is that Palestinian Hebrew in general represents a form of the language which has developed further than has bA from their

14 Revell, 1970, part II.

15 Opinions on the number of '*shewa* phonemes' in the bA pronunciation range from 'none' (Garbell, 1959, pp. 153–4) to 'four' – including all the *ḥaṭef* vowels. The number arrived at depends, of course, on the extent to which such features as vowel quantity and stress level are admitted to the phoneme system.

common original, and is therefore a later form. This has already been argued elsewhere.[16] The following are the main points.
(i) The use of the 'a' signs in classes 3, 5, and 7 and of the 'e' signs in classes 2 and 3 is never completely indiscriminate (see 5 and 8 above). The general pattern suggests that a distinction once made is breaking down.
(ii) The unusual uses of the vowel signs (including the 'a' and 'e' signs) in many cases indicate vowel changes resulting from processes already visible but less advanced in bA, or processes of which the situation found in bA formed the initial stage. This also applies to the use of ⟨o⟩ where bA has *qameṣ ḥaṭuf* (see 2–10 above).
(iii) Some of the individual cases coming under (ii) can be supported by reference to the transliterations of Origen. Moreover, that source does distinguish two 'e' vowels. If Palestinian Hebrew, which does not normally make this distinction, is to represent a stage of the language between that of Origen and that of bA, one must argue that two 'e' vowels were distinguished, then merged, and then were redistinguished in their original positions, which is highly unlikely.[17]
(iv) The theory presented here does not require the postulation of any complicated historical or linguistic situation. It assumes simply that bA records a well-preserved archaic pronunciation, and that that of Palestinian Hebrew is less well preserved. This is supported by the fact that the Palestinian biblical texts are all 'vulgar' types; i.e. their tradition is less well-preserved than is that of bA. There are similar grades of preservation within Palestinian Hebrew. Most noticeable is the fact that biblical texts show a much better preserved form of language than do the non-biblical.[18]

13 In summary, then, it can be said that Palestinian forms have developed further from their common original than have those of bA. Both pointing systems were in use at the same time. Therefore bA records a better-preserved form of the language than does Palestinian. Palestinian Hebrew records a variety of forms ranging from a pronunciation very close to that of bA in biblical texts of class 1, down to what must have been almost the common colloquial pronunciation in liturgical texts of classes 8–11. It is not claimed that these historical levels are absolute. Palestinian mss undoubtedly contain occasional

[16] Revell, 1970, part 1.
[17] Probably impossible. See Hoenigswald, 1960, p. 117.
[18] Such as in their use of the –CV form of the 2ms. pronominal suffix. See Revell, 1970, 1, no. 38; also 23 below.

early forms, and bA texts do contain a few late forms. In general, however, Palestinian Hebrew represents a more developed, and therefore a 'later' form of the language.

THE RELATION OF THE PALESTINIAN POINTING SYSTEM TO THE TIBERIAN

14 The above theory deals with the relationship of the two dialects in terms of morphological development from their common original, and has no significance for the relationship of the two pointing systems used to write them. However, current theories about those systems may be felt to counteract the arguments given above. Díez-Macho has argued that the Tiberian pointing is an outgrowth of the Palestinian, the intermediate 'proto-Tiberian' stage being seen in the mss of the so-called ben Naftali type. Other scholars have accepted this view.[19] The following points can be raised against this theory. (i) No Palestinian ms ever uses a sign comparable in function to Tiberian *shewa*, even though the dialect undoubtedly used '*shewa* vowels' much as did bA (see 11 above). Conversely, I know of no Tiberian ms which does not use *shewa*, however similar its pointing may otherwise be to Palestinian.[20] The conclusion seems inevitable

[19] To the extent that Yeivin can call it a 'highly probable assumption that the Tiberian system developed out of the Palestinian one,' without supporting argument (Yeivin, 1963, p. 127). For Díez-Macho's views, see Díez-Macho, 1960, and works cited there.

[20] This statement is no longer true, since in 1967–68 I found two mss with Tiberian pointing which do not use a *shewa* sign. These are, however, two mss among thousands, and appear to me to represent a *simplified*, rather than a *primitive*, form of Tiberian pointing, so the argument retains its force. One of the mss is Bod. Heb. d33 f. 60–61, a Hebrew-Arabic vocabulary to Exodus on parchment. All Tiberian signs except *shewa* are used. *Qibbuṣ* is rare, *segol* very rare, and possibly secondary, so that *ṣere* represents most 'e' vowels. *Qameṣ* and *pataḥ* occasionally interchange. *Pataḥ* is used where bA has *pataḥ* 'furtive' and 'vocal' *shewa*. *Śin* and *shin* are marked as in bA. *Dagesh forte* and (rarely) *lene* occur, also *rafe* on the '*begad kefat*' letters only. The Arabic words are also pointed with Tiberian signs (*shureq*, *pataḥ*, *ṣere* (rare), and *ḥireq*). Possibly the Arabic pointing system, which has no equivalent to 'vocal' *shewa*, has influenced the pointing of the Hebrew. The other ms is Westminster College (Cambridge), *Fragmenta Hebraica Cairensia Liturgica*, vol. III, no. 34, a liturgical fragment on paper. It uses all Tiberian signs except *shewa* and *qibbuṣ*, with *segol* used where bA would have 'vocal' *shewa*, and shows a strong tendency to interchange *pataḥ* and *segol* (*pataḥ* is rather rare), reflecting (presumably) Babylonian influence. Mss showing this influence not infrequently reserve the *shewa* sign (almost) exclusively to mark (bA) 'silent' *shewa*, while a 'full vowel' sign marks (bA) 'vocal' *shewa* (e.g. TS B14:64). In the Westminster fragment the marking of 'silent' *shewa* has been dispensed with.

that the *shewa* sign was a Tiberian (or Babylonian) invention by the use of which the language could be recorded much more efficiently than was possible in the Palestinian system. It was for the sake of this increase in efficiency that followers of the Palestinian tradition began recording their pronunciation in Tiberian signs, thus producing the 'ben Naftali' and similar types of pointing.

(ii) The mss published by Díez-Macho in illustration of his theory simply use both the Tiberian and the Palestinian systems to point the text. Both systems are usually complete and self-sufficient. The type of Tiberian pointing in such a text may be that of bA, or a divergent 'ben Naftali' type showing a Palestinian tradition. The Tiberian pointing may complement or replace the Palestinian.[21] Mss are found with Tiberian and Palestinian, Tiberian and Babylonian, or with all three systems. Such pointing gives no indication of the historical relationship of the systems involved, but only about the owners of the mss.[22]

(iii) A few mss are found which use a single Palestinian sign in an otherwise completely Tiberian pointing system. In this case the Tiberian system is, in all the examples I have seen, of a non-bA type showing a Palestinian tradition. The obvious assumption is that a change has been made from (native) Palestinian signs to (imported) Tiberian signs because they provided a more efficient medium. A Palestinian sign was retained for reasons of tradition, sentiment, or perhaps (since the sign in question is usually ⟨o⟩) clarity. Undoubtedly the change from Palestinian to Tiberian did occur in this situation, but equally certainly, in my opinion, Tiberian was already in use elsewhere when the change was made. If this were not so, why should the signs be changed at all?

(iv) One ms, to my knowledge, uses a Tiberian sign *(pataḥ)* in an otherwise completely Palestinian system. The probable reason is to avoid confusion with the Palestinian sign for the accent *rebiaʿ*. The ms in question (J.T.S. MS 594, box B, env. 12) also uses a Tiberian

[21] J.T.S. MS 594, box B, env. 12 is an example of a Palestinian text with bA type Tiberian pointing. Such 'bA type' pointing obviously does show a number of differences from the much more carefully pointed model codices, but can be called 'bA type' because it does not show any of the confusion or interchange of vowel signs common in Tiberian pointing related, for example, to Palestinian or Babylonian. This ms is an example of a text in which the Tiberian replaces the Palestinian pointing. TS H2:30 (II.6.C) is an example in which the Tiberian pointing complements the Palestinian. Another example of this (with a few exceptions) is TS NS 249:8+.

[22] See Wallenstein, 1958, p. 558.

accent sign, showing again that the Tiberian system was in use before this ms was pointed, and was copied, rather than the reverse.

15 The problem of the relationship of the Palestinian pointing system to the Tiberian is of significance for the evaluation of TS NS 249:14[a]+ (see II.9). This text is unique in that it shows Tiberian and Palestinian signs used not in two separate pointing systems, but combined into a single system. It might therefore seem extremely important as demonstrating the central stage of the supposed process of transition from Palestinian to Tiberian signs. However, such a view is to be rejected. The *naqdan* was obviously perfectly familiar with Tiberian pointing, which must, therefore, already have been in existence. His curious double system normally uses a Palestinian sign above the line and a Tiberian one below. Where no Tiberian sign was written below the line (i.e., in the case of *shureq*, *ḥolem*, and *dagesh*) the corresponding Palestinian sign was used in this position. Tiberian *shewa* is used, and is the only Tiberian sign for which a Palestinian equivalent does not occur. In view of the importance of the *shewa* sign (see 11 and 14(i) above) this seems a significant exception. Consequently, this pointing is probably nothing more than the result of idle experimentation by a Palestinian scribe who knew the Tiberian system. The fact that *qibbuṣ* is not used could perhaps be significant for the placing of this pointing.[23] It is quite probable, however, that the Tiberian system with which the *naqdan* was familiar was that of bA, since the pointing of the main text (TS NS 249:14+, see II.8) appears to me to show symptoms of bA influence.

16 In summary, then, the relationship of the Palestinian to the Tiberian pointing can be stated as follows. Palestinian pointing must have grown up either earlier than, or in isolation from, Tiberian. A period of contemporary use of the two systems ensued, during which the Tiberian system became increasingly popular. As a result of this popularity, the Tiberian system exerted influence on the Palestinian. This is shown in a number of ways, but most commonly, and most significantly, in the Palestinian attempts to specialize a single sign to correspond in function to Tiberian *shewa* (classes 1, 4, 5, 8,

[23] *Qibbuṣ* is used in some Tiberian mss even where *waw* is used as a *mater lectionis*, e.g. Bod. Heb. d55 f. 17–20 (see also II.6.F). The fact that *qibbuṣ* is not used in TS NS 249:14a+ suggests that the Tiberian pointing with which the *naqdan* was familiar was one in which *qibbuṣ* was specialized for use only when *waw* was not present as a *mater lectionis* (as is true in bA).

and isolated examples in other classes). The final result of the increasing popularity of the Tiberian system was its use by Palestinian scholars to reproduce their own pronunciation, and the consequent disuse of the Palestinian system. It is not considered impossible that the Tiberian pointing should have grown out of some early stage of the Palestinian, but it is considered that this conclusion is not warranted by the evidence at present available. In the opinion of the present author, however, Tiberian and Babylonian are much more likely to have had a common origin than Tiberian and Palestinian.

THE PALESTINIAN DIALECTS

17 In the discussion of the Palestinian vowels, and their tentative assignment to phonemes, in paragraphs 1–11 of this chapter, only cursory attention has been given to the claim that there is not one, but some dozen Palestinian pointing systems, which it was the purpose of chapters III and IV to prove. In those chapters each ms is taken at face value as the record of a pronunciation (see I.2). The division of the mss into classes with consistent characteristics surely demonstrates that this is the correct way to treat the Palestinian mss. There is no more error due to carelessness or ignorance in these mss than is normal in human endeavours. In paragraphs 12–16 of this chapter it has been argued that, although there is evidence of influence of the Tiberian pointing system on the Palestinian, the Tiberian ideas were applied to the better reproduction of the *Palestinian* pronunciation. There is little in any class which can be taken as an attempt to copy the bA pronunciation. Consequently, the vast majority of vowel signs occurring in Palestinian mss reproduce genuine Palestinian pronunciation. If this is so, the existence of some dozen pointing systems presents a problem of great interest.

18 The theory most commonly put forward in explanation of this phenomenon is that the Palestinian pointing underwent a unilinear development from the use of few signs to the use of many, and from a 'Palestinian type' use of those signs to a 'bA type' or 'Tiberianized' use. There are two very strong objections to this theory, one based on palaeography and the other on orthography.

(i) Despite the difficulty of dating Palestinian mss (see, for example, III.2.0) some broad statements can be made on the basis of the science of palaeography. Some mss with complex pointing are definitely earlier than some mss which use fewer signs. For example, TS 16:93 and TS E1:107 (see III.2.0) are earlier than TS H2:30 (see III.6.0).[24] The pointing of some classes was in use over a long period, during which other types of pointing were certainly used. Thus mss of class 2 were produced over a period of some three centuries, during which period most of the mss studied here were written (see III.2.0). Similarly mss with diverse types of pointing were produced at about the same time. For example, TS H16:3+ (class 7) and TS 13H2:11+ (class 6) are of about the same date.[25] While it is certainly not true to say that the date of the script of a ms is a certain guide to the date of its pointing (cf. TS H2:1 recto and verso), the homogeneity of script in some classes of pointing (see III.4.0, 5.0, 7.0) suggests that script and pointing were normally contemporary.

(ii) The argument of unilinear development in the use of the signs would require that the use of all the signs in a class show development from the class supposed to have preceded it. Yet if, of the group 4, 5, 6, and 7, class 4 be seen as the latest and class 7 as the earliest, as supposedly the most 'Tiberian' and 'a-Tiberian' respectively, how can classes 5 and 6 be placed in such a line of development? Similarly, how could the use of ⟨e′⟩ in classes 1–3 (where it normally represents a 'full vowel') have developed from its use in classes 4 and 5 (where it represents a '*shewa* vowel')? Or how could the use of ⟨e⟩ ≑ *shewa* in class 1 have developed from the use of ⟨e′⟩ ≑ *shewa* in class 4, which is closest to class 1 in most other features?

[24] TS H2:29, with a system of five vowel signs (class 11), is certainly among the latest mss described here; see III.11.0, and note there. In any case the argument that a simpler system must necessarily be earlier than a more complex one is obviously fallacious, as can easily be shown for the Tiberian pointing. The British Museum MS Or. 5556D, f. 22^{x}–23 is a sheet of paper containing a letter written in Portuguese. A few psalms were later written on the remaining blank spaces, and pointed with Tiberian signs in a system using five 'full' vowel signs and *shewa*. This is manifestly much later than the far more complex productions of Aaron ben Asher. Further TS Misc. 12:7, a printed text of Rashi's commentary on the Pentateuch, has a similar pointing added in ink.

[25] Probably the early ninth century. Another example is TS 12:195+ (class 3), and TS D1:12 (class 7), both dated *ca.* 700 in Weil, 1962, p. 69, although in my opinion TS D1:12 (with the simpler pointing!) is somewhat later. I consider this chronological point so important that I wrote to S. A. Birnbaum about it. He was good enough to allow me to quote his opinion (although he asked me to state that it is given 'with the very greatest reserve' because he had time only for a very superficial examination). He felt that my opinion of the *chronological relationship* of TS H16:6 to TS H16:7 (in my opinion the earliest and latest mss in class 2) and of TS H16:3+ to TS 13H2:11+ was justified, although he disagreed with the *absolute dates* I suggested.

19 In my opinion, these considerations of palaeography and orthography make any theory of unilinear development untenable. Some new basis for the understanding of the place of the various types of pointing within the Palestinian system must therefore be sought. Since we are dealing with written records of spoken language (see 17 above), we may expect that relationships between different texts will be shown in two areas: orthography and phonology. The mss have already been catalogued into classes on an orthographical basis. The 'full vowel' phonemes represented by the pointing of each class can be listed, on the basis of the discussions in 2–11 above, as in Table 2.[26]

TABLE 2

Class	⟨u⟩	⟨o⟩	⟨a⟩	⟨a′⟩	⟨e⟩	⟨e′⟩	⟨i⟩
1	/u/	/o/	/ɔ/	/a/	/ɛ/	e	/i/
2	/u/	/o/	/ɔ/	/a/	/ɛ ∼ e/		/i/
3	/u/	/o/	/ɔ ∼ a/		/ɛ ∼ e/		/i/
4	/u/	/o/	/ɔ/	/a/	/ɛ/	—	/i/
5	/u/	/o/	/ɔ ∼ a/		/ɛ/	—	/i/
6	/u/	/o/	/ɔ/	/a/	/ɛ/	—	/i/
7	/u/	/o/	/ɔ ∼ a/		/ɛ/	—	/i/
8	/u/	/o/	/ɔ/	—	/ɛ/	—	/i/
9	/u/	/o/	/ɔ/	—	/ɛ/	—	/i/
10	/u/	/o/	/ɔ/	—	—	/ɛ/	/i/
11	/u/	/o/	—	/ɔ/	/ɛ/	—	/i/

20 The differences between the various classes of pointing are, then, partly in the pronunciation which they indicate (e.g. classes 1, 3, 5), and partly in the way in which they indicate it (e.g. classes 4 and 6, 8 and 9). No reason for the two types of difference is apparent if the classes are studied individually. The classes themselves, however, fall into two major groupings, in which the significance of the phonological and graphic differences between them can be seen much more clearly.

21 The major distinction between the two groups (A and B) is most clearly seen in the comparison of classes 4 and 6 with classes 5 and 7. Classes 4 and 5 are superficially very similar. They both use ⟨e′⟩ only where bA has *shewa* and indicate the 'full vowels' with the six other signs only. Classes 6 and 7 appear equally similar. The only

[26] The signs used for the vowel qualities are conventional and not intended to represent any exact quality, although it is probable that the qualities involved were near those suggested by the symbols used. It is thought that the number of '*shewa* vowel' phonemes would be the same for each class. On this see 11 above.

difference between them and classes 4 and 5 is the fact that they do not use ⟨e′⟩. A closer look, however, shows that the classes should not be grouped in this way. The real difference between these four is that classes 4 and 6 use ⟨a⟩ and ⟨a′⟩ much as bA uses *qameṣ* and *pataḥ*, while classes 5 and 7 do not. Beyond this basic feature, mss of classes 4 and 6 on the one hand, and classes 5 and 7 on the other, show so many features in common in the use of vowel signs, diacritics, and even of script, that it is sometimes difficult to tell their members apart. Classes 4 and 6 can, then, be said to belong to a group A, the members of which characteristically use ⟨a⟩ and ⟨a′⟩ much as does bA, and show other signs of a conservative and well-preserved tradition. Classes 5 and 7 belong to group B, the members of which show many divergencies from bA usage, particularly in the case of the 'a' and 'e' signs. It is not difficult to project this classification into classes 1, 2, and 3. Class 1 must obviously belong to group A. Classes 2 and 3 belong to group B. With class 3 this is obvious, and class 2 is assigned to this group on the basis of its use of the 'e' signs, and of various similarities to classes 5 and 7 (see 22 below). Its members do, however, show a number of conservative features, although some of these may be due to bA influence. The projection of the group division into classes 8–11 is more difficult as it must be done on the basis of minor characteristics, of which there is not always adequate evidence. However, it would appear likely that class 8 (which shows a number of conservative – or possibly 'Tiberianizing' – features) and classes 9 and 11 should be assigned to group A, while class 10 is assigned to group B.

22 It is, of course, recognized that some small mss may have been wrongly classified. It is also possible that all mss known should not be fitted into this classification, but that those which show up as outtandingly atypical in the class to which they are assigned belong to groups other than A and B. However, the general validity of the division into two groups is demonstrated by Table 3, which compares their main characteristics according to classes.[27]

23 One further feature of these mss can be taken into consideration here: those uses of signs (apart from the interchange of the two 'a' and of the two 'e' signs) which suggest phonological development

[27] These characteristics are not always entirely without exceptions. These have been ignored for the purposes of the chart, but are in any case in very small proportion.

TABLE 3

The columns of the table indicate the following:

1–4 The 'a' and 'e' phonemes of each class.
5 The Palestinian sign used where bA has *ḥaṭuf qameṣ*.
6 The relative frequency and regularity of the use of ⟨i⟩ where bA has *shewa* before *yod* (F = 'frequent and regular').
7 The method of marking ⟨ś⟩ distinguished as <̲ (שׂ) and o (other).
8 The relative frequency of the marking of '*dagesh*' compared to that of ⟨ś⟩ (F = 'frequent').*

Class	1	2	3	4	5	6	7	8
Group A								
1	/ɔ/	/a/	/ɛ/	/e/	⟨a/o⟩	F	o	—
4	/ɔ/	/a/	/ɛ/		⟨o⟩	F	o	F
6	/ɔ/	/a/	/ɛ/		⟨o⟩	F	o	F
8	/ɔ/		/ɛ/		⟨o⟩	F	o	F
9	/ɔ/		/ɛ/		⟨o⟩	—	o	(F)
11	/ɔ/		/ɛ/		⟨o⟩	F	o	F
Group B								
2	/ɔ/	/a/	/ɛ ~ e/		⟨o/a/a'⟩	—	<̲/o	—
3	/ɔ ~ a/		/ɛ ~ e/		⟨o/a/a'⟩	—	o	—
5	/ɔ ~ a/		/ɛ/		⟨o/a/a'⟩	—	<̲	—
7	/ɔ ~ a/		/ɛ/		⟨o/a/a'⟩	—	<̲(o)	—
10	/ɔ/		/ɛ/		—	—	(o)	—

* In columns 6, 7, and 8, the characteristics of non-biblical mss of group B are taken as the type. Biblical mss may show characteristics closer to those of group A.

away from the bA pattern. These are listed in Table 4. The statistics are rather hard to evaluate, because of the different amounts of material from which the figures for the different classes are taken. However, two facts seem to be definitely indicated. These usages are more common in texts of group B than in those of group A (compare the figures for class 5 with those for class 4), which shows that group A texts indicate a more conservative pronunciation. The usages are also more common in non-biblical texts than in biblical (compare the figures for the two divisions of class 1, despite the fact that there is much more biblical than non-biblical material), which shows that the biblical pronunciation was more conservative than the non-biblical.[28] The following evidence is not used: that of TS 20:53+ for ⟨o⟩ ÷ *shureq* in class 3 (bib.), that of Heb. d29 f. 17–20 for ⟨e⟩ ÷ *ḥireq* in class 7 (bib.), and that of Heb. d63 f. 98 for ⟨e′⟩ ÷ *ḥireq* in class 2 (non-bib.). The reasons for this will be found in the descriptions of

TABLE 4

	Group A							Group B							
	Biblical	Non-biblical						Biblical			Non-biblical				
Usage	1	1	4	6	8	9	11	2	3	7	2	3	5	7	10
⟨o⟩ ÷ וּ	1	1	7	3	—	—	1	1	11	—	13	—	31	24	—
⟨u⟩ ÷ וֹ	—	1	2	3	—	—	1	—	—	2	4	2	4	35	—
⟨e⟩ ÷ ◌ָ	2	1	—	1	—	—	1	—	9	3	3	—	8	5	—
⟨e′⟩ ÷ ◌ָ	—	—	3	—	—	—	—	—	1	—	3	—	3	—	—
⟨e⟩ ÷ ◌ַ	2	—	—	4	—	—	—	—	2	—	6	—	16	16	—
⟨a′⟩ ÷ ◌ֶ	2	1	—	1	1	—	—	—	5	2	3	1	6	2	—
⟨i⟩ ÷ ◌ֶ	1	—	—	—	—	—	—	—	2	2	2	—	4	4	—
⟨a′⟩ ÷ ◌ֵ	2	2	3	2	—	—	—	—	1	1	9	—	4	8	—
⟨a⟩ ÷ ◌ֵ	—	—	8	—	—	1	—	—	4	—	4	—	4	5	1
⟨i⟩ ÷ ◌ֵ	—	1	1	—	—	—	—	1	—	—	5	—	5	18	—
⟨e⟩ ÷ ◌ִ	1	1	17	7	1	—	3	—	8	—	12	—	20	36	—
⟨e′⟩ ÷ ◌ִ	1	1	—	—	—	—	—	—	5	—	4	—	1	—	—
⟨a′⟩ ÷ ◌ִ	—	1	1	—	—	—	—	—	4	1	—	—	5	3	—
Other	4	—	—	1	—	—	—	—	22	6	8	—	11	10	—

those classes. It should also be noted that, for obvious reasons, this list does not attempt to discriminate between a usage reflecting a sound change and one probably caused by the use of a variant form. A considerable number of the usages reflected in the figures for biblical texts probably come from the latter source, so that the figures for those texts are probably slightly inflated in comparison with those for the non-biblical texts. This is particularly true of the figures for 'other usages.'

24 The Palestinian mss can thus be divided into two groups, A and B. The difference between these two groups lies mainly in the pro-

[28] This fact is, of course, demonstrated in a number of other ways. See chapter IV, Appendix; 12 above; and note to Table 3.

nunciation represented. These phonological differences can be summarized as follows:

(i) Where two 'a' signs or two 'e' signs are used, mss of group A invariably use them distinctively. According to the conclusions of 19 above, then, where they use two 'a' or two 'e' signs they represent two 'a' or two 'e' phonemes, showing a strong tendency to preserve the pattern found in bA. Members of group B never show more than one 'e' phoneme, and only in class 2 do they represent more than one 'a' phoneme. This shows that in this group the situation found in bA has to a considerable extent broken down.

(ii) The interchanges of other vowel signs characteristic of Palestinian mss reflect developments which took place in the language after the stage recorded by bA. In group A there are relatively few of these, again showing the tendency to adhere to the older pattern. In group B such interchanges are relatively common, reflecting a dialect which changed faster.

(iii) In group A, with the exception of class 1, ⟨o⟩ is used where bA has *qameṣ ḥaṭuf*. In group B ⟨a⟩ and ⟨a′⟩ are used as well. The use of ⟨a′⟩ shows that this is not a matter of conformity with bA, but a usage deriving (presumably) from the influences which caused the other changes found in this group. The use of ⟨a⟩ in class 1 is probably due to bA influence.

(iv) The use of ⟨i⟩ where bA has *shewa* before *yod* is regular and consistent in mss of group A. This corresponds to the pronunciation,[29] although not the spelling, of bA. The fact that this usage is irregular or non-existent in many mss of group B probably indicates the assimilation of this special case to the typical pronunciation of '*shewa* vowels.'[30] Again this suggests that in group B older patterns preserved in bA have broken down.

(v) The remaining point to be made from Table 3 above is that mss of group A tend to mark '*dagesh*' frequently and ⟨ś⟩ rarely, while mss of group B do the opposite. This may be a purely graphic phenom-

[29] As recorded by a long series of grammarians beginning with the author of the *Diqduqe ha-Ṭeʿamim* and *Saadya Gaʾon*. See Revell, 1970, II, no. 13. See now also Mosheh ben Asher in Allony, 1965, p. 146, ll. 62ff.

[30] I.e. {wiyiqtol} is replaced by {wəyiqtol} because the conjunction is in most cases pronounced {wə}. This process has certainly taken place in academic circles, despite the grammarians (see G-K, no. 10.e). The same sort of process probably caused the replacement by {wə} of {u} as a pronunciation of the conjunction (see Revell, 1970, I, no. 35).

enon, as the method of marking '*dagesh*' and ⟨ś⟩ certainly is. However, it is true that in mss of group B, which mark '*dagesh*' rarely, many sign changes appear to stem from the loss of lengthening ('doubling') in consonants which in bA are lengthened (and therefore marked with *dagesh*), and the consequent quality change ('compensatory lengthening').[31] The tendency of mss of group B not to mark '*dagesh*' may, therefore, reflect a phonological feature of the dialect. If so, this again shows the breakdown of older patterns in group B while they are retained in group A.

25 This analysis shows that the two groups, A and B, represent two strata of Hebrew pronunciation. The difference can be described generally by saying that, while both show evidence of change subsequent to the stage of the language recorded by bA, in group A the patterns found in that stage are largely preserved, while in group B many of them are breaking down, or are lost completely. Despite the appearance thus presented, it is most unlikely that a development bA > group A > group B is involved. The two groups both show the same range of classes with seven, six, and five vowel signs. In some cases the classes have identical distinguishing features (see below). This suggests that the development of the two groups was parallel, a suggestion fully supported by the palaeography of the mss involved. The two groups, then, represent two major divisions of Hebrew pronunciation current in the region of Palestine from the seventh to the tenth centuries. The one division (group A) was conservative, and resisted change. The other (group B) was not conservative, and underwent considerable change, largely, no doubt, under the influence of the various other languages spoken in the area.

26 Once the distinguishing features of groups A and B are isolated, it can be seen that the features distinguishing the classes within each group are largely graphic. The one major exception to this is the number of 'a' and 'e' phonemes used in each class. On the basis of these, group A can be divided into three subgroups.

(i) Class 1: seven vowel signs, each representing a 'full-vowel' phoneme.

(ii) Classes 4 and 6: seven or six vowel signs, representing six 'full-vowel' phonemes. The distinction between the two classes in this subgroup is graphic: the use in class 4 of ⟨e′⟩ ≑ *shewa*.

[31] See Revell, 1970, 1, no. 16.

(iii) Classes 8, 9, and 11: six or five vowel signs representing five 'full-vowel' phonemes. The major distinction between the classes in the subgroup is again graphic: class 8 uses ⟨a'⟩ ÷ *shewa*, while classes 9 and 11 use different signs to mark the 'a' phoneme.

27 If the classes of group B are analysed in this way, they are found to contain only two subgroups:

(i) Class 2: seven vowel signs representing six 'full-vowel' phonemes.

(ii) Classes 3, 5, 7, and 10: seven, six, or five vowel signs representing five 'full-vowel' phonemes. The difference between the classes is graphic. Classes 3 and 5 use seven signs, but in class 5 ⟨e'⟩ ÷ *shewa* only. Class 7 uses six signs, and class 10 uses five signs. These classes were also probably distinguished by the use of the allophones of the 'a' and 'e' phonemes required by their pointing (see 19 above), but it is possible that, in mss using only one 'a' or 'e' phoneme, and one sign to represent it, these allophones were still distinguished in speech but not in writing.

28 The question of the significance of these classes is a difficult one, and probably one that cannot be completely solved with the information at present available. Again it seems unlikely that the different classes represent chronological stages of the language or of the pointing system within either group, although the graphic differences between some of them may represent chronological stages. There does not seem to be any reason why the systems forming the three subgroups of group A should not have been in use at the same time. The following observations suggest reasons for the different systems of pointing.

Group A

(i) Class 1 represents a pronunciation very close to that of bA. The use in this class of ⟨a⟩ ÷ *qameṣ ḥaṭuf*, of a single sign where bA has *shewa* (except in special cases), and of the Tiberian form of *mappiq* in the biblical texts almost certainly derives from bA influence. The mss of this class, then, are probably to be assigned to a period and area in which the bA pronunciation of Hebrew, and the bA pointing system, were recognized as superior. It is, however, possible that some mss of this class could have been produced by a highly conservative group independent of bA influence.

(ii) Classes 4 and 6 differ from class 1 mainly in the fact that they only represent one 'e' phoneme. If the theory presented here is correct, and bA and class 1 do represent archaic pronunciations of Hebrew, then classes 4 and 6 represent a form less archaizing and closer to the common speech. This is not to be considered as a different chronological stage of the language, except in the sense that, while both have been in use contemporaneously, one was better preserved than the other. The difference between classes 4 and 6 is perhaps that class 6 represents an early stage of the development of the writing system of this subgroup. Class 4, in which the specialization of a single sign (⟨e′⟩) to indicate '*shewa* vowels' has begun (and is almost complete in some mss), would represent a later stage of development under the influence of the Tiberian pointing system.

(iii) Classes 8, 9, and 11 would represent a third form of the language in which only one 'a' and one 'e' phoneme were used. This form is presumably the closest to the pronunciation current in everyday speech. Again there are two forms: class 9, probably earlier, and class 8, later, since it has specialized one sign (⟨a′⟩) for the representation of '*shewa* vowels,' probably under the influence of the Tiberian pointing system. The one ms of class 8 shows a number of possible instances of bA influence (see II.8) which would support this suggestion. Class 11 uses a different set of signs from classes 8 and 9, and, therefore, may well derive from a different locality. This is suggested also by its script. Its use of signs, particularly the relatively frequent marking of '*shewa* vowels' in a rather sparsely pointed ms, and the frequent use of '*dagesh*' and '*rafe*' signs, suggests a relatively late period in the development of the Palestinian pointing.

29 The classes of group B can be understood in the same way.

Group B

(i) Class 2 is the only class in this group to retain two 'a' phonemes. This is probably a genuine archaic survival, although some mss in this class do show signs of bA influence (see III.2). Mss of classes 2 and 3 are sometimes hard to distinguish. It is possible that these two classes should be included in a single subgroup with three divisions: (a) the most archaic form of group B retaining two 'a' phonemes and other archaic features found in group A (mss of class 2); (b) a later form in which these archaic features are being lost (mss of class 3); (c) a 'Tiberianized' form in which the graphic distinction of 'a' signs, and some other old features, have been restored under bA influence (mss of class 2). However, the evidence at present is not sufficient to warrant the acceptance of this suggestion.

(ii) Class 3 is the most archaizing form of this subgroup, since it still retains a graphic distinction between the allophones of the 'e' phonemes. On this basis it should possibly be placed in subgroup (i). Classes 5 and 7 represent a less archaic form of the language than do classes 2 and 3. As in classes 4 and 6 of group A, the fact that class 5 has specialized ⟨e′⟩ to indicate '*shewa* vowels' suggests that it is the later, and class 7 the earlier, form of pointing in this subgroup.[32] Class 10 presumably represents a form of the language close to the contemporary everyday speech. However, the use of the ⟨e′⟩ sign to represent the single 'e' phoneme is most unexpected, since ⟨e⟩ is elsewhere used for this purpose. Mss of this class might derive from some locality outside the main Palestinian area, as was suggested for class 11. However, the pointing in mss of class 10 is so sparse that it is possible that the complete pointing system is not displayed in any of the available fragments. These mss may, then, be sparsely pointed examples of class 2 or 3. The script of these mss and in some cases the signs used (Tiberian mark of ⟨ś⟩) suggest that they are relatively late productions.

30 It is suggested here that the reason for the existence of the various classes of pointing is not the historical development of the pointing system, although that was a factor, but the purpose for which a text was pointed. It is for this reason that the classes of groups A and B show parallel types of pointing. Class 1 (group A) and classes 2 and 3 (group B) use seven vowel signs. They represent the most archaizing pronunciations in their respective groups. Undoubtedly these forms of pointing had the highest prestige in their respective groups. The vast majority of biblical mss fall into these classes. Classes 4 and 6 (group A) and classes 5 and 7 (group B) show a less archaizing form of language. Two stages of development can be seen in each group, showing that this form was long in use, and the method of writing it not stagnant but progressive. The same development is found in each group, suggesting that these are forms of language used by two communities in contact. It would be impossible to suggest either that classes 4, 5, 6, and 7 (in any order) are representative of a single line

[32] Mss of both classes use the 'dot' form of the ⟨a′⟩ sign which Díez-Macho regards as original (Díez-Macho, 1957, p. 30). However, this form of the sign cannot be regarded as the earliest (unless the development of the entire Palestinian system from the system of classes 5 and 7, which it would be very hard to argue plausibly, is envisaged). The 'dot' form of ⟨a′⟩ must be taken simply as characteristic of the *naqdanim* who produced the mss of classes 5 and 7.

of development, or that classes 1, 2, and 3 developed out of (or into) the pointing of classes 4 and 5. Classes 4–7 show, then, a form of pointing separate from that of classes 1 and 2, and most probably used at the same time for different purposes. It was probably the standard form for literary language. Most of the liturgical texts fall into these four classes. Classes 8, 9, and 11 (group A) and class 10 (group B) show forms of language probably very close to that of everyday speech. The pointing here also (at least in group A) shows evidence of internal development, and therefore of long use. However, few mss fall into these classes, and most of those that do are sparsely pointed. Probably most mss using these styles of pointing did so from motives of economy, pointing, for the most part, only the few words that might otherwise give rise to ambiguity.[33] This would be the form of pointing with the least prestige, and it is probably significant that no biblical texts fall into these classes.[34]

31 The analysis of the Palestinian pointing system thus shows that there were, in the 'Palestinian' area, two major dialect groups. There is no evidence as to the communities who spoke these dialects, but the suggestion that they existed is not inherently improbable. Group A, for example, might represent the Jews of Palestine, whose pronunciation still had much in common with the equally 'Palestinian' (although better preserved) pronunciation of bA. Group B might represent the Jews of Egypt, whose pronunciation would be open to a greater variety of foreign influences. In each dialect group, a number of forms of language were used. These 'subgroupings' (see 28 and 29 above) were probably in use at the same time for different purposes.[35] These subgroups do show linguistic development within the dialect groups, but are not to be thought of as chronological stages, or as 'dialects' except in the restricted sense of literary pronunciation of varying degrees of archaism. They probably do not represent a form of the language that was ever used in everyday speech.[36] The classes of pointing within the subgroup show differences which are merely

[33] TS NS 249:14+ is, of course, an exception.

[34] Biblical texts using only five 'full-vowel' signs do, however, occur with Tiberian pointing in a Palestinian tradition (e.g. TS NS 42:1), although they are very rare.

[35] For the use of different pronunciations for biblical and non-biblical texts in other communities, see Morag, 1963, Introduction, p. 14.

[36] Presumably the bA pronunciation also was never used in everyday life – to the extent that it is the product of a compromise among a number of traditional pronunciations with minor differences.

graphic. These indicate chronological development of the system of pointing used to write the pronunciation of the particular subgroup. The situation thus envisaged may seem chaotic to one who thinks of written Hebrew in terms of the relative uniformity resulting from the general acceptance of the bA system (or the complete uniformity imposed by the authors of introductory grammars). However, comparison with the situation in most written languages before – and for some time after – the introduction of printing suggests that it would be more surprising if this much diversity did not exist in Palestinian Hebrew.

VI

List of Texts

All Hebrew texts with Palestinian vowel signs mentioned in this book are listed here, with the exception of those that use a single Palestinian sign in a pointing which is otherwise Tiberian. Those of this type that I know have either been published by Dr. Díez-Macho, or were drawn to my attention by him as texts of which he was proposing to publish a study. Such texts, although interesting and important, cannot be classified by the methods used in this study, and so are not listed here. For similar reasons texts that use Palestinian accent signs, but no vowel signs, are also omitted from this list.[1]

Each fragment is listed under its library number. Fragments deriving from the same ms are also listed together under the number of the first fragment of that ms to be published, or, if none are published, that of the first fragment in the ms. All information about such fragments is given in this combined listing. An exception to the rule of priority has been made in the case of the 'Levias' fragment, as it is no longer available for study. Fragments of that ms are therefore listed under H.U.C. MS 1001. Throughout this study the fragments are referred to by their library numbers. Where several fragments of the same ms are known, they are referred to by the number used for the combined listing, followed by a + sign (e.g. H.U.C. MS 1001+). In a few cases the library number of a ms has been changed since its

[1] Bodleian MS Heb. c18, f. 17–22, a Midrash text described in Allony, 1963, p. 31, as having 'much (Palestinian) pointing,' appears to combine these characteristics, as it has a thoroughgoing (though simple) Palestinian accentation, and occasional use of the Palestinian ⟨o⟩ sign. Tiberian accents are also used, though not throughout, as is a Tiberian pointing system with some interesting features. Consequently, although there is a considerable amount of Palestinian 'pointing,' the Palestinian 'vocalization' which it shows does not warrant its being listed.

publication. Such mss are described under the old number marked with an asterisk, with cross-reference under the new number.

If a ms has been published or described previously, references are given. The content of unpublished mss is described. An attempt has been made to give references to other known texts of *piyyuṭim* occurring in these mss, but because of my unfamiliarity with this field, my researches have extended little further than Israel Davidson's *Thesaurus of Mediaeval Hebrew Poetry*.[2] This work is referred to throughout this chapter as D. In order to give as much help as possible to the student of literature, an index of the first lines of the poems found in the unpublished texts is given as an appendix to the chapter. For mss found in 1967–68 and included here, no first lines are given, and the pointing classification is given in parentheses.

As was stated in the Preface, many of the unpublished mss listed here were discovered by Dr. Dietrich, and formed the original basis of this study. Others were discovered by Dr. N. Allony, by Dr. A. Díez-Macho, and by Dr. I. Yeivin, who very kindly drew them to my attention. I have indicated these mss by means of footnotes.

A MANUSCRIPTS IN THE CAMBRIDGE UNIVERSITY LIBRARY

(i) *Taylor-Schechter Collection, 'Original Series'*

TS 12:189 + 12:208. Taylor, 1900, pp. 93f., and plate XI. Palimpsest, Hebrew over Greek. Midrash on Genesis with occasional Palestinian pointing, too sparse to classify.

TS 12:191. Lewis and Gibson, 1900, no. XVIII. Mandelbaum, 1962, description p. 13, photograph (recto) p. 28 (both as TS 12:1a1). Dated (p. 13) ninth or tenth century. Palimpsest, Hebrew over Western Syriac. *Pesiqta de Rav Kahana* with pointing of class 2.

TS 12:195 + 12:196 + NS 249:3. Kahle, 1930, MS L (TS 12:195 + 196), Dietrich, 1960, MS Cb 8. Photograph Kahle, 1930, plate 10, also Birnbaum, 1954–57, plate 91*. In the temporary 'List of Facsimiles' accompanying the latter work this text is dated *ca.* 700–800 (changed by hand in my copy from *ca.* 600–700). Parts of Psalms (51–55, 69–72, 74–77) with pointing of Class 3.

TS 12:196. See TS 12:195+.

[2] Published by the Jewish Theological Seminary of America, New York, 1924–33.

TS 12:197. Kahle, 1930, MS K, and plate 9. Parts of Jeremiah (1–2). Mixed pointing, see IV.12.

TS 12:208. See TS 12:189+.

TS 12:210. See TS NS 249:14+.

TS 12:210[a]. See TS NS 249:14[a]+.

TS 12:744. See TS 16:322+.

TS 12:745. See TS 16:322+.

TS 16:93. Allony and Díez-Macho, 1959[a], with some photographs. Complete (and excellent) photographs are given in Taylor, 1900, plates IX and X. Palimpsest, Hebrew over Greek. Dated by Allony and Díez-Macho (p. 58) to the eighth or ninth century, by Mandelbaum, 1962, p. 13, to the tenth or eleventh century. *Pesiqta de Rav Kahana* with pointing of class 2.

TS 16:96 + NS 208:23 + NS 301:75. Kahle, 1930, MS J, and plate 8 (TS 16:96). Parts of Daniel (9–12) with pointing of class 3.

TS 16:322 + 16:323 + 16:324 + 12:744 + 12:745 (probably also Bod. Heb. b13 f. 12–13, Bod. Heb. e73 f. 42-3, and Cambridge Or. 1080, Box 4:65). Lewis and Gibson, 1900, nos. ii, iii, v, xii, xxiv, and plates II and III (TS fragments). Various parts of *Bereshit Rabba* dated by Dr. Schechter (there) to the tenth or eleventh century. Palimpsest, Hebrew over Western Syriac. Occasional Palestinian pointing, too sparse for certainty, but probably of class 2.

TS 16:323. See TS 16:322+.

TS 16:324. See TS 16:322+.

TS 16:327. See TS 16:351+.

TS 16:351 + 16:327. Lewis and Gibson, 1900, no. XV (16:327). Palimpsest, Hebrew over Western Syriac. *Torat Cohanim*, with occasional Palestinian points, too sparse to classify, but probably of class 2 or 3.

TS 16:383. See *TS NS 249:8+.

TS 20:52. See TS 20:53+.

TS 20:53 + 20:52 + 20:54 + 20:58.[3] Murtonen, 1958, MS c (see also Murtonen, 1964, pp. 16f.). Allony and Díez-Macho, 1958a (20:53 + 54), 1958b (see also 1959b) (20:52 + 58). Photographs in both editions, also Kahle, 1959, plate I. Allony and Díez-Macho did not assign all these fragments to the same ms. However, the

[3] Recently I was kindly informed by Dr. I. Yeivin that MS 273 (E.N.A. 3550) of the Jewish Theological Seminary in New York is a fragment of this ms. As this text is notoriously difficult to read from photographs (and as the pointing appears sparse), I have not included it here.

only real difference between the fragments as far as the pointing is concerned lies, I think, in the use of the 'a' signs. In TS 20:54, 41 of the 43 uses of ⟨a⟩ are in open final syllables; in TS 20:53, 16 out of 20; in TS 20:58, 3 out of 7; and in TS 20:52, 1 out of 3. These differences seem to be outweighed by the similarities between the fragments, some of which are unique in this ms: for example, the small number of accents, frequent use of ⟨o⟩ to mark consonantal *waw*, irregular use of 'e' signs in segolate nouns (see Revell, 1967, I, no. 11). Consequently I have treated these fregmants as part of the same ms. Parts of Psalms (26–33, 35–46, 52–62) with pointing of class 3.

TS 20:54. See TS 20:53+.

TS 20:58. See TS 20:53+.

TS 20:59 + *TS 2nd 1:125. Kahle, 1930, MS H (20:59) and plate 7. Dietrich, 1960, MS Cb 5. Parts of Ezekiel (1–2, 13–16) with pointing of class 3.

TS 20:182. Lewis and Gibson, 1900, nos. i and viii and plate 1. Palimpsest, Hebrew over Western Syriac. Liturgy for Tabernacles. Badly preserved. Dated by Dr. Schechter (there) to the tenth or eleventh century. Sparse pointing of class 3.

TS A39:9. See J.T.S. MS 504 f. 2+.

TS A43:1. See Bod. Heb. e30 f. 48–9+.

TS B17:25. Yeivin, 1963, pp. 121–4. Parts of Isaiah (11, 53, 56, 63), Hosea (10), Micah (7), with pointing of class 7.

TS D1:12. Weil, 1962 (also Kahle, 1927, p. 29). A fragment of *'Okla we'Okla*. Dated by Weil (p. 69) *ca.* 700. Pointing of class 7.

TS D1:19. Two fragments of a lexical work, Hebrew and Arabic, with annotations in Arabic script. Tiberian pointing, with a few Babylonian signs, as well as the occasional Palestinian signs, too sparse to be classified.[4]

TS E1:107. Allony, 1963 (also Kahle, 1927, p. 28). Mishna, parts of *Baba Batra* and *Sanhedrin*. Dated by Allony (p. 32) to the eighth or ninth century. Pointing of class 2.

TS E2:76. Listed in Kahle, 1959, p. 70, n. 2. Two small leaves of parchment. Mishna, parts of *Sanhedrin*, *Makkot*, *Shebu'ot*. Sparse Palestinian vocalization of class 6.

[4] This ms was kindly drawn to my attention by Dr. N. Allony, who has also generously encouraged me to make use of other mss, such as those in TS NS box 301, which he was the first to find.

TS H2:1. Zulay, 1936, p. 322. Recto contains poems by Yannai (Zulay, 1938, MS 1, p. 283) with pointing of class 1. Verso contains the first three parts of the *qeroba* שיר השירים אימרת צרופה (see D, no. ש 943; צרופה of H2:1 v1 was corrected to צפה, as in D's listing). The pointing of the verso is of class 7.

TS H2:2. See TS H16:3+.

TS H2:29. Ms 11, class 11.

TS H2:30. Ms 6, class 6.

TS H2:44. An incomplete leaf of parchment containing the poem אהללה אלהי אשירה עוזו (D, no. א 1494; see H2:61) from the second *gimel* stich to the third *taw* stich. Few variants from H2:61. Sparse pointing of class 3.

TS H2:45 + H2:58. Two fragments forming most of a leaf of parchment. Passover liturgy, containing the title סלוק חורן v24. Sparse pointing of class 2.

TS H2:55. A leaf of parchment with one corner and the inside margin torn away. Part of a *qeroba* on Exodus 15:22 f. Initial lines of poems are אומן כראם מלינים (r19), אנוסים כפופים רדו אל סוף (v11), איום בחן וביאר כל עצי מדה (v26). Tiberian vocalization confusing *qameṣ* and *pataḥ*. Palestinian vocalization of class 6.

TS H2:58. See TS H2:45+.

TS H2:61. A fascicle of six leaves of parchment containing liturgy for various occasions. The following poems are found: המאמירים באימה ואומרים (1r15) by Yoḥanan haKohen (D, no. ה 736); אפס אין בילתך (1v16); אות יום משפט (2r3); אפתח פי ברנן (2r13), each stich ending with מלוכה; אהללה אלוהי אשיר עוזו (2v5) by Yose ben Yose (D, no. א 1494; cf. TS H2:44); אנא ממליך ומיסיר אול (3v19), each stich ending with מלוכה (the poem is incomplete, but space was left to finish it); אחוז נא במשפט ותימלוך (4r9), each stich ending במ׳ ות׳; אפחד במעשיי (4v9) by Yose ben Yose (D, no. א 7117); את לן [ ] תיזכרנו (5v19), each stich ending with תיזכרנו; אב לא חסך בנו (6r11); זוכרינו בזיכרון טוב (6v4). Various prayers are interspersed between the poems. Occasional Tiberian signs. Sparse Palestinian pointing, provisionally assigned to class 11.

TS H2:72. Zulay, 1936, p. 322; 1938, MS 2, p. 17. Poems by Yannai, pointing of class 4.

TS H2:75 Zulay, 1936, p. 369; 1938, MS 127, p. 273. Recto contains poems by Yannai for Passover, verso contains a *shibaʿta* on the Song of Songs, evidently by some other author. Pointing of class 7.

TS H3:4. Liturgy for the Feast of Weeks (class 1).

TS H5:25. Edelmann, 1934, MS D_1. Liturgy for the Day of Atonement by Yoḥanan haKohen. Assigned by Edelmann to the same ms as H16:10 (class 1), but since the four uses of the 'a' and 'e' signs in this ms show one case of ⟨a⟩ ≑ *pataḥ* and one one of ⟨e⟩ ≑ *ṣere*, this is not justified, at least as far as the pointing is concerned. The pointing is too sparse to allow more than a provisional assignment to class 9.

TS H5:222. Two pieces of parchment sewn together to form a scroll. Liturgy for the Day of Atonement. Badly preserved. Sparse pointing of class 3.

TS H6:28 + NS 116:37. Part of אתה כוננתה by Yose ben Yose (class 2?).

TS H6:29. An incomplete sheet of parchment. Liturgy for the Day of Atonement. The following initial lines of poems are found: אין לנו לא אשים ולא אשם (r6; see D, no. א 3050), לולי אדונינו מעט הותירנו (r27), או״א בהיות אר[ון] בית קודש הקדשים (v11; D, no. ב 175), אופל אלמנה תאיר (v23; D, no. א 4805). With various rubrics, some, as the poems, still in use. Pointing of class 10.

TS H6:38. Most of a sheet of parchment containing liturgy for the Day of Atonement. The initial lines of poems on the recto are lost. Those on the verso are: אין לנו מזבח לכפר (v5), כתועים ואין לבקש (v16; D, no. כ 574), תנות צרות לא נוכל (v24; D, no. ת 401). TS H6:97, which contains the same liturgy, follows this with כי ארבנו זה לזה (v17) and תבעתה ולא הישגחנו (v26). With various rubrics, some, as the poems, still used. Pointing of class 1.

TS H6:39. A sheet of parchment forming two leaves, somewhat damaged. Contains the *'Aboda* אזכיר גבורות by Yose ben Yose, from the end of the *'alef* verse to the end of the *resh* verse. Sparse Palestinian pointing of class 7.

TS H6:40. Most of a leaf of parchment containing liturgy for the Day of Atonement. The initial lines of the first poems are lost. The first one visible is או״א אל תעש עמנו כלה (r16; D, no. א 4808). After this the following titles and biblical passages are quoted:

recto

23 אׄינו ואׄי א[בׄו] אופל אלמנה (D, no. א 4805) כׄכׄ עׄיׄנׄ והביאותים (Isa. 56:7)

24]אׄינו ואׄי אבׄו תבוא לפניך ת[ ]אתה רחום (כׄכׄ) עׄיׄנׄ שובו[

25]זדונות והשגגות וגׄו מה[ ]לפניך וגׄו אתה יודיע רזי וגׄו[(D, no. א 8808)

26 [נו ואי אבו שתכפר לנו ע] [עוונותינו] [מחול ותסלח]
27 [עבור על פשעינו ועל חט שחט וגו ודויד עב]
28 ומאהבתך יי אינו את ישר ע וגו (D, no. ו 328)

These are followed by the poem יום אדיר לאל רם (r29), each of whose verses is introduced by יום, with the initial letters of the following words forming a double alphabetic acrostic. The verso contains the poem through the first *pe* verse. Pointing of class 1.

TS H6:51. See TS NS 117:7+.

TS H6:97. Most of a leaf of parchment containing liturgy for the Day of Atonement, for which see TS H6:38. Pointing of class 7.

TS H7:1. A leaf of parchment containing liturgy for Tabernacles by Qalir (cf. the title שמונה עשרה הושענא ד̄ר אלעזר r15). Initial lines of poems preserved are: אדמוה רבו אות במועד גש דרישת (r2), אם צרותיה (r6), הושענא אל אמונה אום שרה (r16), הינוו אתנו לך (v9), ומראשית שנה לכן אכוונה שני לבבות (v18), לשבט אם לארצו (v14), ועד אחרית שנה (v23), ונגילה ונשמחה בישועתך (v26). Sparse pointing of class 9.

TS H7:2.[5] A sheet of parchment folded to form two leaves, somewhat damaged, containing liturgy for Tabernacles. Initial lines of poems preserved are all on fol. 1: או״א אם תחנה תבל תפקוד בגשם (1r16), עלי מחנה (1r24), אביבי אדמת ארץ אמץ בברכת גשם (1v18, alphabetic acrostic, each line ending בבר׳ ג׳). Folio 2 contains a long poem in verses of three rhyming stichs followed by a fourth ending מים. The initial letters of each verse form a double alphabetic acrostic. A few Tiberian signs are used, apparently much as bA. Occasional Palestinian signs, too few to permit classification, but probably (cf. ⟨i⟩ ≑ *shewa* before *yod* (2r13), שׁ marks ⟨ś⟩ as in 1v9) of class 6.

TS H7:7. Ms 12, class 12.

TS H7:15 + NS 272:2. A leaf of parchment with most of the outer half torn away. Liturgy for Tabernacles by Qalir. The recto contains the second half of Qalir's poem אקשטה כסל וקרב להביע בעד מים (D, no. א 7419), followed by תיכנס לארץ וחוצות לחצות מים (r26; D, no. ת 267). The latter poem ends at v19. No further initial lines are visible. Sparsely pointed with Tiberian signs used much as bA. A few Palestinian signs of class 3.

TS H7:44. A torn leaf of parchment containing liturgy for Tabernacles. Poems on the recto are תיקרא לה עוד אחת (r1, '*tashraq*'

[5] See note 4.

acrostic to *lamed*), אני ארעה (r15, each stich beginning with אני, ending with מחצתי ואני ארפא, and containing two letters of an alphabetic acrostic), אדום אמרה אן קץ (r23, by Qalir; D, no. א 476). The writing on the verso is much faded, and contains no initial lines of poems which can be made out. The pointing is sparse, of class 9.

TS H15:69. Liturgy for *Parashat Para* by Qalir (class 2).

TS H16:1 + NS 249:1. Edelmann, 1934, MS F (H16:1). Ms 7, class 7.

TS H16:2. See TS H16:3+.

TS H16:3 + H16:2 + H2:2 + NS 249:12[6] + Bod. Heb. d63 f. 82–9 + Mosseri P171/2. Kahle, 1927 (with photographs of the Bodleian fragments), and 1956, pp. 38–47 (TS H16:2, H16:3, and Bod. Heb. d63 f. 82–9). Zulay, 1939, pp. 113–18 (TS H2:2 and Mosseri P171/2). TS NS 249:12 is a fragment torn from the sheet catalogued as TS H16:3, and so completes much of the missing material from (Heb.) pp. 1 and 2 of Kahle's edition. Contains *qerobot* on the 24 'priestly courses.' The pointing is of class 7.

TS H16:4. Murtonen, 1958, MS e with photograph (no. 4). Poems by Yannai with pointing of class 4.

TS H16:5. Edelmann, 1934, MS G. Liturgy for Tabernacles with pointing of class 7.

TS H16:6. Edelmann, 1934, MS A. Liturgy for Passover with pointing of class 2.

TS H16:7 + Leningrad Ant. 369. Kober, 1929. Poems by Yannai. In Revell, 1967, these two fragments were treated as belonging to different mss on the grounds of differences in their use of the 'e' signs. These differences were quantitative, and no longer seem to me significant, since the pointing of both fragments falls into class 2.

TS H16:8. Edelmann, 1934, MS B. Liturgy for the New Year with pointing of class 5.

TS H16:9 + Bod. Heb. d55 f. 4r–7v, 9r–12r. Edelmann, 1934, MS C (TS H16:9). The Bodleian ms is published in Murtonen, 1958, as the first part of MS a. It is separated from the second part of his MS a on account of differences in pointing which are apparent from the descriptions of the mss (see III.2 and 5). Murtonen, 1958, (Heb.) p. 60 gives some corrections to Edelmann's edition of TS

[6] This ms was discovered by Dr. Dietrich (see Dietrich, 1968, p. 9, where in the list of liturgical texts, TS NS 249:8 is accidentally written for TS NS 249:7).

H16:9. Bod. Heb. d55 f. 4 is photographed in Kahle, 1959, plates 2 and 3. Liturgy for various occasions. Class 5.

TS H16:10. Edelmann, 1934, MS D. Liturgy for the Day of Atonement. Class 1.

TS H16:12 + Bod. Heb. c20 f. 5–6. Described and partially published in Zulay, 1936, pp. 222f. See also p. 362.[7] *Qerobot* by Shimʿon haKohen on Genesis 24:42, 25:1, 27:1, 27:28, 28:10, and 29:31. Sparse pointing of class 6.

TS K25:108. See Bod. Heb. e30 f. 48–9+.

TS K26:1. Dietrich, 1960, MS Cb 2. Parts of Ezra (3–4) with pointing of class 7.

TS K26:8. See Bod. Heb. d44 f. 1–4+.

TS 10H5:7. See Bod. Heb. d63 f. 98+.

TS 10H7:1.[8] A sheet of parchment, somewhat damaged, folded to form two leaves. Liturgy for the New Moon day. Folio 1 contains part of a long poem in verses of two rhyming stichs. Folio 2 opens with the end of a poem, followed by כֹּכֹ וקרא. The next poem (2r16) opens כבודו חודש במגן ושמש and is followed by the rubric לעוֹמתם (2r26). The final part of the *qedušša* opens מֹמ יופיע על עמו (2v1). This is followed by a poem on the word אחד beginning שש[ה] דברים בם ניתאששה (2v11), followed by טומאה יעביר לטהרה (2v23). Occasional Tiberian signs. Sparse Palestinian pointing of class 6.

TS 10H10:7. A sheet of parchment folded to form two leaves. Headed (1r) קדושתא זכור. Contains the first five divisions of the poem, with acrostics as follows: (1) [אמר העדה (1r1 alphabetic); (2) תקיפה ניראית ככפ] (1r24 '*tashraq*'); (3) אדין בערב חימ] (2r4 '*atbash*'); (4) אספר נא נעשה (2v3 alphabetic to *mem*); (5) איתייעט עמלק בצאתו מצוען (2v9 alphabetic). Much of the text is written in a Hebraized Aramaic. The pointing is of class 9.

TS 13H2:10. Murtonen, 1958, MS d. *Qerobot* by Yannai with pointing of class 4.

TS 13H2:11 + 13H2:12. Zulay, 1936, p. 323; 1938, MSS 5 and 6, p. 192. *Qerobot* by Yannai with pointing of class 6.

TS 13H2:12. See TS 13H2:11+.

[7] See now Schirmann, 1965, pp. 5–8, where TS H16:12 2r31–2v end is published, and the Palestinian vowel signs (with a few errors and omissions) noted.

[8] See note 4.

(ii) *TS 'Second Series'* (Usually called *T.S. 'Miscellaneous'*; for current library numbers read 'Misc.' for '2nd')

*TS 2nd 1:44. Dietrich, 1960, MS Cb 4. Parts of Numbers 32 to Deuteronomy 1, with pointing of class 1.
*TS 2nd 1:125. See TS 20:59+.
*TS 2nd 1:130. Dietrich, 1960, MS Cb 6. Parts of Isaiah (11, 49, 63) and Hosea (10) with pointing of class 7.
*TS 2nd 2:71. Dietrich, 1960, MS Cb 7. Parts of Ezra (16–18, 27–30) with vocalization too sparse for classification.

(iii) *TS 'New Series'*

TS NS 67:1.[9] Two fragments, originally the upper inside part of two pairs of conjugate leaves of parchment. Contains parts of Exodus 27–30, Deuterononomy 12–14, 18, 20, written in two columns. Occasional Palestinian vowel signs, too few to classify.
TS NS 81:2.[10] Fragment of a leaf of parchment containing parts of Song 2–3. Sparse Tiberian pointing. One Palestinian sign (⟨e⟩, but the fragment is too small to permit the statement that this was the only Palestinian sign used in this text. The pointing cannot, of course, be classified.
TS NS 116:15^{b}.[11] A sheet of parchment folded to form two small leaves, the writing on 1v and 2r much faded. Poems for Hanukka, apparently by Yannai – at least in part. Folio 1r contains a poem תבל ומלואה לא יכילוך (with '*tashraq*' acrostic) which introduces the blessing « מחיה ». Folio 1v opens יקרנו במשכן and continues as a poem typical of the third division of a Yannai *qeroba*, with acrostic ינ״י. Two following poems on this folio open כמראה תבנית משכן שמים (1v8) and אוהל מועד אֱלוה עומד (1v14). The upper part of fol. 2r is obscure. At 2r9 there is a title סלוק מנשה את אפרים ואפרים את מנשה. The following poem opens שקול מנשה כאפרים and is continued on fol. 2v. Folio 2 is pointed with Tiberian signs in a style which confuses *qameṣ/pataḥ* and *segol/ṣere* (note also בִּיוֹם 2v13). Folio 2r has extensive corrections, probably by the Tiberian pointing hand. Folio 1 has sparse Palestinian pointing of class 10.
TS NS 116:37. See TS H6:28+.
TS NS 117:6[12] + NS 123:2. Ms 4a, class 4.

[9] This ms was kindly drawn to my attention by Dr. A. Díez-Macho.
[10] See note 9. [11] See note 6. [12] See note 6.

TS NS 117:7[13] + H6:51. Ms 10, class 10.

TS NS 117:13. A leaf of parchment, somewhat damaged. Liturgy for the Day of Atonement. Contains the following poems: כי אמרנו אין רואה (r4) and אריאל בקומה אכוף (r12), both with alphabetic acrostic. These are followed by two titles: הזדוֹנ[ ]וגו׳ and על חט שחטאנ[ו (r19). The following poem, אב[ינו ש]מע תחנונינו (r20), is composed in verses of four stichs, the initial letters of which form a quadruple alphabetic acrostic. The text breaks off at the fourth *qof* stich (v29). Sparse Palestinian pointing of class 9.

TS NS 118:38.[14] Ms 2, class 2.

TS NS 119:42[15] + NS 301:66. Ms 3, class 3.

TS NS 119:43. A sheet of parchment folded to form two small leaves, partially damaged. Liturgy for the Day of Atonement. Folio 1 contains a poem composed in verses of four rhyming stichs, the last of which alludes to or quotes a biblical passage which is given in full at the end of the verse. The stichs of a verse normally begin with the same letter, but the initial letters of the verses כהלחייה׳ע do not appear to be in any significant order. Folio 2 contains four rhyming stichs introducing the blessing «מגן», followed by a poem, תוחלת[ ]נמהרה טן טף מלילה (with '*tashraq*' acrostic), all the stichs of which have the same rhyme. Occasional Tiberian signs. The Palestinian pointing – almost entirely confined to a few lines on fol. 2r – is of class 6.

TS NS 123:2. See TS NS 117:6+.

TS NS 172:11. See TS NS 249:6+.

TS NS 208:23. See TS 16:96+.

TS NS 246:22. Díez-Macho, 1967. Part of II Chronicles (13–15). (Class 1.)

TS NS 249:1.[16] See TS H16:1+.

TS NS 249:2.[17] Ms 1, class 1.

TS NS 249:3. See TS 12:195+.

TS NS 249:5. See Bod. Heb. e30 f. 48–9+.

TS NS 249:6 + NS 172:11. Dietrich, 1960, MS Cb 9 (NS 249:6). I hope to publish NS 172:11 shortly. Part of I Chronicles (2–6) with pointing of class 2.

TS NS 249:7.[18] See H.U.C. MS 1001+.

*TS NS 249:8 + NS 281:2. Dietrich, 1960, MS Cb 10 (NS 249:8).

[13] See note 6. [14] See note 6. [15] See note 6.
[16] See note 6. [17] See note 6. [18] See note 6.

This ms is now listed as TS 16:383. Díez-Macho, 1963a (NS 281:2). Parts of Judges (6–9) with pointing of class 3.

TS NS 249:9. See Bod. Heb. e30 f. 48–9+.

TS NS 249:11.[19] A small fragment of a leaf of parchment. Passover liturgy. [א]ויב היקשה ערפו (v4) is the only initial line visible. Scant Palestinian pointing of class 6.

TS NS 249:12.[20] See TS H16:3+.

TS NS 249:13.[21] A damaged leaf of parchment inscribed in two columns with parts of Genesis 33–35. Occasional Palestinian pointing, possibly of class 11, but more probably the whole system is not represented. Both ש and שׂ mark ⟨ś⟩, e.g. עשׂה Gen. 34:7. ⟨i⟩ ÷ *shewa* before *yod* Gen. 34:16, 21. Note also וישׂב Gen. 33:16, אתם Gen. 34:8. Probably class 2 or 3.

TS NS 249:14[22] + 12:210. (Main hand) Ms 8, class 8.

TS NS 249:14^{a}[23] + 12:210^{a}. (Marginal hand) Ms 9, class 9.

TS NS 249:15.[24] Two pieces of parchment sewn together to form a scroll. Parts of five columns of writing, at right angles to the length of the scroll, are preserved, containing parts of Deuteronomy 28–29. Occasional Palestinian signs, too few to classify.

TS NS 272:2. See TS H7:15+.

TS NS 281:2. See *TS NS 249:8+.

TS NS 301:28. See H.U.C. MS 1001+.

TS NS 301:29. See Bod. Heb. e30 f. 48–9+.

TS NS 301:63. Liturgy for Passover (class 8).

TS NS 301:66. See TS NS 119:42+.

TS NS 301:75. See TS 16:96+.

(iv) *TS 'Miscellaneous'*

See TS 'Second Series' under (ii).

(v) *Oriental Manuscripts*

Or. 1080, Box 4:65. See TS 16:322+.

B MANUSCRIPTS IN THE BODLEIAN LIBRARY, OXFORD

Bod. Heb. b13 f. 12–13. See TS 16:322+.

Bod. Heb. c20 f. 5–6. See TS H16:12+.

[19] See note 6. [20] See note 6. [21] See note 9.
[22] See note 6. [23] See note 6. [24] See note 9.

Bod. Heb. d29 f. 17–20. Dietrich, 1960, MS Ob 1. Photograph, Kahle, 1961, plate 19. Parts of Joshua (14–21) with pointing of class 7.

Bod. Heb. d37 f. 38–9. See Bod. Heb. d44 f. 1–4+.

Bod. Heb. d41 f. 11–15. The text is described, and fol. 15v, 15r1–15, published, in Bar, 1936. The text (but not the pointing) is published in Davidson, 1928, pp. 8–35, with a photo of fol. 12r (wrongly captioned 'Heb. d14 ...') as frontispiece. Poems by Yannai and Samuel with pointing of class 7.

Bod. Heb. d44 f. 1–4 + Heb. d37 f. 38–39 + TS K26:8. Dietrich 1960, MS Ob 2/Cb 3. Parts of I Kings 16 to II Kings 10, Isaiah 32–37, 54–58, with pointing of class 2.

Bod. Heb. d55 f. 4r–7v, 9r–12r. See TS H16:9+.

Bod. Heb. d55 f. 12v–14v. Murtonen, 1958, MS a, second part, with photograph (no. 1), which is also given in Kahle, 1959, plate 4 (12v not 12r). Separated from the first part (the preceding listing) on account of the differences in pointing between them (see III.2 and 5). Part of the *'Aboda* אזכיר גבורות by Yose ben Yose with pointing of class 2.

Bod. Heb. d63 f. 82–9. See TS H16:3+.

Bod. Heb. d63 f. 97. See Bod. Heb. d63 f. 98+.

Bod. Heb. d63 f. 98 + f. 97 + TS 10H5:7. Folio 98v is published in Murtonen, 1958, as MS b with photograph (no. 2). Liturgy for the Day of Atonement (by Qalir) and for *Simḥat Tora* with pointing of class 2.

Bod. Heb. e30, f. 48–9 + TS A43:1 + TS K25:108 + TS NS 249:5 + TS NS 249:9 + TS NS 301:29. The fragments designated by the first two numbers form Kahle, 1930, MS M, and were published partly there, and partly in Kahle, 1901. The remaining fragments are published in Dietrich, 1960, as MS Cb 1, save for TS NS 301:29, which is unpublished. Photograph, Kahle, 1930, plate 11. Parts of Exodus (28–29), Leviticus (13–14), Isaiah (5–13, 41–48, 53–64), Jeremiah (23–29), and Ezekiel (31–36) with pointing of class 1.

Bod. Heb. e73 f. 42–3. See TS 16:322.

C FRAGMENTS IN THE GASTER GENIZA COLLECTION OF THE JOHN RYLANDS LIBRARY, MANCHESTER

The only fragments I know of from this library are those listed in Díez-Macho, 1956, pp. 4–8. Unfortunately, most of these were not available for photography when I requested photostats. However, Dr. Díez-Macho has kindly assured me that the pointing of all these fragments is sparse.

J.R.G.G. fr. 5. A small piece of parchment with parts of Leviticus 23. From the photograph I cannot see sufficient pointing to classify.
J.R.G.G. fr. 18. Liturgical. Class 7.
J.R.G.G. fr. 21. Liturgical. Class 7.

D MANUSCRIPTS FROM THE LIBRARY OF THE JEWISH THEOLOGICAL SEMINARY OF AMERICA, NEW YORK

J.T.S. MS 504 f. 2 + TS A39:9 + Leningrad Ant. 260, 339, 816. Scattered folios of Kahle's MS Eb 10 (see the introduction to BH^3). For J.T.S. MS 504 f. 2, see Díez-Macho, 1954, pp. 253–60. Information on the other folios of this ms is given in Yeivin, 1963, pp. 124–7. Sparse pointing of class 1.
J.T.S. MS 594, box B, envelope 12. Described in Díez-Macho, 1954, pp. 249–53 (see also Díez-Macho, 1957, pp. 28f.). Published by Díez-Macho and Kahle, with notes by Murtonen, in Kahle, 1959, appendix III, and plates 5 and 6. Parts of Ecclesiastes (11–12) and Lamentations (1) with pointing of class 2.
J.T.S. MS E.N.A. 2020 f. 23. Described in Díez-Macho, 1956, p. 7; 1957, p. 30. Ms 5, class 5.

E MANUSCRIPTS IN THE LIBRARY OF THE HEBREW UNION COLLEGE, CINCINNATI

H.U.C. MS 1001 + 'Levias' + TS NS 249:7[25] + TS NS 301:28. The text of H.U.C. MS 1001 was partially published (with an inadequate transcription of the pointing, and a photograph) in Sonne, 1944. The 'Levias' ms was published in Levias, 1899. This edition was copied, with some improvements, but also one or two printing errors, in Kahle, 1927, the ms having been lost by that time. These, with the TS fragments, form ms 4, class 4.
H.U.C. 'Levias.' See H.U.C. MS 1001+.

[25] See note 6.

F MANUSCRIPTS IN THE ANTONIN COLLECTION OF THE M. E. SALTYKOV-SHCHEDRIN STATE PUBLIC LIBRARY, LENINGRAD[26]

Ant. 222. Murtonen, 1958, MS f with photograph (no. 5). *Qerobot* by Qalir, with pointing of class 7.

Ant. 260. See J.T.S. MS 504 f. 2.

Ant. 339. See J.T.S. MS 504 f. 2.

Ant. 360 + 361.[27] A sheet of parchment folded to form two leaves numbered 360 and 361. Leaf 360 is considerably damaged, but the writing is clear. Initial lines preserved are ייחדתה לך הר 360r8, and אז טרם נוסדו ארץ ושמים 360v19. The latter poem continues, onto 361 recto and verso. Occasional Tiberian signs. Sparse Palestinian pointing, probably of class 6.

Ant. 361.[28] See Ant. 360+.

Ant. 369. See TS H16:7+.

Ant. 816. See J.T.S. MS 504 f. 2+.

Ant. 912. Ormann, 1934. Liturgy for the Day of Atonement, with pointing of class 12.

Ant. 959. Edelmann, 1934, MS E. Liturgy for the Day of Atonement, with pointing of class 3.

G MANUSCRIPT FROM THE MOSSERI COLLECTION (Originally in Cairo, location now unknown)

P171/2. See TS H16:3+.

APPENDIX 1

Initial Lines of Poems in Texts Described

TS H2:29, 1v28 (VIII.11)	אאמירם לאיומה אבוננם להתחכמה
TS H16:12, 1v15	אב לעת זיקנה פרח יריכו
TS H2:61, 6r11	אב לא חסך בנו
TS H16:12, 1v5	אב מנערותו בטח בבריתו

[26] Through the courtesy of the Director of this library I have received photographs of Ant. 222, 360–361, 369, 912, and 959. The analysis of these texts is not based on these photographs, since they arrived when this book was almost finished, but they have been used to check the unusual usages noted. The pointing of Ant. 360–361 (unpublished, and kindly drawn to my attention by Dr. N. Allony) is not discussed in chapter III.

[27] See note 4. [28] See note 4.

אבה מפ[	Bod. Heb. c20 f. 6v31
אביבי אדמת ארץ אמץ בברכת גשם	TS H7:2, 1v18
אביו ואמו קראוהו גדול	Bod. Heb. c20 f. 5v8
אבן מאוסה בריאיון	TS H16:12, 2r32
אב[ ]מע תחנונינו: אל נא	TS NS 117:13, r19
אדום אמרה אן קץ	TS H7:44, r23
אדום אשר[ ]א אימתני	TS NS 249:7, 2r20 (VIII.4)
אדון חקק בכסאו דמות שור	J.T.S. MS E.N.A. 2020 f. 23v13 (VIII.5)
אדוני חיבבך באהבה	TS H16:12, 1r8
אדין בערב חימ[	TS 10H10:7, 2r4
אדמוה רבו צרותינו	TS H7:1, r6
אדמוני איש האדום	TS NS 249:7, 2r11 (VIII.4)
אהללה אלוהי אשיר עוזו	TS H2:61, 2v5; TS H2:44 (part)
אודד[ ]החניי[	TS H16:12, 2v26
אדמת קודש המקדשת	TS NS 249:7, 1r1 (VIII.4) (end)
אוהב לשוקדיי אני הוא	Bod. Heb. c20 f. 5r30
אוהב מבין ש[נואים] קניתה	TS NS 117:6, 1v16 (VIII.4a)
אוהל מועד אֿלוה עומד	TS NS 116:15b, 1v14
א]ויב היקשה ערפו	TS NS 249:11, v4
אומן כראם מלינים	TS H2:55, r19
אומץ חלק בחתולות	Bod. Heb. c20 f. 5v31
אופל אלמנה תאיר. עי׳ אלוהינו ואלוהי אבותינו אופל וגו׳	
אורך החצר כפל חמשים	TS NS 119:42, v23
אורחות תם יישרתה	TS NS 249:7, 2v11 (VIII.4)
אות במועד גש דרישת	TS H7:1, r2
אותיות משפט	TS H2:61, 2r3
אז טרם נוסדו ארץ ושמים	Leningrad Ant. 360+, v19
אזכיר גבורות	TS H6:39 (part)
[אחדים] אחודים אימרה [אחת	TS NS 117:6, 1r15 (VIII.4a)
אחדים בשיח מילליהם	TS NS 117:6, 1r1 (VIII.4a) (end)
אחוז נא במשפט ותימלוך	TS H2:61, 4r9
אחז צדיק נתיבו	TS H16:12, 1r23
איווה לאכול מטעמים	Bod. Heb. c20 f. 5r16
איום בחן וביאר כל עצי מדה	TS H2:55, v26
איום ונורא יום העשור	TS NS 249:2, r11 (VIII.1)
[איום] ונורא מוראך	TS NS 249:7, 1r25 (VIII.4)
איילים חיילים ומושע[	TS NS 249:7, 1v25 (VIII.4)
אימצתה אומץ אהבה	J.T.S. MS E.N.A. 2020 f. 23r16 (VIII.5)
אימצתה ריפיון עגומה	TS H16:12, 2v14
אין לנו לא אשים ולא אשם	TS H6:29, r6

אין לנו מזבח לכפר	TS H6:38, v5; TS H6:97, r17
אירשה ארוש רחשון	TS NS 249:14, v7 (viii.8)
איש אשר כמלאך הוסר	TS H16:12, 2r10
איש אשר נימשל באש משקת	TS NS 249:7, 1v17 (viii.4)
איש חלק בצאתו	Bod. Heb. c20 f. 6v19
איש קראוי פעמיים	TS H16:12, 1v28
איש תם בטוב אסמתה	Bod. Heb. c20 f. 5v16
אישרתה כישרון גואל	Bod. Heb. c20 f. 6r20
איתייעט עמלק בצאתי מצוען	TS 10H10:7, 2v9
אל מלך בעולמו	TS NS 117:7+, r29 (see viii.10)
אל תעש עמנו כלה. עי׳ אלוהינו ואלוהי אבותינו אל וגו׳	
אלוהינו ואלוהי אבותינו אופל אלמנה תאיר	TS H6:29, v23, H6:40 r23 (title)
או״א אל תעש עמנו כלה	TS H6:40, r16
או״א אם תחנה עלי מחנה	TS H7:2, 1r16
או״א טל תן ברכה בארצך	TS 12:210, v17 (viii.8)
או״א שתכפר לנו ע[ ]עוונותינו	TS H6:40, r26 (title)
או״א תבוא לפניך ת[	TS H6:40, r24 (title)
אליך כליווה[	TS NS 117 : 6, 2r14 (viii.4a)
אלים ביום מחתן	TS 12:210, r and v (viii.8) (parts)
אם לשבט אם לארצו אם לחסד תת פידיון	TS H7:1, v14
אם תחנה עלי מחנה. עי׳ אלוהינו ואלוהי אבותינו אם וגו׳	
אמר תנין יאורו לרדוף עם	TS H2:29, 1r14 (viii.11)
אנא ממליך ומיסיר אול[	TS H2:61, 3v19
אנה אב בקיהיון	Bod. Heb. c20 f. 5r5
אנה חדש פזמות לאב	TS NS 119:42, v17
אנוסים כפופים רדו אל סוף	TS H2:55, v11
אני ארעה[	TS H7:44, r15
אני ומלאכי עימך	TS NS 249:7, 1r5 (viii.4)
אספר נא נעשה[	TS 10H10:7, 2v3
אפחד כמעשיי אדאג בכל עת	TS H2:61, 4v9
אפס אין בילתך	TS H2:61, 1v16
אפתח פי ברנן	TS H2:61, 2r13
אקשטה כסל וקרב להביע בעד מים	TS H7:15, r1 (end)
אריאל בקומה אכוף	TS NS 117:13, r12
ארקא קצרה וקפצה	Bod. Heb. c20 f. 6v3
אתה יודיע רזי עולם	TS NS 249:2, r10, TS H6:40, r25 (title)
אתרוג הדומה ללב	TS 20:182, r33
א[ ]משוטטים	TS NS 117:6, 2v15 (viii.4a)
]]אמר העדה	TS 10H10:7, 1r1

TS H2:61, 5v19	[ ]את ל[ ]תיזכרנו
TS NS 249:14, v4 (viii.8)	בדעתו אביעה חידות
TS H6:29, v11	בהיות אר[ון] בית קודש הקדשים
TS NS 249:1, r5 (viii.7)	ביום הראשון יהודה
TS 20:182, r8	בסוכה אשען ת[
TS NS 249:14, r13 (viii.8)	בעשר מכות פתרוסים הפרכתה
J.T.S. ENA 2020 f. 23r8 (viii.5)	בׄ(רוך) שׄ(לום) דו[די ה]יצצתה מחרכים
TS NS 249:7, 1r19 (viii.4)	בתמימים תותמם
TS H2:30, 1r16	דפקו וסובכו ולילות תבכו
TS H7:1, r16	הושענא אׄל אמונה אום שרה
TS NS 117:13 r19	הזדוׄנ[
TS H7:1, v9	הינו אתנו לך בארבעת הילולים להללך
TS H2:61, 1r15	המאמירים באימה ואומרים ײ אׄלהינו
TS H6:40, r27 (title)	ודויד עב[
TS H2:29, 1r2 (viii.11)	ויושע אברהם בראש
TS H2:29, 2r4 (viii.11)	ויושע אדיר הוגיא תעודה
TS H2:29, 2v11 (viii.11)	[ויושע] אסונים אשל פאר ניטעם
TS NS 119:42, r13	ויעלוז צור במקדשו
TS H2:29, 2v24 (viii.11)	וירא ת[ ]מש מיודעות
TS 20:182, r49	ולמה[ ]שבעה
TS H6:40, r28 (title)	ומאהבתך ײ אׄינו את ישׄר עׄ
TS NS 249:7, 2r29 (viii.4)	[ומן בית יעקב א]ש יצמח אנש
TS H7:1, v23	ומראשית שנה ועד אחרית שנה
TS H7:1, v26	ונגילה ונשמחה בישועתך
TS H2:61, 6v4	זוכרינו בזיכרון טוב
TS NS 249:1, v1 (viii.7) (end)	חנוכת אוהל אהליבה תאיר
TS 10H7:1, 2v23	טומאה יעביר לטהרה
	טל תן ברכה בארצך עי׳ אלוהינו ואלהי אבותינו טל וגו׳
TS NS 249:7, 1v7 (viii.4)	יׄה לא תדום אם פינו ידום
TS NS 249:7, 2v22 (viii.4)	יׄה משלם גמולים משלם
TS H6:40, r29	יום אדיר לאׄל רם
TS NS 118:38, v12	יוטף אויים פי שניים
TS H5:222, r26	ײׄ אלהינו בימינך[
Leningrad Ant. 360+, r8	ייחדתה לך הר
TS NS 116:15b, 1v1	יקרנו במשכן
TS 10H7:1, 2r16	כבודו חודש במגן ושמש
TS NS 117:13, r4	כי אמרנו אין רואה

כי ארבנו זה לזה	TS H6:97, v17
כמו שברתה כור ברזל	TS H2:45+, v1
כמראה תבנית משכן שמים	TS NS 116:15b, 1v8
כתועים ואין לבקש	TS H6:38, v16; TS H6:97, r29
לולי אדונינו מעט הותירנו	TS H6:29, r27
ליל א]	TS NS 249:14a (VIII.9)
לכן אכוונה שני לבבות	TS H7:1, v18
לסוסתי ברכבי עם לועזים	TS H2:1, v14
לעולם הטל סימן תחי]	Bod. Heb. c20 f. 6r28
מאגד ברבות הכלולות הוד	Bod. Heb. c20 f. 6r8
מהרה באה השמש	Bod. Heb. c20 f. 6v8
מה[ ]לפניך	TS H6:40, r25 (title)
מוחץ וגם רופא	TS H16:12, 2v4
מוצב ארצה סולם אווה	Bod. Heb. c20 f. 6v23
מיהרתה פדות אמוניי	TS H2:29, 1r27 (VIII.11)
מילול מך אף מישיב	TS NS 249:7, 1v1 (VIII.4)
מכל [פר]ה ומכל בהמה	J.T.S. MS E.N.A. 2020 f. 23v10 (VIII.5)
מ̄מ יופיע על עמו	TS 10H7:1, 2v1
מ̂מ נם לחלק שוב שבתי שבותך	TS NS 249:7, 1r22 (VIII.4)
מ̂מ נם לתם אם תראה לאח	TS NS 249:7, 2v8 (VIII.4)
מנער ועד זקן	Bod. Heb. c20 f. 5v13
מנת שפר חבלים	Bod. Heb. c20 f. 5v22
מעקיד ערפו על אחד ההרים	Bod. Heb. c20 f. 5r8
מעשה הרעה מצליח מהרה	TS H16:12, 1v7
מ̇(עשי) א̇ד(ם)]א	TS NS 117:7+, r1
מצרים]א	TS NS 249:14, r1 (VIII.4) (end)
מקום נחלת מקנה	TS NS 249:7, 2v17 (VIII.4)
מריח גן עדן מברך היריח	Bod. Heb. c20 f. 6r1
משליך עליך יהבו תאזרנו כוח	TS H16:12, 2v18
[מ]שמים לשמי שמים	TS NS 117:6, 1v2 (VIII.4a)
[מ]לף[ ]פילגשיו	TS H16:12, 1r28
נפלאות אז צור ערכך	TS 20:182, v13
על חט שחטאנו	TS H6:40, r27; TS NS 117:13, r19 (titles)
על ישראל איומי אמונך	TS H5:222, r13
עצתך אין לידע	TS NS 249:7, 2v4 (VIII.4)
פאר אלביש לרוקע	TS NS 118:38, r6 (title)
צאתנו ובואנו שמרתה	TS H16:12, 2r6
קורות בתינו פיתוחי פרקים	TS H2:1, v27

TS NS 249:7, 1v11 (VIII.4)	ריבותיים מלאכי צבאות
Bod. Heb. c20 f. 5r1	שביל זה אין לדחות
TS H2:30, 1r3 (see VII.6)	שבת חסד אמונת שימור ליל
TS H16:12, 1r17	שוכן עד דרכו הצלחתה
TS NS 249:7, 2v26 (VIII.4)	שומר ישראל[
Bod. Heb. c20 f. 6v15	שומר רגלי חסידיך
Bod. Heb. c20 f. 5v27	שושנת עמק תפרח
TS H16:12, 2v10	שיפרתה השנואה
TS H2:1, v1	שיר השירים אימרת צרופה/צפה
TS H16:12, 1v2	שנית יד תוסיף
TS NS 119:42, r3	שפתו הוד תביע
TS NS 116:15b, 2r10	שקול מנשה כאפרים
TS 10H7:1, 2v11	שש[ה] דברים בם ניתאששה
	שתכפר לנו ע[. עי׳ אלוהינו ואלוהי אבותינו שתכפר וגו׳
TS NS 117:6, 1v11 (VIII.4a)	[ ]שפה ופה ולשון
TS NS 116:15b, 1r1	תבוא לפניך ת[עי׳ אלוהינו ואלוהי אבותינו תבוא וגו׳
	תבל ומלואה לא יכילוך
TS H7:2, 1r16	תבל תפקוד בגשם
TS H6:97, v26	תבעתה ולא הישגחנו
TS NS 119:43, 2r4	תוחלת[ ]נמהרה טן טף מלילה
TS 12:210a (VIII.9)	תיכן בראשן עטרה
TS H7:15, r26	תיכנס לארץ וחוצות לחצות מים
TS H7:44, r1	תיקרא לה עוד אחת כעוד נגע
TS H6:38, v24, TS H6:97, v9	תנות צרות לא נוכל
TS NS 249:7, 1r17 (VIII.4)	תצמח ותצליח תבוא ותביא
TS NS 249:7, 2r27 (VIII.4)	תקיפה ועתיק יומיה
TS 10H10:7, 1r24	תקיפה ניראית ככס[
TS NS 249:7, 1r11 (VIII.4)	תשיבנו מכל שערים

APPENDIX 2

Authors of Poems in the Unpublished Texts

Qalir	TS H7:1, H7:15, H7:44, H15:69, Bod. Heb. d63 f. 98+
Shimʿon haKohen	TS H16:12+
Yannai	TS NS 116:15b (?)
Yehuda Zebida	TS H2:29
Yoḥanan haKohen	TS H2:61, TS H5:25
Yose ben Yose	TS H2:44, H2:61, H6:28, H6:39

VII

The Content of the Texts

This chapter describes the contents of the texts which are published in chapter VIII. Dr. Dietrich and I had planned, in our joint work (see the Preface), to give translations of all the texts we published if they were not too fragmentary. However, because of the peculiar problems of this type of poetry, it is unlikely that translations of this sort, made primarily as adjuncts to a grammatical study, would be of any value to specialists in *piyyuṭ*, or, indeed, to any who have passed beyond their initial studies in the field.

Any poetry (I suppose) depends for part of its meaning on a 'context of ideas,' a 'sphere of thought' common to the author and his readers. For this reason it is virtually impossible to translate any poem from its original language into another, and still call to the mind of the reader all the ideas and images which might have been derived from a reading of the original. This is true of the *piyyuṭim* translated here – perhaps to a greater extent than with other types of poetry. Each line, of course, has a simple meaning *(peshaṭ)*, one might say a literal meaning. This literal meaning is often based on a particular haggadic tradition, which may be more or less openly referred to. In addition to this, by a careful choice of the words of the line, the poet may refer to one or more verses of the Bible, each of which may again represent a haggadic tradition which he wants to call to the mind of his readers. In this way the few words of a single verse may call up echoes from the entire range of Hebrew literature. It is these echoes from the biblical and the rabbinic literature, and the ingenious way in which they are worked into the poem, which make the poems so fascinating, and so difficult to translate.

1 TS NS 249:2 (Liturgy for the Day of Atonement)

This fragment opens with prayers (r1–5), followed by the quotation of Deut. 4:30 (r5–6). Another line of prayer (r7) follows, then the quotation of Hos. 14:2–3 (r8–9), and *Shebu'ot* 1:6 (r10). This is followed by אתה יודע רזי עולם, the title of a well-known prayer,[1] and then by]על, possibly the opening word of the prayer על חטא שחטאנו. The following poem is איום ונורא יום העשור,[2] which runs from r11 to v25. The acrostic shows that r29, of which traces are still visible, was the last line on the recto. The few words visible in v26 and 27 are insufficient to show the character of the next item in the liturgy.

A text of איום ונורא צום העשור with Palestinian pointing (Ant. 912) is published in Ormann, 1934, pp. 24–27. The present text shows few variants from that one.

2 TS NS 118:38 (Liturgy for the Feast of Tabernacles)

The text of this small fragment appears to open with a poem (r1–5), but too little remains for any structure to be visible. On line 6, Deut. 16:3 (?) is quoted, followed by a poetic line (or perhaps a title) פאר אלביש לרוקע. This is followed (r7) by the quotation of Lev. 23:39. Lines 8–10 contain a short poem followed by the quotation of Neh. 8:18. This is followed (r11) by the title מוספה הושענה[. The remainder of the recto contains a poem composed in verses of (probably) five stichs each. The initial letters of the first four stichs form a simple alphabetic acrostic. The fifth was followed by, and probably alluded to, a 'blessing.'

The verso opens with a poem composed in verses of four (or five?) stichs. The initial letter of each stich in a verse is the same, and the initial letters of the verses form an alphabetic acrostic. The first stich of each verse is preceded by הוש̄(ענה), and the fourth (?) by למ̄(ען ?). The final stich is followed by הוש̄(ענה) and בׄ(רוך). The first three (or four) stichs have the same final rhyme. Lines 1–10 of the verso contain the *samek* to *taw* verses of this poem. Line 11 carries the title שבעה שמיני עצרת. The following poem opens יוסף אוים פי שניים

[1] Already mentioned in *Yoma* 87b, and still in use. See Davidson, 1924–33, no. א 8808.

[2] See Davidson, 1924–33, no. א 2673, with the more common reading of צום for יום.

(v12). It appears to be written in verses of six (or five?) stichs. Each stich has the same initial letter and the same final rhyme. The initial letters of each verse form an alphabetic acrostic. The first stich of each verse is preceded by one word from a quotation: יוסף יי̄ probably from Isa. 11:11.

3 TS NS 119:42 + TS NS 301:66 (Liturgy for Various Occasions)

The recto contains poems for the New Moon Day.

(i) Lines 1–4 contain the last part of a poem ending]בי נוטה אליה כנהר שלום בֹּ.

(ii) The next poem (r4–25) is composed in ten verses of four or five stichs. The first word of the first stich forms part of the quotation על הנחל יעלה על שפתו מזה ומזה כל עץ מאנל (Ezek. 47:12, BH[3] ועל), and the first letter of the following word forms part of an alphabetic acrostic to *yod*. The first word of the third stich is בחדשך, and the first letter of the following word forms part of a '*tashraq*' acrostic to *mem*. The first two verses have a fifth stich introducing a 'blessing' (מגן, מחיה). In verses 3–5, the place of the fifth stich is taken by quotations from Num. 10:10, Ps. 98:1, and Ezek. 47:12. Of the remaining verses, only the eighth has five stichs.

(iii) The following poem, ויעלז צור במקדשיו (r25–28), is composed of six rhyming stichs, followed by כֹּכ וקרֿא.

(iv) Following this are three verses forming a *qedusha* (r29–34). They appear to be composed of four rhyming stichs, the third of which begins with בֿח(ודש). The beginnings of the verses are not preserved. The first is followed by the rubric לעו(מתן), the second by פע(מים), and the third by]לֿחיות.

(v) The remainder of the recto contains fragments of eight lines. It would seem that they formed a poem composed in verses of four stichs, with each stich followed by בֿ(רוך), and the initial letters of each stich forming an alphabetic acrostic, but the text is too broken for certainty.

(vi) The reverse opens in the third verse of a poem for the '18 benedictions' for the seventeenth of Tammuz. It is composed in verses of four rhyming stichs. The first letter of each verse forms part of an alphabetic acrostic from which *ṣade* was omitted, permitting the author to use the letters קדש as initials for the first three stichs of the last verse. The third stich of each verse begins בתֿמ(וז).

(vii) The remaining text contains poems for the ninth of Ab. Line 28 contains the title א̂ב. The liturgy opens with a poem beginning אנה חדש פזמות לאב composed in verses of four rhyming stichs. The initial letters of each verse form an alphabetic acrostic. The third stich of each verse appears to have begun באב. The first two verses are followed by (בָ(רוך, and the last stich of these verses alludes to the following blessing (מגן, מחיה). The third verse is followed by the quotation of Isa. 43:18–19 (v33–34).

(viii) Line 23 contains the beginning of a second poem, אורך החצר כפל חמשים, composed in short stichs. The initial letters of each stich form an alphabetic acrostic. The last traces of text (v42) belong to the *resh* stich.

4 TS NS 249:7 (*Qerobot* of Yannai on the weekly *Sedarim*)

Folio 1r opens at the *pe* line of the sixth poem of the *qeroba* on Gen. 31:3, continuing directly from the last line of H.U.C. MS 1001 fol. 1v (see Sonne, 1944). This *qeroba* is completed at 1v23. The text contains the complete *qeroba* on Gen 32:4 (1v24–2v9), and the *qeroba* on Gen. 33:18 to the middle of the fourth poem. The text of this *qeroba* continues in H.U.C. MS 1001 f. 2r1. Zulay (1938) published part of the *qeroba* on Gen. 32:4. The rest of the poems are, I believe, hitherto unknown.

The structure of the poems is typical of the *qerobot* of Yannai as described by Zulay. Many of the linguistic peculiarities typical of this poet and others of the period are represented here, such as:

(i) Masculine form nouns are derived from feminine forms,[3] e.g. רגם (1v16) from רגמה (Ps. 68:28). מחן (1v16) is derived from מחנה in a similar way.

(ii) 'Biliteral' forms of ל״ה verbs occur,[4] e.g. כנת 1r18.

(iii) Absolute forms occur in place of constructs,[5] e.g. פה 1v13.

(iv) 'Inverted' construct structures are used,[6] e.g. נצח מדון (1v9) = מדון נצח, ישועות חוסן (2v13) = חוסן ישועות.

(v) Prepositions are used with verb forms,[7] e.g. כסחתי 1r3, כנם 1r23.

(vi) נא is used as an 'emphatic' to fit the acrostic,[8] e.g. 1v2, 2v17.

[3] Cf. Wallenstein, 1956, p. 12.
[4] See Zunz, 1920, pp. 381f.
[5] Cf. כלה Zulay, 1938, p. 4, l. 58.
[6] Cf. Sonne, 1944, p. 205, l. 7, and note there.
[7] See Zunz, 1920, pp. 383f.
[8] See Zulay, 1945, p. 207.

The midrashic traditions to which the poems allude are mostly recorded in the *Midrash Rabba*, although some, of course, only appear in other collections. Some are very early, being already in the Pseudepigraphic literature, e.g. the tradition that the dead will rise first in the land of Israel (2 Baruch 29:2, 40:2, 71:1, IV Ezra 9:8, 13:48–9 – and note that 1r3 contains an almost direct quote from *Talmud Jerushalmi Kilaim* 9:3 on this subject), and the tradition that God will revive the dead with dew (cf. Isa. 26:19) (2 Baruch 29:7, 73:2, and cf. *Jerushalmi Berakot* 5:2). Some interpretations do not seem to occur in any Midrash; thus 2r8–9 refers to Isa. 5:20 and connects כאכל קש לשון אש of Isa. 5:24 with it, interpreting קש as Esau (cf. Obad. 18). Such cases (supposing that a collection in which they do occur has not been overlooked) could be examples of 'lost Midrashim'[9] or individual interpretations by the poet. (This particular connection is made in *Talmud Babli Soṭa* 41b, but for a different reason.)

4a TS NS 117:6 + TS NS 123:2 (*Qerobot* of Yannai on the weekly *Sedarim*)

The five fragments which are all that remains of this ms belong to two folios. The first contains parts of Yannai's *qeroba* on Gen. 11:1 (recto, and verso lines 1–15). The text preserved covers lines 58–86 and 112–22 of this *qeroba* in Zulay's edition (1938), and also contains part 9 of the *qeroba*, which was unknown to Zulay. Lines 16–18 of fol. 1 verso contain parts of the opening poem of the following *qeroba* (on Gen. 12:1, lines 1–5 of Zulay's edition).

The second folio contains parts 6, 7, and 8 of a *qeroba* on Gen. 18:1 (2r1–13), ending [כ]כֹּ וקֹרא. Part 9 was not included. Part 7 of the poem describes members of the top hierarchy of angels. Similar descriptions occur from an early date, e.g. in III Enoch. Note that, in this poem, *he* is used in place of *ḥet* in the acrostic (2r8), as occasionally elsewhere (e.g. Bod. Heb. d63 f. 89v25).

The following poem is the first of a qeroba on Gen. 19:1, opening ?]אליך כליווה[. Traces of most of the twelve stichs, and of the biblical quotations following, are preserved. The verso of fol. 2 contains parts of poems 4, 5, and 6 of the same *qeroba*. Poem 6 breaks off at the

[9] See Klar, 1939, p. 290.

ḥet verse. From the scanty remains, the poems on fol. 2 appear to belong to typical Yannai *qerobot*. They are, I believe, hitherto unknown.

5 J.T.S. MS E.N.A. 2020 f. 23 (Liturgy for Passover)

This text was originally discovered among the manuscripts of the Jewish Theological Seminary of America in New York by Dr. A. Díez-Macho, who described it[10] and was planning to publish it in collaboration with Dr. N. Allony. Dr. Dietrich wished to include it with the fragments he had found, so these scholars very kindly gave up their intention to publish it themselves. It contains the following poems:

(i) A poem (r1–7) composed in verses of four short rhyming stichs. The second stich is followed by בׄ הׄמ, which appears to refer to a historical event, and the fourth by בׄ הׄס, which appears to refer to a future one. The poem looks forward to the time of the Messiah. The initial letters of the stichs form a double alphabetic acrostic (our text begins with the *mem* verse). The *shin-taw* verse is followed by a final verse which appears to contain the acrostic שמעון בן שמואל. As far as I know, no poet of this name is known from a period sufficiently early to permit ascription of this poem to him. The poem is followed by a quotation from Deut. 16:16 and the rubric אינו בׄ מׄק.

(ii) A poem בׄ שׄ דו[די ה]יצצתה מחרכים (r8–13) composed in three verses of four rhyming stichs. Each verse is introduced by בׄ(ליל) שׄ(מורים) and followed by בׄ(רוך) (the last by בׄ עושה). It deals, in highly figurative language based on the Song of Songs, with the spiritual significance of the events of the Passover.

(iii) The final poem on the recto, אימצתה אומץ אהבה, is headed (r15) קדושתא שור או כש[ב]. The initial letters of the stichs form an alphabetic acrostic, and all have the same rhyme.

(iv) The first few lines of the verso are virtually illegible. Lines 5–9 contain a series of biblical quotations, ending with the rubric אל נא. Lines 10–12 contain a prose passage dealing with the Passover sacrifice.

(v) The final poem, אדון חקק בכסאו דמות שור (v13), is composed in verses of two rhyming stichs, the initial letters of which form an

[10] Díez-Macho, 1956, p. 7; 1957, p. 30.

alphabetic acrostic. It deals with Abraham, Isaac, Jacob, and Joseph under the figures of bull, ram, lamb, and goat (cf. *Bemidbar Rabba* 14:5). This poem also occurs in the British Museum MS Or. 5557Q f. 20a, among poems by Yannai.[11]

6 TS H2:30 (Liturgy for Passover, part of a prayer book)

Folio 1 of this text opens with the end of a poem. Line 3 of the recto contains the title ז׳ שבת ליל שימורים. The following poem, שבת חסד אמונת שימור ליל (1r3–15), is composed in three verses, the first of six, and the second and third of seven rhyming stichs. Each verse is followed by בׄ(רוך). This poem is followed by אתה בחרתה, the opening of a prayer (1r16). The remainder of fol. 1 is taken up with a poem דפקו וסובבו composed in verses of four rhyming stichs. The first letters of each verse form a double alphabetic acrostic (דדההו״ו etc.) which starts with the first *daleth* verse and runs to the first *ṭet* verse. The poem deals with the significance of the Passover festival.

Folio 2 contains part of a single poem, also composed in verses of four stichs with the initial letters of each stich forming a double alphabetic acrostic. The acrostic runs from the first *gimel* verse to the second *lamed* verse, which was probably the last of the poem. The first three stichs of each verse rhyme, the last always ending with לילה. Occasionally a verse is composed of five stichs, in which case the last two may rhyme. The poem is divided into three equal parts. The first, verses *(ʾalef)* to *dalet*, deals with specific instances of God's salvation of Israel on the Passover night (cf. 9 below) and prays that God will continue to save his people. The second part, verses *he* to *ḥet*, poses questions about the ritual actions done 'on this night.' The third part, verses *ṭet* to *lamed*, gives the traditional answers to these questions. The last verse refers to the Passover as the first feast taking place in the first month, and is followed by the quotation of Lev. 23:4. The poem is unified by the use, in every second verse, of the word הבדיל to give the theme of the poem. God has divided 'this night' from other nights, and Israel from other nations (cf. Lev. 20:26).

11 See Zulay, 1936, p. 356. The three lines preceding the poem in the J.T.S. text also appear in the British Museum text.

7 TS NS 249:1 (Liturgy for *Ḥanukka*)

This fragment forms the upper part of the leaf of which TS H16:1 (Edelmann, 1934, MS F) is the lower. The recto of the present fragment probably opened with the end of a poem corresponding to poem 5 of the typical Yannai *qeroba*. This is followed (r4) by [אל נא] לעׄ תעׄ, and then by a poem ביום הראשון יהודה based on Num. 7:12ff. This poem is completed in TS H16:1, and followed by another introduced by ובכן [זאת] חנוכת המזבח (Num. 7:84), which is completed in TS NS 249:1 v1–5. These two poems probably correspond to poems 6 and 7 of a Yannai *qeroba*. They are followed by two further poems forming a *qedušša*. TS NS 249:1 v13 contains the four letters missing from the title שמונה עשרה חנוכה which introduces a new *qeroba* in the first line of the verso of TS H16:1.

8 TS NS 249:14 + TS 12:210 (Liturgy for Passover)

TS NS 249:14 contains the following:

(i) A poem dealing with the ten plagues of Egypt and the corresponding punishments to be meted out to Israel's enemies in the future (r1–13). The text opens halfway through the third verse of the poem.

(ii) Qalir's poem בעשר מכות פתרוסים היפרכתה[12] (r13–v2) introduced by ובכן, and followed by כֹּכ וקֹרא. The text in this ms shows many variants from ancient and modern editions. The sign ‹ (at the end of r21) appears to indicate the omission of part of the poem.

(iii) The first two verses of Qalir's poem בדעתו אביעה חידות[13] (v4–7) preceded by the title טל ד[רֹ] לעז[ר] (v3).

(iv) These verses are immediately followed, as in printed prayer books, by Qalir's poem אירשה ארוש רחשון (v7–27) introduced by the title נטילת רשות (v7). The two verses of (iii) are separated by בֹּר(וך). The first verse shows some variants from printed texts, while the second differs widely from them, and from the Paris ms published by Elbogen.[14] The text of (iv) also contains many variants from printed texts. The end of the verso is taken up with biblical quotations and rubrics.

[12] Davidson, 1924–33, no. ב 1157.
[13] Davidson, 1924–33, no. ב 162.
[14] Elbogen, 1926, p. 222.

TS 12:210 contains:

(i) Parts of Qalir's poem אלים ביום מחסן.[15] The text opens at the biblical quotation following the *gimel* verse, and runs on the recto to the end of the *ṭet* verse. The verso contains the text from the *'ayin* verse to the end of the poem (v17). The text of the poem contains numerous variants from printed editions, and also differs from the text found with Palestinian pointing in TS H16:6.[16]

(ii) The remainder of the verso contains the opening verses of Qalir's poem אלוהינו ואלוהי אבותינו טל תן ברכה בארצך. The usual form of this opening line is לרצות ארצך,[17] a form which is used in TS H16:6.[18] As this suggests, the few lines of this poem preserved in TS 12:210 contain a number of variants from ancient and modern editions.

The chief source of the first poem of NS 249:14 is of particular interest. The poem itself is formed of verses having four rhyming stichs. The first word of the first stich is מצרים, and that of the third צרינו. The first letters of the following words of these stichs form an alphabetic acrostic. The poem is based on the tradition that the enemies of Israel (צרינו called – as is more common – אדום in the *'alef* verse, presumably representing the Byzantine church and state) will suffer in the future the same punishment as Egypt (מצרים) suffered in the past. The tradition is recorded in the *Pesikta de Rav Kahana*,[19] *Pesikta Rabbati*,[20] *Midrash Tanchuma*,[21] and elsewhere. The first two stichs of each verse of the poem refer to one of the 'ten plagues.' The last two allude to a biblical verse held to show that the same punishment will fall on 'Edom.' The biblical verses are those usually adduced in support of this tradition, but the poem must have been based on a defective tradition, such as that represented by the 'Carmoli' ms of the *Pesikta de Rav Kahana* in the Cambridge University Library. In this ms, the proof adduced for the future punishment of 'Edom' by 'rash' is Ezek. 38:22. This text should refer to punishment by 'hail,' as in other mss, but the Carmoli ms omits that

15 Davidson, 1924–33, no. א 5126.
16 Edelmann, 1934, Hebrew p. 1.
17 Davidson, 1924–33, no. א 4823.
18 Edelmann, 1934, Hebrew, p. 2.
19 Mandelbaum, 1962, no. 7:11 (p. 133).
20 Ed. M. Friedmann (Wien, 1880), no. 17 (p. 90a).
21 Ed. S. Buber (Wilna, 1913), Exodus, *Bo'* 6 (p. 44).

plague.[22] Lines *ṭet* to *lamed* of our poem deal both with 'rash' and with 'hail,' but omit the proof text for 'rash' (Zech. 14:12). They thus represent a compromise between the author, who followed the biblical listing of the plagues, and his midrashic source, which omitted the reference to 'hail.'[23] The poet's midrashic source cannot, however, have been identical with that of the Carmoli ms, for that ms, as well as the other sources mentioned above, adduces Ezek. 39:17 as proof for the smiting of 'Edom' with 'locusts,' whereas our author used Isa. 33:4 (r8). The tradition omitting the plague 'hail' must, then, have been current in several forms.

9 TS NS 249:14ª + TS 12:210ª (Poems for Passover)

This text is represented by the writing in the lower margins of the fragments named. That in TS NS 249:14 contains part of a single poem celebrating the events which took place on the night of the first Passover and its anniversaries. It is composed in verses of four rhyming stichs. The first stich of each verse begins with ליל, the third with הוא הלילה. The first letters of the following words form an alphabetic acrostic. The first two stichs of the verse refer to events of the first Passover night, the last two to important events in the subsequent history of Israel which were also held to have taken place on the night of Passover. The particular events mentioned in the poem are connected with the Passover night in various midrashic sources (*Midrash Rabba*, *Midrash Tanchuma*, *Pesikta Rabbati*, *Pirqe de R. Eliezer*), but I have not found one source that contains all of them. They are all mentioned, however, in Yannai's poem אז רוב ניסים.[24]

The text on TS 12:210, recto, opens at the *'ayin* stich of a poem in which the initial letters of each stich form an alphabetic acrostic. The poem appears to be composed in verses of four rhyming stichs,

[22] See Mandelbaum, 1962, p. 133, and, for a description of the various mss and their relation to each other, the introduction, pp. 8–19. The same plague is omitted from *Pesikta Rabbati* (Friedmann, 1880), but this cannot have been our poet's source, as the order of the plagues there differs from that of the poem. The omission was no doubt due to confusion of ברד with דבר. The two plagues are not only written with the same consonants, but also have the same proof text.

[23] It is interesting to note that TS 16:93, a ms of *Pesikta de Rav Kahana* with Palestinian pointing, did contain the correct proof text for 'rash,' and the reference to 'hail.' See Allony and Díez-Macho, 1959a, p. 65, frag. 2, v6.

[24] Zulay, 1938, p. 92.

the last verse being followed by two extra *taw* stichs which rhyme with those of the preceding verse. This argues some irregularity in arrangement earlier in the poem, since, if the verses were all composed of four stichs, the *pe* to *resh* stichs should compose a verse. The poem deals with the destruction of Israel's enemies, and the setting apart of God's habitation, and of his people, as holy. It is followed by a quotation from Num. 15:40 (?) to which the last line of the poem seems to refer. This is followed by בׄ(רוך) הטוב. The verso of this fragment contains five rhyming stichs dealing with the coming of salvation to Israel.

10 TS NS 117:7 + TS H6:51 (Liturgy for the Day of Atonement)

The opening poem on the recto contrasts the wondrous acts of God with the insignificant acts of man. It is composed in verses of four rhyming stichs, the first letters of each verse forming an alphabetic acrostic with two *taw* verses. The poem is preserved from the *he* verse to the end. The first verse, and every second following verse, has מׄע(שי) אׄ(לוה)ינו before the first stich and (?) וה(שם) ית(ברך) before the fourth. The second verse, and alternate verses following, has מׄע(שי) אׄד(ם) before the first stich[25] and (?) ואׄ(לוהינו) ית(ברך) before the fourth.[26]

The following poem on the recto is אל מלך בעולמו.[27] Another text of this poem with Palestinian pointing appears in Leningrad MS Ant. 959.[28] The text of the present fragment differs both from that text and from the early printed editions, but is closer to the printed editions than is that of Ant. 959. The present text is exceptional in that it gives the quotations from 1 Chron. 16:8–36 in full.

The verso of this scroll contains part of an *ʿaboda* composed in verses of four stichs, each of which begins with the same letter. The second and fourth stich of each verse is preceded by עד לא. The initial letters of the verses in lines 1–16 form a '*tashraq*' acrostic running from *ḥet* to *ʾalef*. Line 17 is blank. The same poem continues with

[25] Before the *nun* verse (r15) מׄע אינו is written, presumably in error.

[26] This was omitted in the *ḥet* verse (r7), and also in the *ṣade* verse (r21), where it was inserted above the line.

[27] In printed texts, but not in this ms or in Ant. 959 (note 28), אמרו לאלוהים precedes each verse (Davidson, 1924–33, no. א 5860).

[28] Edelmann, 1934, Hebrew p. 20.

a complete alphabetic acrostic (v18–64). The poem is interrupted by the quotation of Lev. 8:34 (v4) and by the following rubrics:

v44 וכך היה א[ומר אנה] השם עויתי וגו
v49 וכך היה אומר עויתי וגו
v56 וכך היה אומר עוו וגו

Lines 65 and 66 contain the following rubric:

ויום טוב היו עושים לכל אוהביו·]
בצאתו בשלום מן הקו: כן יהי רצ]

11 TS H2:29 (*Qeroba* for the seventh day of Passover)

The text is headed ויושע ליהודה זבידה. I have been unable to find any information on this author, save that a poem of his is contained in the *Seder Ḥibbur Berakot*.[29] Poem 5 of the present *qeroba* appears in slightly different form as part of a *yoṣer* for the seventh day of Passover published by Davidson.[30] One of the preceding (unpublished) poems in the text from which the *yoṣer* was taken contains the acrostic יהודה חזק, which suggests a possible connection with our author. Davidson has also published a poem ויושע אשל נטעם[31] with which poem (vii) of the present text, ויושע אסונים אשל פאר נטעם, definitely has connections, but only to the extent that they use some of the same key words.

Eight of the poems of this *qeroba* are preserved, as follows:

(i) Ten verses, each of two stichs, preceded by the first word (or words) of the verses of the 'Song of Moses' (Exod. 14:30–15:8). The stichs all have the same rhyme. The initial letters of the stichs form an alphabetic acrostic to *resh*. The poem is followed by biblical quotations, and a 'seal' *(ḥatimah)* of four rhyming stichs, the last of which alludes to the following blessing (מגן). The poem deals with the events at the Red Sea.

(ii) The second poem is identical in structure with the first, save that the verses are preceded by the first words of Exod. 15:9–18, and the acrostic is '*tashraq*' to *gimel*. The last stich of the 'seal' refers

[29] A *qeroba*, published in Davidson, 1931, pp. 266–75. On this author see now Schirmann, 1965, pp. 87f. Various reasons are given there (p. 88) for doubting whether Yehuda Zebida actually did write the poems of TS H2:29.

[30] Davidson, 1928, pp. 54–55.

[31] Davidson, 1928, pp. 123–4.

to the blessing מחיה. The subject is much the same as that of the first poem.

(iii) A poem composed in verses of four stichs. All the stichs of the first three verses rhyme, and the initial letters of these verses form the acrostic משה. The stichs of the fourth verse have a different rhyme, and their initial letters form the word חזק. This verse is followed by biblical quotations followed by a 'seal' of four rhyming stichs each of which begins with *qof*. The poem emphasizes God's help in the past, and asks for his help in the present.

(iv) The fourth poem is composed in verses of three stichs. The initial letters of the first two stichs are the same, and these initials form an alphabetic acrostic. All three stichs of a verse rhyme. The third stich consists of the first few words of the verses of Exod. 14:30–15:18, which may be changed slightly to fit the rhyme. The last verse of the poem, which contained both the *šin* and the *taw* of the acrostic, appears to consist of four stichs, and does not use a biblical quotation. The same four stichs, in a different order, were inserted between the *gimel* and *dalet* verses. The use of the sign< after every three verses suggests that this verse may have been used as a refrain. The poem deals with the events at the Red Sea as a prototype of God's salvation of Israel at other times.

(v) A poem introduced by the quotation of Exod. 13:17, which represents God as explaining his actions on behalf of Israel 'lest they return to Egypt.' It is composed in verses of four stichs, each of the first three stichs opening with a first person singular imperfect verb form. The second letters of these words form an alphabetic acrostic. The fourth stich of each verse is פן ישובו מצרימה. All the stichs of the poem rhyme.

(vi) A poem composed of verses of four rhyming stichs. Each verse is composed as follows. The first stich opens with ויושע. The next word (or two) comes from the beginning of the verses of Exod. 14:30–15:18. The first letter of the following word forms part of an alphabetic acrostic. The second stich opens with ביום ההוא. The first letter of the following word forms part of an alphabetic acrostic. The third stich opens with ולעתיד. The first letter of the following word forms part of the acrostic וולבון בירבי שבתי, a name I cannot trace. The fourth stich opens with ביום ההוא, which is followed by a biblical quotation dealing with Israel's future triumph. The last verse does not follow the same pattern. The poem deals with God's salvation of Israel at the Red Sea as a prototype of his final salvation of Israel in the future.

(vii) A poem composed in rhyming stichs of which the first letters form an alphabetic acrostic. Each stich (save the last two) is preceded by the first word(s) of the verses of Exod. 14:30–15:18. The poem deals with the events at the Red Sea. It is followed by a verse of three rhyming stichs.

(viii) A poem on the same subject as the preceding, identical in structure save that the acrostic is '*tashraq*,' and the verses of the 'Song of Moses' are taken in the order 14:31–15:18 + 14:30.

The extreme complexity of the structure of these poems, which is also found in the *qeroba* published by Davidson (1931, p. 266), suggests that they are relatively late in the history of Palestinian *piyyuṭ*.

12 TS H7:7 (Part of a *Qeroba* for *Shemini 'Aṣeret* by Yannai)

This text has already been described and published by Zulay.[32] Since this text is only given as an example of pointing clearly done by hands of two classes, I have only printed the verso (lines 39ff. in Zulay's edition).

[32] Zulay, 1936, p. 323; 1938, MS 3, p. 342.

VIII
Texts

Of the texts printed here, nos. 1, 4, 4a, 5, 7, 8, and 9 are the product of the collation of the independent reading of Dr. Manfried Dietrich with that of the present author. Texts 2, 3, 6, 10, 11, and 12 represent the reading of the author only. A final check of the transcription was, in all cases, made from the original texts.

The transcription of the vocalization involves a small amount of interpretation, since some signs in a ms may be carelessly written and capable of more than one reading (for example, the 'i' sign is often slanted to one side or the other, and so may be confused with either of the 'e' signs). However, on the assumption that any questioning of the reading given here would be done on the basis of the text or its photograph, no attempt has been made to reproduce the individual forms or positions of signs. Signs which are considered to represent the same grapheme are represented by the same printed symbol, placed above the letter they follow. For the same reason, texts with only occasional words pointed are not printed in full.

Where its reading is uncertain, the consonantal text is printed with an underline. Lacunae – represented by square brackets – are restored without an underline where the reading of another text is used, and with an underline where the restoration is the editor's. Letters in a text appearing in unusual forms – as in partial writings, ligatures, etc. – are not distinguished in the transcription.

The line numbering of the original is given for all texts, and is used throughout this work for reference. Large texts, however, are here set up to display the structure of the poems they contain. In these texts, line endings are marked by a vertical line. Small fragments, in which this practice would result in many blank lines, are reproduced line for line as in the original.

After some deliberation, it was decided not to list variants between the texts published here and other editions of the same poems. The present writer does not have ready access to a library containing the early printed prayer books, although he has been able to use them in the libraries of other institutions. The biblical quotations differ from BH[3] almost solely in orthography. Few are considered of sufficient interest to note. This refers, of course, only to biblical quotations given as such. Variant quotations occurring within a poem are considered as changed to suit the author's purposes: either to fit rhyme or acrostic,[1] or to recall a particular interpretation or some related biblical verse.[2]

1 TS NS 249:2

recto

נבין את שגיא[ ]ינו ולא נזקור את חטאנו ו[
ליזדונותינו וא[תה] ארך אפים וטוב וסלח מכל[
על התשובה ותתן תיקווה ליכנעים מפני חרונך [
ישר צעדינו ללכת בתורתך והט אורחותינו לשוב ע[
ותמוך יד אבודים ואל יטבעו בשחת ככ בתו[3] בצר ל[ך
באחרית הימים ושבת עד יי איך ושמעת בק[
ואתה רחום ומקבל תשובה ועד התשובה מאז היבטח[תנו
ככ עינ[4] שובה ישראל עד יי איך כי כשלת בעו קח[ו
אימרו אליו כל תשא עוון וקח טוב ונשלמה פרים[
[5]הזדונות והש[גגות] וגו אתה יודע רזי עולם וגו על[
איום ונורא יום הע[שור לכל הי]צורים אין תלות פנים בושת לכל פנ[
אשר צדק תענה[חותם]ך אמת: הנשמה לך והגוף פעלך[
בערכך משפט תקרא ל[שמ]ים לי[תן] הנפש בכן אל הארץ תקרא[
בעת ידריש[ו מי חטא לי]תען וזה לזה יוכיחו הנשמ[ה

[1] E.g., the quotation of Exod. 15:1 in TS H2:29, 1v7.

[2] E.g., the use of נישוף for ינשוף in TS NS 249:14, to connect the ינשוף of Isa. 34:11 with נשף of Isa. 40:24.

[3] Deut. 4:30. [4] Hos. 14:2–3. [5] *Shebu'ot* 1:6.

גולם יענ[ה בהיות בי הנפש] היא הירשיעתני גם הייתה לי כמיכשול[
גם בעופפה מני השלכתי לר]ימה כמו אבן דומה]
דיברה הנפש הלוא זכה אני כמו אש נופחתי דמיתי בגול[ם
דין להחטיאיני בכל כחש וגיזל לפניו ולא מילאני]
הבשר יען נפש הידריכתני נתיב עקלקלות הירהור[
הוסעה מני לא ת[ואר ולא] שיח ולא עוון לי[
והנפש תאמר איך [תרשי]עיני למ[ען תצדק] ואת[ה
ומעת פרשי ט[רף לא טעמתי] הנ[ני]]
זה ממרום על[יהם
זומנו זה בזה יש[ימו
חשובים הם שנימו[
חש מלך להודיע כ[חשם
טובך ידוע לאין[
ט[
....]

verso

א]ל [חיים יהי וא]ל[ימו]ת הנשמה[ ] הנשמה לך
ניכ]ספנו ק[נו]ת כי לא היבננו מה באחריתינו[ ]לבוא לתוכחת
צ]דקה תעשה הנשמה לך
]כמעשיך: למען תיוורא דין כל הייצורים שופט ערבתה
]חי יודוך הנשמה לך
]לכן נוצדו: מה בצע בדמינו שחת אם נרד מי יודה לך
נוב]ע מקור חיים הנשמה לך
]שבנו אל תבישינו: נפשות לך הנה יוצר כל נפש אדון כל נשמה
]לעד יברכוך הנשמה לך
עצ]מות להוכיח בשר: שמחה בו נפ[ש כ]ישאור ל[עיסה כ]מלח לשמר תפל

11 נחשבי]ם כאיין ואם יחד יודוך   הנ[שמה לך   ]
12]לתולעת והגוף לרימה עליפת נפש [אם תקולע בקלע] על אודות רשע
13 תתיכם] כחלב תקפיאם כזכוכית   ה[נ]שמה [לך]
14 לבט]ח בלי פחד   פי[קדו]ן נפשם ביצרור [החיים כי לכן] שוו
15 ב]כבוד יעליזו   הנשמה ל[ך
16 לתק]ן: צקתנו כחומר ונשברנו כחרש] ולך יכולת לחדש
17 להש]יבך   הנשמה לך
18 אס]ירים: קומו מעפר בואו מבשן שובו מימצולות
19 יכ]ירו   הנשמה לך
20 ריב]בות אלפינו המון מיספ[רינו י]עמוד לפניך
21]הנשמה לך
22]גויי [רשע יר]קב ו[יבלה   ]שירשיך
23 [
24]טומאה
25 [
26]ומאהבתך ומאהבך
27]ם סליחה לכל
28]....

2 TS NS 118:38

This text contains the following vocalized words:

verso

2 עִיתֹר

3 פִּנָּה

5 לְנוֹךְ

6 נֹסַב, לשִׁיווּעִים

9 שתוליך(?)

10 תְּשבִי

recto

12]בׂ, שְׁבוּעִים

13 מִ]גֵן

14 ונָפֶש

16 כַּנֹם (÷ כְּנָם?)

3 TS NS 119:42 + TS NS 301:66

This text contains the following vocalized words:

recto

4 כנה̄ר

7 הנח̄ל

8 שׂק̇̈י

9 נ̇ץ, לש̈מחה

10 ר̇נן

12 ה̈תאוה

15 כ[̈]ש

20 עלב̇ל

31 כ̇[ ]חבל

verso

3 הנ̈קדש, בע́ם

5 ק́ר̇ב

6 ד̇לה, מ̈מ̄שואות

7 ה̈יקר̇יב, חר̇ב, ותקר̄ב

8 ע́ר̇ב

9 ית̇ד, ובשב̈יעית

11 למ̈תעננים, ר̈פאות, ע̇צ̇ב

17 ואו̇ר

19 מ̈קמ̂ינו, וס̇יב[, ת̈גרע

20 נו́ו̇ה

21 סח̇י̇ביירא̇ה

22 נ̈שמעה

23 עטרינ̈ו, ש́ב̂ת

29]̈אב

32 מ̈גדל, חד̇ש̱

34 תצמ́ח

35 כ̇פ̇ל

36 גר̈ור(?)

40 חד̇ש

42 ר̇יע̇יה̱

In addition, שׂ is used frequently to mark ⟨ś⟩.

4 TS NS 249:7 + TS NS 301:28

TS NS 249:7, fol. 1, recto

ו

1 [6][פיריה ויבולה] | נותנת   לך ולזרעך נית[נת]
[צד]קתך בה לא מתמתנת   חורה בך לא מתחתנת: |

2 קיבוע אבניה ברזל ניקצב   והרריה נחושת נחצב:
3 רוץ ודלג שור ובה תוצב | כסחתי לך ואני עליך ניצב:

ששמה ארץ החיים   כי מיתיה תחילה חיים: |
4 תחוללתיך עד הם בחיים   ויוסיפו לך שנות חיים:

ז[1] ובכן [7]ואהיה עמך |
5 אני ומלאכי עימך   בל אעתק מעימך
גאון אח לפניך יימך   דרך שלום אחכימך |
6 הון ונפש לא ייחסר ממך   ותחלה פני אביך ואמך:
7 זך ומוצל מילוחמך | חנון כמו מראה חלומך:
טוסה והתהלך בתומך: ימינך בימיני תותמך |
8 כיסא כבודי בו אחתמך   לעד לא אתימך:
9 מה טובו אוהלי מקומך | נצח בהם אקימך
סיח היטיף נואמך   ערב בקול נויי טעמך
10 פקדתיך ברחמים לרחמך | ציויתי ישעך לרוממך
קדוש אתה ולא אאשימך   רודפך בידו לא אשלימך |
11 שמי ערבתי בשמך   תשוב למולדתך בשלומך

[6] Restored from H.U.C. MS 1001. [7] Gen. 31:3.

ז[2] ובכן

12 תשיבנו מכל שערים | שערים טבעו רומם ר כפופי קומה
13 ק וקוממיות צייננו צ לראש פינה | פ ויקרת עליון
ע על כל שימנו ש ולכל ראש נשאינו נ ונטלינו מרום |
14 מ מראשון לינה ל עימנו בתוך כפרים כ מכפרים בעד יקרים
15 י נכבדים טעינו | טעינ בארץ חמדה ח ותאות זבת
16 ז חלב ודבש ודבש בלי בו הקאה | ה ובל תקיא דריה
ד אשר הם גדיריה ג ומוסדי בריתה ב כרותה לה אמת |
17 א מתוכה תצמח

ח

18 תצמח ותצליח תבוא ותביא תשוב ותשיב תקרב ותקרב | תקום ותקים
שבי עדיך אשר הם עידיך ובני עבדיך
19 ביראה עובדיך כנת | קדושיך כינוי מקדישיך
ככ וקרא

ט

20 בתמימים תותמם ובקדושים תוקד[ש]מידים
ואומ קקקק
ק מתמימי דרך ק ממיישרי הילך ק משפויי היפך |
21 [ק] לתם תום דרך לפי תומתו
ק ייׄשר לו יושר הילך לפי ישרותו
22 ק | [ ]פי הילך לפי שפיותו
וגו לעו כל
ממ נם לחלק שוב שבתי שבותך |
23 [ממ ה]שיב לו תשובת אש[']שרתי
ממ השיבו ושובבו כנם והשיבותיך
וגו פ |

24 וישלח יע̲[קב מלאכים] [8] |

א

25 [א̲י̲ו̲ם̲] ונוֹרא מוֹראך: בכֹן מי לא יי̇ר[א̲ך̲]

[ג ד]ע̲ מנּו יריאך : |

26 [ה] מאוד מתפּחד: ותמיד היה מ[

ז] ח |

27 [ט] נשׂא פניו יהיר בשׁומעו הן לפ[נ̲י̲ו̲

28 [כ | ל ש]ל̲ו̲חים לפניו

ככי [8] וישלח

ונ [9] מעק̲[|

29]ונ [10] אשרי אדם ונ [11] תחנונים[|

TS NS 249:7, fol. 1, verso

1 חרבך אדום תרוה מאדום ותמגינו אדון [

ב

2 מילול מך אף מישיב: נא | חלק לשׂעיר הישיב:

סער עליו פן ישיב: עז עזו̲ת לבל יקשיב:

3 פיצח לשון רכה: | ציפצף ושפל עד דכה:

קושבו דבריו ביכה: רבת צררוני פץ ולך חיכה:

4 שר | וזה עולם שלו: שיוע ושוחד לימד לו:

5 תחכמונים אשר שילח לו: תלאותיו | ציוה לתנות לו:

[8] Gen. 32:4. [9] Isa. 42:16 (?).
[10] Ps. 32:2 (?). [11] Prov. 18:23.

ככ[12] ויצו אתם

ונ[13] מה תאמרי כי יפקוד עליך ואת לימדת אותם עליך אל[פים]

לר[אש] הל[וא] חב[לים] יאחז[וך] כמ[ו] אשת לידה: ונ[14] רבות רעות צדיק

6 ונ[15] | התרפיתה ביום צרה ונ[16] רבת צררוני ונ[17] לא יקרא עוד לנבל

7 שוע תשעשעינו | ואל תרשיעינו ובטל לתחי הושיענו ב

ג

8 יה לא תדום אם פינו ידום | להיפרע מאדום וירשה תהיה אדום:

9 נצח מדון ומצח זדון תעביר אדון | ותריב ותדון:

ירדו לאבדון וידעו שדון ותנטה כידון על צור וצידון:

10 ישולח | בם רזון ויהיו לאש מזון וצעקתינו תאזון כהודעתה לעובדיה חזון

11 ככ[18] חזון | עובדיה

ונ[19] ועלו מושיעים

וא ק אל נא

ד

12 ריבותיים מלאכי צבאות | ציויתה לאיש תם בתוצאות

13 דרכיו ללוות אורחותיו לנוות ואותו לחוות את | פה הוות

פן תחנה עליו מחנה וירא וייתירא מלא ירא

14 הם המלאכים אשר | היו עימו בצאתו מבית אביו ואמו

15 והם ראה בסולם בחלומו והם סיעדוהו | בבית חותנו

והם היו בצאתו והם היו בבואו· והם פגעו בו

16 והם שולחו בשליחותו | אל אח ובם פגש אח

מחן מלאכותיך ורגם מלכותך קדוש |

[12] Gen. 32:5.
[13] Jer. 13:21. The quotation from עליך to the end was written above the line and in the margin by a secondary hand.
[14] Ps. 34:20. [15] Prov. 24:10. [16] Ps. 129:1.
[17] Isa. 32:5. [18] Obad. 1. [19] Obad. 21.

ה

17 איש אשר נימשל באש משקת   בן והנה העת למשול קש שוחקת:

18 בתיו | חילק פן שלל יחולק   איש החלק כבוד לו נחלק:

19 גם לדרכו הי[ה] ולקראתו לא | היה   ודרך ארץ תם עש ועל כבוד קונו חס:

20 דברי כיבושים וריכוכי שיעה | שילח אליו לגבול רישעה:

21 העשרתו והחזקתו ודברי ענייות שילח אלי[ו ובדברי] | רכות שילח אליו:

ושמע ונזכר יום מכירתו   ובא לקראתו אחוז מ[כרתו

22 [זה] | אדון עולמים נם לו אדונך אני ולא האמין ונם כה תאמרון ל[אדוני

23 [חלף כן] | לבניו בעלום אדונים   זולת אדון אדוני האדו[נים

24 טוב סח לו [י]צרתיך לע[בד לי] | עבדי אתה וס[ח כה אמר עבדך

25 [יען כן] עבדים בנו מעבידים   איליך[ ] | עינינו כעב[דים

ו

איילים חיילים ומושע[|

26 [ב] משעים כי מחניפים לרשעים

[ג |

27 [דבר]י שלום לאין בם כבוד   ולא נא[|

28 [ה]מה בצע בדמי:

והיצילו מיד[|

29 [ז] יועצו לעריץ   להרפותו מעור[

TS NS 249:7, fol. 2, recto
+ TS NS 301:28, recto

1 [ח] | תפילה לעת מצוא   חן בעיניו אולי למצוא:

2 טענות רכות לקש במדומה   [ ] | שלום והם למלחמה:

יום להכחיש בו אימה   כי מענה רך ישיב חימה:

3 כל צרות | אשר ראתה עינו בבית חותנו אשר בו צרה עינו:

4 לבל יבוא במ[ח]נו ויך ואינו | לא עליו תחוס עינו:

מלאכים ממחנות אשר לו הראה אל אשר אליו ניראה |

5 ניתחכם על איש אין בו יראה וראשית חוכמה היא יראה:

6 סיח רצון לאיש קשה | לרפס מקורו בידו פן ירפס:

עז אשר הוא הכל מרפס וברצי כסף הוא מתרפס: |

7 פיתויים לאין לו חיסה על אבות ובנים פן ירוטש אם על בנים:

8 צעק לך מרחם | כאב על בנים פן תילקח קינו אם ובנים:

9 קידום מנחה וכל טוב לאיש רע האומר | לרע טוב:

רץ להפרידו מהנה מה טוב ומשכיל על דבר ימצא טוב:

10 שלוחים לישר | את עקוב פני עקוב עקובות לנקוב:

11 תינה כה אמר עבדך יעקב ונאמר לו אל | תירא עבדי יעקב›

ז[1] ובכן[20] ארצה שעיר

12 אדמוני איש האדום: | בז בכורה במאכל אדום

גיא ירושתו גבול אדום דבוקיו מאודמים כדם א |

13 הוא אהב דם לכן שמו א והוא עשו והוא אדום

14 זכור יה לבני א | חורבן אשר עשתה בת א

טבח גדול בארץ[א יקי]דת אש בשדה א |

15 כמהנו לך דוד צח [וא] להיראות בלבוש א

16 ממרום תפיל שר א | [נע]לך תשליך על א

שימה נקמתך בא עוד תאבד חכמים מא |

17 [פרוס מצודה] בארץ א צוד תצוד לאיש צייד אבי א

[20] Gen. 32:4.

18 קרנות עשר גדע מא | [רם הפוך]ה כס והדום
שיתה מהפכה כסדום שליפת חרבך תרוה מא |
19 [תופיע ונאמ]ר מי זה בא מאדם תיסוב לך מלוכה מאדום

ז[2] ובכן |

20 [אדום אשר]א אימתני בחיוותא לא התפרשת בשם
21 גושמה מתיל בחזיר גיבר | [דחילה בחבר]תה חזות דמיונה
הלא כנהר פרת המייה ומהשנייא מן כולהין ותקיפה |
22 [זערה היא ורבר]בן הם זוועתה חיוה רביעאה ויתירה חייל:
23 טיפרה די נחש טיבה[21] | [יע שינה] די פרזל יכיל
כל ארעה אכלה כדנה לה התיהב חזוי לילה |
24 [מדא ואכ]לה שאר מאכלה ניגוח עשר קרנין ניכתרה:
25 סום קרן זעירה סלקת | [עינין כעיני א]נשה עלוהי:
פומה ממלל רברבן פתיח: צניף מלכותה בצרה צירה |
26 [קרב עבדה ע]ם קדישין: רישיונה עשרה מלכין רשים:
27 שם מלך אחרן שני | [תלי מלין לצד]תקיפה:

ז[3]

תקיפה ועתיק יומיה יומיה יקרבון ויום יאתה
28 יא | [קטילת] חיוותה ה והובד גושמה
ג ליקידת אשא אש אכלה אשא: |

ח

29 [ומן בית יעקב א]ש יצמח אנש
ועם ענני שמיה יטוס ועד עתיק יומייה ימטי |

TS NS 249:7, fol. 2, verso + TS NS 301:28, verso

1 [ויתי]הב ליה שולטן עלם: ויקר ומלכו יחאחסן

[21] Read טיבחה.

2 שֻׁולטָנֹה די לא יֶעדֵי | וִיקְרֹה | די לא יִפסֹק   וֹמלכֹותֵיה די לא תִתחֹבֹל

3 וֹעמֹמֹיה ליה ישֹלמֹון   וֹאומֹיה ליה | ישֹתעבדֹון ולישֹנֹיה ליה יפלחֹון

4 וֹמלכֹותֹה ושֻׁולטֹנֹה ורֹבותה תֹתיֹהב לעֹם | קֹדישֹין המקֹדִישים שֹם הקֹודש
    כֹכ וֹקרֹא

ט

5 עצֹתֹך אין לֹידע   כוחֹך | אין לבֹלות   שמֹך אין להֹחליף
    יֹענו ויֹאמרו קֹקֹק

6 קֹ מבֹעלֵי עֵיצֹה   קֹ מבֹעלֹי | כוח   קֹ מבֹעלֹי שֹם ומעֹשֹה
    קֹ הֹשלים את עצֹת יעקב והֹפר את עצֹת עשׂו |

7 קֹ הכביד תֹשֹות כֹוח יעקב והֹתיֹש כֹוח עשׂו
    קֹ הֹיטֹיב שֹם יעקב ממעשֹה עשׂו |

8 וֹגֹו לעֹו כֹל

מֹמֹ נם לתֹם אם תֹרֹאֹה לֹאֹח לא תֹיתֹירֹא

9 מֹמֹ נם לו אם תֹעבֹור | בֹמֹים לא תֹשטֹף
מֹמֹ נם לו אֹם תֹלֹך בֹמֹו אֹש לא תֹיכֹוֹה
וֹגֹו פֹעֹ |

10 [22]וֹיבֹא יעקב שלם |

א

11 אֹורֹחֹות תֹם יֹישֹרתה: בֹֿואֹו וצֹאֹתֹו שֹימֹרתה:

12 גֹֿאֹון עֹוֹזֹֿו אֹישֹרתה: דֹיגֹלֹי | מֹחֹנֹותֹיו הֹיכֹשֹרתה:

    הֹוא זֹרע בֹדֹמעֹת חֹסד: וֹברֹינֹה קֹצר לפֹי חֹסד:

13 זֹומֹנֹו לֹו | ישׁועֹות חֹוֹסֹן: חֹמדֹת בֹרֹכות אוֹסֹם:

---

[22] Gen. 33:18.

14 טס עליו שר וישר: יוסר בהצלעת גיד | אשר יוסר:
כעת נרפא]]ל[ ]ק[ ]במוסר: לשלם בא שלם ולא מחוסר

ככ[22] ויבא |
15 ונ[23] וידעת כי שלום ונ[24] יה ישמר צאתך ונ[25] הזורעים [בדמ]עה
16 ונ[26] הלוך ילך ובכה | ונ[27] שלום רב

מכשול לא יבוא לנו בצאתינו ובואינו בצל מגינך[ ]באיפ[|

ב

17 מקום נחלת מקנה נא חלק בה קנה:
18 סלה לניניו היקנה: עיר[|] ניתקנה:

פנה ונח בה כי בן בה: צפנת כי ינוח בה:
19 קסיטות מא[ה] | אשר כשדה היפיח בה:

שלום שר בחילו: שליו ושקט בחיילו:
20 ת[ ] | בנוחלו: תיכן ונטה שם אהלו

ככ[28] ויקן
21 ונ[29] אים דבר בקדשו ונ[ ] | ונ[30] להנחיל אוהבי יש
ונ[31] יבחר לנו את נחלתינו סלה
22 ברכת שמך [ ] | בטל תחי יבורך שמך ב

ג

23 יה משלם גמולות משלם פרע[ ] | למחריבי שלם:
24 נחז סוכך בשלם בבינין שלם וכתם הבא שלם[ ] | נשלם:

[23] Job 5:24. [24] Ps. 121:8. [25] Ps. 126:5.
[26] Ps. 126:6. [27] Ps. 119:165. [28] Gen. 33:19.
[29] Ps. 60:8. [30] Prov. 8:21. [31] Ps. 47:5.

ישולמו תשלומים לגוי רע משלמים ותיקרא שנת שילומ[ים |

25 יחלוך בשלמים עם לך מושלמים ויהיו משולמים רבים וכן של[מים]

[ככ[32]] | אם שלימים

26 ונ[33] יה תשפות שלום

וא ק אל נא

ד

27 שומר ישראל[ ] | כי מכל רע שמרו

אהי ישראל שמו היקים לנו נואמו

28 וכונן על[ ] | תם התימו[34] כיהילך בתומו

בצאתו ובואו ומובאו שומרו וצילו[|

29 שלם השיבו ושלום הישיבו שליו יישבו וברכות השאיבו

ל[

4a TS NS 117:6 + TS NS 123:2

TS NS 117:6, fol. 1, recto

1 .....

2 לקנ[ן ברום מק[ום

3 יחד פה אחר: וש[נו

4 חפצ[ו וכ]פי כסיל מ[חתה

5 נופצו [טע]מו לעשות[

6 עליליה זדו ופקו פליל[יה

7 ניפצם כאבן אל א[שר

8 על עושה כל באומר: נ[תגדל יו]צר[

9 בחנייתם ובינסיעתם לשון שבעים ב[שיחתם: על] ענו[תם נבלה בשפתם

[32] Nah. 1:12. [33] Isa. 26:12.

[34] A later hand suggests, in the margin, the reading התמימו.

[ב]עבור כן נבלה שפתם: פלגה ניקרא[דורם כי פל]גו במגדל דירם [צור פילגם
[ופ]רץ גדירם ופלגו זה על [זה בדיבורם קריאת] שפתותם אשר חלקו וכי[קריאתם
[כן] לקו: רגשו ובערו [וד]לקו ובא[חד חטא]ו בה לקו: שיווי שפו שפה [אחת
[וישיב]תם ישיבת נחת: ת[אבו רום וישנאו תח]ת וניתעב מרום ונוסחו [מתחת
] ובכן [[35]ודברים אחדי]ם
[אחדים] אחודים אימרה [אחת אווילי אדמה בי]זו ביזו בבוחן ביטויים ב[אמרם
[ג גיברו] גרי גיא גי[דופי גאווה דברו] ד דהרו דאו דרוד[
[המה הש]מימום הותל היט[ם הפכפך ונואלו] ו ונאלמו ונעלמו[
[זולות זומ]מו זורבו זועמו ז[ורו חוץ ח ח]ניית חמ[דתם
[טפו ט ט]פשו טורדו טורפו[

TS NS 117:6, fol. 1, verso

]נתך א יז[
מ]שמים לשמי שמים
ממ]עונה לשחקים משחקים
]ידמה מי ישווה מי ראה
]יקשה מי יעיז מי יהרהר
כר]וב ודיאתך על רוח
ושביל]ך במי[ם וש]לוחך באש אלפי אלפים וריבי
]אנש[ים] נ[עשים נשים] נעשים רוחות נעשים זיקים נעשים כל
[דמות ועו]שים כל שליחות [באימה ב]יראה בפחד וברעדה ובריתית בזייע
[יפתחו] פה להזכיר שם קודשך[ככ ו]קרא׳
[ ]שפה ופה ולשון ביברירות וב[ ]בינקיות יענו ויאמרו קקק[
[ק] מברורי לשון ק מנקיי פה[ ]רי שפת אמת הנכונה ק[
]לימודי דת ק חשק ב[ ]וקדושה וגו לעו ׳ ממ[
]שר שפה אחת[ ]ן שלישי כדור ל[

[35] Gen. 11:1.

15]ג כדור חדיפה[ ] [

16] אוהב מבין ש[נואים]קניתה: ברואים אותו [הקניתה

17 דר]כי לבו ח[קרתה: הן] כבת יחידה הנחיתו[

18]תועני בלא בוא[

TS NS 117:6, fol. 2, recto
+ TS NS 123:2, recto

1]עה כי ני[

2 להרחיץ במים[

3 כל עץ: רוענן ויש[

4 ולפניו במדבר הו[

5 קורבנות לחם›[ ]מים

6 ו בכנפיהם רוח בדע[ ]לא[ ]ב[

7 ו הוד עיניהם כלפידי אש[ ]ודגלותם כעין קדם

8 ו הלל קולם כהמון[ ]שים ו טסים[ ]ששים

9 ו כמראה בזק מאוששים ו לא[ ]שים ו מגבורו[ ]ס[]פים

10 [ו] נוראים ואימים וקשים[ ]קדשים ו עושים שליחו[יות]משים

11 [ו פ]אים וניפלאות רוחשים ו צק[ ]לגדיית לוחשים ו קול דממה דקה[ ]שים

12 [ו רצי]ם ושבים ולא נופשים ו ש[ ]בים אל מקודשים ו תמודים ומכתירים ומקדישים

13 לקד]ש הניזכר קדוש כ[כ]וקרא ›

14]ויבאו שני המלאכים[36][ ]אליך כליווה[ ]לש[ ]כשלחתם הם חגרו

15]גיבורים אשר כבזק[ ]רשת השלוחים לש[ ]ה[ ]נו מיהלך

16]דברך לא ימירו:[ ]תשלח וימהרו ח[ ]שן ביקשו ויאחרו:

[36] Gen. 19:1.

17]כלא ראו: יקרים[ ]כאנשים נראו[מל]אכים נראו ולא נחבאו

18 מל]אכותם סדומה כ[כ[36] ויבאו] שני ונ[ ]א[37] ונ עושה מלאכיו

19]ונ[38] הללוהו כל מל[אכיו]ונ[39] השולח אמרתו[

TS NS 117:6, fol. 2, verso
+ TS NS 123:2, verso

1]מ[ ]אבי[

2]תידון במכבידי זדן

3]כאב זריותם דרכם

4]יצא וצדיק לא נימצא

5 מלאכי שלו[ ]נעשו מלאכי חימה

6 לעשות רע[ ]תאמין וקוום בכל העולם

7]ימין ב[ ]ברצוא ושוב: גזירה עד

8 לא תצ[ ]ב וטף[ ]חי[ ]דבר שליחות אחת בשניים

9 לא תיש[ ]ה ושתי שליחויות[ ]: הלא כל אחד שליחותו יעש א[

10 לכ[ ]ם לרע אם לרצון אם ל[ ]משמע מקדימים במשלחם[

11 ובסדום ניתמתנו בשליחותם: זכות[מה]מחפש אבהמון להם כי היה ע[

12 ומתחנן [ע]ליהם: חיכו כי כלימודך על[יהם]אנחם על אכזריים כדובר[

13 טיסה אח[ ]י העולם יעשו ומינווה [אברהם] מהלך יום אחד עשו: יל[

14 משפ[ ]רש[ ]ם בערב על כן נכנסו לס[דום ב]ערב: לעולם [40]ויבא[ו שני

15 אילי פ[ ] ופחד משוטטים ביקצה רו[ ]: ברקים הנשלחים[

16 אחד ואח[ ]ש[ ]ת אחת: גיבורים גויי[ ]שיש אשר ניפנו ס[

17 דליקה לסדומה ל[ ]ש הדולקים ואין[ ]יש האחד למלט[

[37] Ps. 104:4. [38] Ps. 148:2. [39] Ps. 147:15. [40] Gen. 19:1.

ואחד לערער הערים]]לבייש יד ה[ ]שורש הרים: זומ[
צהריים כי היה צידקו]]צהריים[ ]ערביים כי מה[

5 J.T.S. MS E.N.A. 2020 f. 23

recto

מצרים פחדו מואבים רעדו ב המ[
סוכת בן ישי סמוך ירצה שיי ב הס ע[
פלגי מים נחצו פדויים עברו ועלצו ב המ צפחו[
קומם עיר קרית מלך תעיר ב הס ריפדות ק[ ]ים רינה[
שירה בים שוררו לאל רם ב המ תורה לימינו תע[
שובב מהרה עוזך ועין בעין נחזך ב הס שעינו מימעונך ותן אמת ל[
ככ בתו[41] שלוש פ אינו ב מק]
ב ש דו[די ה]יצצתה מחרכים להצמיח [יש]ועה למחכים לה[ע
להיתרצות בזכים ורכים ב
ב ש הוצגתה אחר כותל והיסעתה גפן [ש]תל והיש[ ]תה גוי מסתל
תפליא ונודך על תל ב
ב ש ושלחתה יד מן החור ותלשתה קו מן החול רבבה כצמח מס[ ]קול
ותן לנו תשועה וברכה וחיים ושלום ב עושה

קדושתא שור או כש[ב]
אימצתה אומץ אהבה באום לך אהיבה[ ]ועיבה
דרשת ליישר לה נתיבה הקדמתה א[ ]ליכפרה
זה לחש היבנתה תמורה חילוי רצון ש[
ייקרם הימירו בשור היות לו ע[
]תה ל[ ]קרי[

[41] Deut. 16:16.

verso

1]ה נהם והים ומלואו רעם נעשה

2]וע ק[ ]תים בחרבו ליפסוע ועמו

3]קי כמו שה ל[ ]ם על מכסת שה פסוח וגנון

4]ליסבי[ ]ת שה[ ]ורעי מחסר תעודה לימד לחוג את זאת

5]נריו בתודה לכבדו בזיבחי תודה ככ[42] וכי תיזבחו זבח

6 [תו]דה ליי לרצנכם תיזבחו ונ[43][זי]בחו זיבחי צדק [ובט]חו אל יי ונ[44]

7 [זוב]ח תודה יכבדנני ושם [דרך] א[רא]נו בישע אים ונ[45]בואו שעריו

8 [ ] בתודה חצרותיו בתחיל[ה] הודו לו ברכו שמו ונ[46] כציפור עפות

9 כן יגן יי צבאות על ירושלם גנון והציל פסוח והמליט אל נא

10 מכל [חי]ה ומכל בהמה מכל רח[לים] לקרבן רצון מכל אילים ומכל מריאים

11 נזבח שה לפסח לאל אשר פסח הכל שלו ואם תתן לו מידו לו מה תועיל

12 לו א[ ]ק כי שלו כי אם הריח אשר בשיי ירח[ ]יח ומשרתיו
יאריח וכתמר יפריח [ ]יח[ ]ק[ ][47]

13 אדון חקק בכסאו דמות שור בעד תבנית שור אם יגעה שור

14 גדול ערב לו ריצוי השה דודיו לבקש אם תעו כשה

15 היות שה תמורה בעד שה פזור[ה]ובכן ייזכר שה מורייה

16 זכותם דרש ב[ ]זיכר עושה עורות גדי עז

17 תייש[ ]טבילת דמו ריצוי לדר שבעה

18]חצבה עמודיה שבעה

19 .]ת שה היות שוחטים

[42] Lev. 22:29. [43] Ps. 4:6. [44] Ps. 50:23.
[45] Ps. 100:4. [46] Isa. 31:5. BH³ כצפרים.
[47] From משרתיו on, this passage is written in the left-hand margin.

6 TS H2:30

The text of fol. 1 is not given, since there is little vocalization. The following words are pointed:

שַׁבָּת 1r3, זמר 1r10, שמור 1v2.

fol. 2, recto

גם בחשבו להאבידי · נְזכר אשכול הכפר לעודדי ·
והפיר את מחרידי · בהקראות ספר בל ׃
גם פיענח רזים · לשלוך בכור עזים · וה לדיראון
לועזים · ולחיי עולם עליזים בל ׃
דן מתחרי אחוז מלוכה · ונתהלך על סבכה · יען
עיקל הליכה · הועדה בי בל ׃
דרך נתיב רְשעה · וּמְפעלות ממלכות הרשעה ·
גל והבדיל עת תשועה · להזמין בזה לילה ׃
הכי לכן אייחלה · ולהורים אשאלה · מה פעל רב
עלילה · מופת בזה לילה ׃
הזיית שתי פעמים · מה על סף ומשקוף מתאומִים
ומה הבדיל אֱל תָּמִים · מלילות זה לילה ׃
וביעור הסאור · מה לי לְבדוק לאור · ומופתי נאור ·
להזכיר בזה לילה ׃
וצלי מה לוכל · מצות מאכל · ומה הבדיל נכר
מִילוכל מְתשורת זה הל ׃
זיווג דשאים מה לי להזכיר · חזרת וחרוסת
ותמכה להכיר · צביעת שילוש מצה בלי להנכיר
בזכר פעולות לילה ׃
זְמרה מה אפגוש[·]והלל למה ארגיש · ומה
הְבדיל והגיש · לגואלי בזה לילה ׃

fol. 2, verso

חִילוּיְ ארבעה מְלפחות · עד מסוכֿן למֿחות · שִׁיעוּרֿם
מה לי לֿיאחות · כי ארבעת פחות · נֿידֿפו בזה ל׳.
חוֹק עבודה זו לִנצור · מה יש לי לעצור · ומה הִבדיל
שומר נצור · עד סערה חצות לילה ׳.
טובי לֵב ומשכילים · יָשִׁיבֿו לחוֹות סכלים · רָז גבורות
יגידו לעוללים · מה נעשׂה בזה לילה ׳.
טבילת שני דמים כי · טֿהֿרנֿו משנֵי כתֿמים · והֿבדיל
צור עולמים · בינינו לבֵן עמים בֿל ׳.
יסֿידֿת חֿמֿץ · כי אֿפס המֿץ · ואכילת מצוֹת · כי על
שלוש מצוות ניגאלנו בזה לילה ׳.
ישיבת צלי אֵש מְלהותיר · כי נכחדו צרים באין
מותיר · והֲבֿד אֵל יֵשַׁע מכתיר · ללוֹ יעתיר בֿל ׳.
כינֿוי חֿרת כי חיֿזרו עול · וחרוֹסֶת כי חרֿסֿונֿו
מחשבי בצור למעול · ותמֿכֿה כי תָמכֿו בִי בחוֹזֶק
תְצוֹד · לולי מושיעי אץ ליסעוד בֿל ׳.
כְשְׂרוֹן מרורים · כי הִמְרִירֻונוּ כִימרור מרורים ·
והִבְדֿיל גולה סתרים · והמס אֿוֹנֿיהֿם בֿל ׳.
לְספֿור כוסות ארבעה · ככוסות ישועות לרבֿעה
עלי רביעית להתרוֹעעה לשוללה כרגע בֿל ׳.
לתילשה כִישלוש שֲׁלֵשון · להבעות מצפּוניה
באימשון · להבדִיל מועד זה ראשון · בעצם
חֿדש ראשון בֿל ככֿ[48] אלה מועדי יי׳

[48] Lev. 23:4.

7 TS NS 249:1

recto

...
]ם יופי מ[
]ם לכן זה קרבן כמי[
] לע תע]
ביום הראשון יהודה אציל שבטו נחשון וטוב[ ]נחשו לעם לא מנ[
בן עמינדב[ ]ו תחילה[ ] ומרכבות עמי נדיב ישב כבת[
ב השני יששכר גביר שבטו נתנאל ושכר נתן לו אל בינת מתת[
בן ציער דברי דת בצער ומב[ ]צהר ליורשים למ[
ב השלישי זבולן הדר שבטו אליאב ואדון לו אל ואב לכן ל[
[בן] חילון וניתחייל חילו ואומץ חילו כי הינחילו[
[ב]הרביע[י ראו]בן זיר שבטו אליצור ונם אלי צור המיניק[
[בן שדיאור]ל[ ]אור אשר היה כע[ו]ר
]ל[ ]שלום ש[לם

verso

...
]ח נ[ ]נמהר[
]ח פירי פינתך תפ[
]תקרא ח רום רבתי תרים ח שע[
ח [ת] תלפיות תתש[ ]
]יהיה כי בית [ש]למים יהיה[ ]ו ל[ ]ובפאת ישפט
]בו נרשן תירינו לא יכבה ואור עול[ ]ה ז[ ]
]תעים לך קדושה[ ]אשת ככ וקרא
] מגיה חדרו בזוק[י]ן ארנן בהילו ב[ ]ם אופנים[ ]לעי
]ממשכנו בתוכי יגיה חשכי איחדו בטעם חיכי

11]ו שיבעתיים ו[ ]י יי אורי משמיעי[

12

13 שמונ]ה עשר[ה חנוכה

8 TS NS 249:14 + TS 12:210

TS NS 249:14, recto

1 צרינו פקוד נחליהם ואיפרם כזפת וגפרית להחפירם:

2 מצרים עו[ ] ערוב: | על כי [ ]יבע[ ]פעם לעדו[

3 [צרי]נו סגר בנישוף ועורב לארוב: [ ]סגרו דגי | לרוב

מצ נוגפו [ב]מכת הדב[ר נ]שפטו כמו חללים שוכבי קבר:

4 צר[ ]שפט | דם ודבר: מקום המוכן מאז לקבר:

מצ לוהטו ברוח עוועים: בשחין רע [וא]בעבועים |

5 צר כלה והשחין בם חלאים רעים: ככלי יוצר המרועעים:

6 מצ יריתה באבני ברד: | יחד מהם חסכתה ייראו ונחרד

7 צר טיט יוון יטבעם במורד: טרודים באלגביש | ושלג וברד

מצ חי[ ]במיני חגבים חגב וארבה שטר גובים

8 צר זעו[ ] | כמשק גיבים: זדון ארבע חיות היות ניג[ע]ים

9 מצ וימש חושך ועיי[ ] | נחוהו: ו[ ]הדין עלימו מתחוהו:

10 צר החושך וערפל כסוהו: [ ]יי[ ] | תוהו ואבני בוהו:

מצ דרשו רעוץ בן בכור: דועכו[ ]בראש און כל בכור

11 [צר] | גיל[וי] ערוה לראימים זכור: גזור דינם לח[

12 [מ]צ בלי עוד | נזכיר בהעלותך צפונים פלאיך נכר:

13 צר [ ]ת[ ]ר מדמם שכר אדום בגוים | בקול קורא תבכר

ובכן

בעשר מכות פתרוסים היפרכתה:

14 וארכה | במו הארכתה:

לשלח ב[לא עכובים עם אשר ב]רכתה:

ובאלה כמה בם התרתה[49]:

15 [וכ]יליון עליהם | [ל]א גמרתה:

[עד כי גמ]רו ר[שע]ם כאשר גז[רתה]

וניאצו למול ציר אשר בחרתה: |

16 [ונם מ]י יי אש[ר אמרתה]

[ל]שלח את עם דיברתה:

ואתה לעומם קינאה אזרתה:

17 וכמי |]

וכלי קרב הגרתה:

בארצם עברתה:

ובכוריהם פיגרתה:

18 ראשית | א[ונם הדבר]תה:

להביהם שיברתה:

ושיפטי שפטים אותם סיגרתה:

19 לילה חציתה | [ראש מח]צתה:

תנין רעצתה:

ראש ליוייתן ריצצתה:

וכל גיאותו ניפצתה:

20 למען | ספר [ש]מך עצתה:

חמש מאות רצתה:

ובסוף לחומו היפצתה:

[49] Corrected from התריתה.

21 וכל שאונו בסאה | סא[ ]תה: בססאה[50]

על ההרים קיפצתה:

ולישע עמך קיצאתה:

ואו[ו]תם בזרוע הוצאתה› |

22 [ואתה בחצי ל]יל פסחתה על פתחים:

באוכלם זיבחי פסחים:

ובעצם היום יצאו שמיחים: |

23 ל[עין פתרוסי]ם וכסלוחים:

והוצתו קוצים כסוחים:

ושושנים כלוקטו מבין חוחים: |

24 דצו[ ] מסוחחים:

תודה וקול זימרה פוצחים:

ואת[ה ב]שמחתם שמחתה: |

25 וישועתם [הושע]תה:

ויצאתם יצאתה:

כי בעוניים נימצתה:

ובנוחם מנוח מצאתה: |

26 וציבאותיך אשר במעל הוציתה:

להודיעם כי במו נימצאתה:

27 ובשלם גיא ודוק | יצרתה:

ובקרבם ניסגבתה וניערצתה:

ובפאיר מעל פיארם[51] אימצתה:

28 וכשירות | מרום שירותם חפצתה:

וכקדושת עליונים קדושתם חפצתה:

[50] This reading is noted in the left-hand margin. See Isa. 27:8 (and Sanhedrin 100a).

[51] Read פארם; cf. v22.

29 ובכינוי שם גבוהים | שמם חצצתה›
אלים בשם אלים:
אים בשם אים:
מחנות בשם מחנות:
30 מחצות | בשם מחיצות:
שמות בשם שמות:
אין כאל בשם מיכאל:
גבור אל: בשם גבריאל: |

TS NS 249:14, verso

1 בני יע[קב בשם א]להי יעקב:
קדושי יעקב: בשם קד[ו]ש יעקב:
2 משלשי קודש בשם | משל[ישי קדוש]
כׄכ וקרא |

3 טל ד[ר] לעז[ר] |

4 בדעתו אביעה חידות:
בעם זו בזו בכן להחדות:
טל גיא ודשאיה לחדות:
5 דבר | גבורות בנים להודות:
[א]ות ילדות טל להגן לתולדות: ב

6 תהומות הואגרו בעלי | [
[ ]גדי פ[ ]יח נאספים:
טל זיכר מראש מוסיפים
[ ]ת[ ]לגישת מוספים |
7 [ ]נקוקי סעיפים

נטילת רשות

אירשה ארוש רחשון: בארש | [ניב ולשון]
8 אתחין חין[52] לחשון: דיבבי מרעשון:
בעד נצורי כאישון: א[פגעה] בלי לשון: |
9 [בק]שה כ[שי] נחשון: אירצה בראשון:

גרו[ני] בל יונטל: מקרוא לרם ונ[טל]:
10 גיווי בל | [יוט]ל: מהזכיר גבור[ות טל]
[ד]יעי לא יבטל: רשות מליטל:
11 דודי יתנטל: בש[יח] | תפילת טל:>

[המון לו נ]כסף [לעדת] אל אאסף:
12 הוא איתם יתאסף: ולמעשיו | יכסף:
ואתייצב בסף: לחלות [פני] יסף:
ואימרת טל אחסף: לחברינה למוסף:> |

13 זבד משאת בר: ואביב נשיקות בר:
זעק [פי יגבר] ושיח לשוני יוגבר:
14 חן וחסד | יחובר: לחנני על דבר:
חשרת מים [י]עבר: כי ה[נה הסתו ע]בר:

15 [טעם ר]ינון: ושאג | שינון:
טל תיתו בתחנון: את פני [חנו]ן:
ישישיי לחנון [ב]זיכ[ר יין לבנון]
16 ידועיי ליגנ[ו]ן: | בפסוח וגנון:>

כשרים כחוללים: אהלל כבחלילים:
כמפי עול[לים אשורר חללים] |

[52] חין is written above an original חק, which was crossed out.

17 לישא דיע פלילים: צגתי במסלולים:
להזכיר בפילולים: שבע גבו[רות טללים]› |

18 מטעם זקינים: אתבונן עד זקונים:
מורים תיקונים: כדת מתוקנים:
19 [נפת] | נבונים: בינות עם מבינים:
נטעות דרבונים: תיוכוני בין שנ[י] לוחות אב[נים] |

20 שפתיי בשווע אפתח: כאילם[53] המפותח:
שיחות בפי אפתח: כאיתון אש[ר נפ]תח: |
21 עוז בכוח לי ימתח: כדוק אֲשֶׁר נפתח:
עב טל ייפתח: וחורב לא יורת[ח]

22 [פני ר]ם | ונישא: עיין בחין אשא:
פאירו לנוססה: כמו בטל נוסה:
23 צבאיו לו א[גיסה   וא]תם | אתגייסה:
צעק בעדם אתנגשה: ולא ברוח גסה:›

24 קמתי ממשפתַ[ים   להפגי]עַ | לניב שפתיים: [54]ליש בְּעַד לָנֵי
[קו]ל מה אתן בשיפתותיים: והן אני ערל שפתיים:
25 [רון בלי עצל]תיים: | ערכתי במחנותיים:
רחשתי גישות שתים: בעד שאילות שתים

26 [שחר]ית חיננתי | למטר: בלקש גיא לעטר: [54]ליש בְּלָקְשׁוֹ
שבתי לקחי לנטר: עוד מתבוע [ער]ף מטר:
27 תפילת גבורות | טל: חלתי בצוהר לנטל:
תיזל אמרתי כטל: לקיוויי רסיסי טל:

53 אילם was changed to אולם by a second hand.
54 These readings are noted in the right-hand margin.

28 ככ בתו[55] | יערף כמטר:

יי שפתי[56] ב׳ למדני חוקיך[57]: |

TS 12:210, recto

1 כ]כ ע י נ והיה[|

2 [דפקי דלתיך לשור]גיע עיגל מישור:

טל דוק למו חשור: עד קץ לחיכת שור |

3 [דגלי אסור מתענה] גיא דשאיה תענה:

ט דשאימו יחנה: כטל סביבות המחנה |

4 [ככ בת]ו[58] ויהי בערב ותעל |

5 [הפגעת טל תרון] [מ]ול מכון שבת מכוון

ט הטפה עב תיתכוון: כמתן טל סיוון: |

6 [הילול קודש תירושי] מגיד לי בטללי קידושי

7 טל הלנת קציר שורשי: ילין בטל | [להשרישי]

[ככ בד] ק[59] שורשי פתוח |

8 [ ]ג[ ]בד[ ]מון לצחצית כתמים

9 ט וותיר לתמימים: להיאחות כמו | [תאומים]

[ורד] עם אל להכן: ונשם מנשי לתכן

10 ט וויעד ציר לשכן: איתו בנס | [לעשות כן]

ככ ע י נ[60] ויעש אים כן בלילה |

11 [זעקי בל תבוז להט]ללי מעוץ ומבוז:

ט זימנתה לרימוז: לחתיל בו כאב תמוז: |

12 [זרע בן עתים חפש] לעד בל יואפס

[55] Deut. 32:2.

[56] Ps. 51:17, BH[3] אדני. Cf. the use of יי in TS H2:29, e.g. 1r29.

[57] Ps. 119:12, etc. [58] Exod. 16:13.

[59] Job 29:19. [60] Judg. 6:40.

ט זורר על פס: כמדבר דק מחוספס |

13 ככ בתו[61] ותעל שכבת |

14 חבר משוד סטן: פוסחים בלי ליסטן:

ט חיים יורטן: לפסוח בגיא סרטן: |

15 חוף ימים בו ציינו: מראות טללי ניצונו:

ט חשור לרבץ צאנו: וכטל על עשב רצונו: |

16 ככ בד קו[62] נהם ככפיר |

17 טל ישע אשאב: במשוש משאב:

ט טעם אב: יטעימנו אל באב:

18 טילול ירידות | שוכני: ישכון לבטח לשכני

ט חשור משכני: ישקוט כעב במכוני

19 ככ ע י נ[63] | כי כה אמר יי אלי אשקטה |

TS 12:210, verso

1 [עלות שכבת מפרחת באיבי נחל מארח]ת:

2 ט עלי עיין מר[ום ומתחת ומתחום רבצת] | תחת

ככ בתו[64] וליוסף אמר |

3 פירחי חלד תשליו: בטל שאנן ושליו:

ט פירות להדגין ולה[שליו צמחי תנוב כסלו] |

4 פקוד בחורב בציאיון: לטללם מחורב ציאיון:

5 ט פירות לבר[ך בצביון כטל חרמון] | שיורד ע ה צ

ככ בד[65] כטל חרמון |

6 צייה אים מולקשת: ומלקוש אים מבקשת:

[61] Exod. 16:14. [62] Prov. 19:12.

[63] Isa. 18:4. אשקטה is unusual in being a 'defective' variant as it reflects the *qere*.

[64] Deut. 33:13. [65] Ps. 133:3.

ט צק עבים תח[א מאוששת כבענינת קשת] |

7 צימאון צהריים: בל ישזוף עדנים אחוריים:

8 ט צל[יחת אתוי נהרים תצליח בו] | יהודה ואפרים

ככ ע י נ[66] מה אעשה לך א[פרים] |

9 קלי בטל יוצבט: בלי בחורב יולבט:

ט קרח בלי לבט: לזרע[ני טבת ושבט]

10 [קראיך] | לטוב תיקוב: להסיר מהם עקוב:

ט קמות בלי לעקוב: לשכון[בטח בדד עין יעקב] |

11 ככ בתו[67] וישכן יש |

12 רישע מר מדלי: מיצילם החדילי:

ט רסיסים תוחיד לי: להזי[ל לגדאי כמדלי] |

13 רשף ניצתם באור כחדק: בצול צלמון צורם לחדק:

14 ט רח[ף עלי זו בצדק] | ושחקים רעפו ויזלו צדק

ככ בד[68] בדעתו |

15 שפר אסמי טל דר: בקודש נאדר:

ט שתולים יהודר: החנוטים מאדר |

16 תדגיא תנובת שנה: בשער דגים מדושנה:

17 ט תרסיס איבי שינה: להפריח בט[ל] | שושנה:

ככ ע י נ[69] אהיה כטל לישראל

אינו ואי אבו |

18 טל תן ברכה בארצך: שיתינו בריבצך:

19 רוב דגן ותירוש בהפריצך: קומם עיר בה | חפצך: בטל

(טל) ציווה בשנה טובה מעוטרת: פרי הארץ לגאון ולתפארת:

עיר כסוכה [נותרת שימה בידך עטרת בטל]

[66] Hos. 6:4. [67] Deut. 33:28.
[68] Prov. 3:20. [69] Hos. 14:6.

9 TS NS 249:14ª + TS 12:210ª

TS NS 249:14ª, recto

31 ליל ואין לו רֵיעֵו׃ היבדלתה לצר לפורעו׃
הוֹא הֹל זרח בחוזק זרועו וינגע יי אֹפ·

32 ליל חצתה בהֻופָּעת חֵילֵךְ׃ | הֹב עֶזֶור בני מלך׃
הֹ הֹ טרף בשֵׁילֵךְ׃ בחלום לאבימלך׃

לֹ יצאתה מחומר להקימי׃ הֹיב זירועים חמשה להטעימי׃

TS NS 249:14ª, verso

29 הוֹ הֹל | כָשָׁל אומר מי׃ ובו ויֹב אֹל אל ל האר·

לֹ לֵוד היכחדתה[70] בסֵלף׃ הֹב רוות שְׁנִינָת שֵׁלף׃
30 הֹ הֹ מלאך הך סביב צלע האלף׃ | מאה ושמונים וחמ אלף׃

לֹ ניתן לראש׃ הֹב חורשים לחרוש׃
הֹ הֹ ספרים אץ לידרוש׃ נדדה שנת אחש·

31 לֹ ערכתה | לצר מכה׃ הֹיב זיכר לענוגה ורכה׃
הֹ הֹ פרס ביכה׃ קטיל בלשצר מלכא·

לֹ צָרו צָעדֵי כְּמָרִים׃ הב קחת מצות ומרורים׃ |
32 הֹ הֹ קוטלֵו חמֻורים׃ ונישמר היות לדורות ליל שימורים
כי[71] אלה מ

[70] **היכבדתה** was originally written. *Ḥet* was written over the *bet*, and then again above the line for clarity.

[71] Lev. 23:4.

לׄ רׄדׄה בָעֲשֶׁרֶת ענמים: רְמָׄסָם כׄגׄת בעיגעֵוג דׄמִים |
33 (הׄ הׄ) לרׄב בן שני עולמים: רׄד ופדה עׄם מעמים:
ביירא‍ה וברעד יעבדוך עמים בׄ

לׄ שלח יד מֵירוּם שמים: שֶׁולְחָוּ]

TS 12:210[a], recto

19] [עִיתֵד לוויתן ובהמות:
פריסת סעודת נעימות ציווה והׄב בׄ שׄ <u>עול</u>[<u>מות</u>] |

20 קׄירׄה רׄום לכׄם קודש: רִיהֵׄב תחת הדום לפעמי קוׄ:
שָׁקָד וׄהׄ בׄ קׄ לק: תִיכֵן עָרָבות לׄקדוׄש:

תׄוכׄו יקדישו קדישין קדוש: תׄר לׄהׄ קדוש
כׄכׄ[72] והייתם

TS 12:210[a], verso

20 <u>תִ</u>יכן בראשן עטרה:
תשועה להחיש בו לנוטירה:
להבדיל בן טומאה לטהרה:
תָאָה בחצות כעב קל לָמהֵירָה:
כן יחיש שלום אין קץ למרבה המישרה |

21 חזק נׄ צׄ טׄ תׄ

[72] Num. 15:40. Following this, בׄ הטוב is written in a different script.

10 TS NS 117:7 + TS H6:51

This text contains the following vocalized words:

recto

7 לעפר (?)

9 הנה

39 ברחמים (?)

40 כמוהם, להגיהם

41 חטאת

43 טען, שען

44 כל (verb, Isa. 40:12)

62 ביסדו

63 דרך

64 נועד

verso

7 סגן בלישכת, הופקד

9 דהר

12 גשו, ובאר

14 תנומה

16 רבוע

18 אשנבי

verso

21 מסווים

22 שיטים

23 במותנים

27 הירצה

29 וייפה

30 כאריה (? ⟨e′⟩)

31 זיר

37 עיטר

48 שבטו

51 עילם

52 החיצון

57 בקרב (בק׳? or) קרב

58 איברים

61 שיכן (÷ שֶׁכֶּן?)

64 תמימים

ש marks ⟨ś⟩ in r35, 55, v22, 31, 43, 47, 48, 55, 65. Tiberian *ṣere* (r39, 41, 43, 64), *pataḥ* (r62, 63, 64), and *ḥolem* (v18?) also occur.

11 TS H2:29

fol. 1, recto

1 ויושע ליהודה זבידא |

2 ויושע[73] אברהם בראש ומאש פ[ר]עו: בהעקד יחיד מחרב הושיעו:

[73] The words beginning the verses of poems א and ב are those beginning the verses of Exod. 14:30–15:18.

3 וירא ג[וי] | גדולת יד מושיעו: דילגו שלושתם על הים ומיד קרעו:

4 אז ישיר היאמן | כהוליך לימינו זרועו: ועדרו על הים בהיוושעו:

5 ע[זי ז]ר[ ] | והיכניעו: חס על עמו להושיעו:

6 יה טס מזויין ברוב[י] | לו שם ימים בקורעו:

7 מרכבות כוש ופוט ומצרים בהכניע[ו: ל] | ולאחור הירתיעו:

8 תהומות מי ים לידידיו בקורעו: ניעור ב[ ] | בילעו:

ימינך סיגרה רוב פרי ניטעו: עוללתה לו כרוב ניגעו:

9 ובר[ב פ] | בא על עם לייגעו: צר[74] בבבת עינו בנוגעו:

10 וברוח קל כסוס נקבה לנחותם[ ] | ריבו ששים בשלח פרעה:

ככ[75] ויהי בשלח פרעה

11 ונ[76] שלח אותות ומפ[תים] | ונ[77] וינחם בענן יומם: ונ[78] יבקע צורים

12 במדבר וישת כתהומות ר[בה] | ונ[79] שלח משה עבדו:

ונ[80] מוליך לימין משה ›

13 עולם שיני יחדש | למענכם: שילא יחיש ויביא בימיכם:

14 תיתו רחמיו על כולכם: יה צבאות יגן | עליכם: ב

אמר תנין יאורו לרדוף עם שלישיו לחלק את יגיעם:

15 נשפתה [ר] | מידה במידה לפורעם: קפץ תהום וכעופרת טיבעם:

16 מי כמוך צורר מים[ ] | פוררו בעוזך מיקרקעם:

17 נטיתה עישיתה לודים לבלעם: סעתה לנ[ ] | יצועם:

נחיתה נידפים קוממיות להסיעם: מנוחה ונחלה להרגיעם:

18 שמעו [ל] | לאומים חיל שימעם: כדונג נמסו ותוארם הועם:

19 אז יראו[ ] | טירותיהם נותצו וזורר ריבעם:

תפול חרב בגיזעם: זדו ע[ ]ם: |

20 תביאמו וויעודיך בית עולמים להנחיל זרעם: המיופה בש[ ]גיעם: |

74 Read כבבת? 75 Exod. 13:17.
76 Ps. 135:9. 77 Ps. 78:14.
78 Ps. 78:15, וישת, BH³ וישק. 79 Ps. 105:26.
80 Isa. 63:12.

21 יֿה   דֿרֿך ים סוף הודיע<u>ם</u>:   גרֿרֿם ויסב את העם:

ככ[81] ויסב אֿים את העם |

22 וֿנ[82] ויֿסֿע כצאן עמו: וֿנ[83] ויֿסֿע משה את ישר[אל] |

23 וֿנ[84] ויוציא עמו בששון: וֿנ[85] ויֿה הולך לפניהם יומם |

24 וֿנ[86] וֿנֿשמע וֿיֿמס לבבינו⁖

25 מתחת בֿדבֿרו מיתים מח[ייֿה] | מֿיתֿו מֿיאֿחֿינו מֿתֿיי יחֿיֿיֿה:

26 אור טל יֿשלח כל רדומים להֿחיֿיה יֿה מֿמֿ[יֿת] | ומחייה: ב

מיהרתה פדות אמוניי: יצאתה ליציאת אמוניי:

27 ענן הירכֿבֿת<u>ה</u> | לפניי: וניסיך ראו המוניי:

שפוך חימה על מעֿנֿיֿי: וצרח לאבד מוניי:

28 והעל | מארץ קציניי: הנֿבֿלעים ברעש מיֿנבוניי:

29 הושעתה מפרך חסוניי: ולך בכל | לב שפכתי חינוניי:

ושוררתי בניגוניי: ויושע יֿה:

30 חספתה צר וצורריי | בעֿברה: זורקו למצולות בנעירה:

fol. 1, verso

1 קידשו [ויֿשֿיֿ]רו עם נביאה   [ככ] | [87]וֿתשר דבורה

וֿנ[88] אז ישיר משה וֿנ[89] אז ישיר יש[ראל] |

2 ק[ ]חתה ברוח להֿחניק מצרים: קל רכבתה להכר[וֿיֿ]ת מֿצֿירים:

3 קניתה ידידים מעם | מֿ[ ]חֿיֿם: קצפתה על רשעים להמיס לב מצרים:

כֿכֿ[90] משה מצרים

4 וֿנ |]   :[ ] | וֿנ]   [יֿה   וֿנֿ[91] ואתה קֿ יֿו תהֿי ישראל |

5 [א   ]   אֿל מושיע נשאתי עיניי: ויושע יֿה:

[81] Exod. 13:18.   [82] Ps. 78:52.   [83] Exod. 15:22.
[84] Ps. 105:43.   [85] Exod. 13:21.   [86] Josh. 2:11.
[87] Judg. 5:1.   [88] Exod. 15:1.   [89] Num. 21:17.
[90] Isa. 19:1.

6 [ב] בנטותו על אויביהם יד: וירא יש א היד:

7 [ג] גדול וקטון רש ועשיר: מושה אז ישיר:

8 [ ]בעשותו פלאיו למי זאת: שיבחו יונקים על זאת: את השירה הזאת: לקדוש|›

9 [ד]ח לאבות תשועה: דיברו יונקים בשוועה: עזי וז יה ו ל ליש:

10 [ה]צרים חימה: הדור כיצא למלחמה: יה איש מלח:

11 [ו]כל האבן יאורה לשקעו: ומידה במידה לפורעו: מרכבות פר:›

12 זידים לשוטפו כנועדו: זולעפו ובשטף אבדו: תהומות יכס:

13 חיי בהיתיש באויב כוח: הייללתי נועם בכל כוח: ימינך יה נ בכ:

14 טרפתה מתקוממיך: טיבעתה בשועל נוקמיך: וברוב ג ת קמ:›

15 יהירים בזעפיך: יוקשו באמרי פיך: וברוח אפיך:

16 [כ]ם עשן לנדוף: כולם כאחת לשדוף: אמ או ארדוף:

17 [ל]לים: להצלילו בעימקי ים: נש ב כס ים:›

18 [מ]שאון גלים: מעביר בים גאולים: מי כמוך באילים:

19 [נ]שללי ייריץ: נועיר בתוך ים בחיריץ: נטית ימ ת ארץ:

20 [ס]ך עם עזו: סלול יישרתה לעמך על זו: נחית ב ע זו ›

21 עשותך נפלאות ע[ ]מים: עוברינו שני תהומים: שמעו עמים:

22 פירחי דומה בו מלו: פלצות אוחזו והוזחלו: אז נבהלו:

23 צרים[ ]ינו ביעתה: צוררתה באפך בעיתה: תפול ע אימ ›

24 [קו]ל אגנ[ן] כסהר: קירייה שלומה כנהר תביאמו ות בהר:

25 [ר]להועילם: רוחשים מעולם ועד עולם: יה ימ לעולם:

26 [שיבחו יו]נקים על זאת: תהילה נתנו בזאת: את השירה הזאת: בעשותו›

27 [ ]אל נא לעולם תוערץ ›

פן ינחם העם בראותם מלח ושבו מצריימה›[92]

28 [אאמי]רם לאיומה: אבונם להתחכמה:

אגאלים ימין רוממה: פן ישובו מצרימה:

[91] Ps. 22:4. [92] Exod. 13:17.

29 [אד]ריכם דרך לא עקומה: אהיה להם חומה:

אובילם בחוזק ביד רמה: פן יש מצ

30 [אזר]זם בתקומה: אחוננם דיעה וחכמה:

אטעימה סוד תעלומה: פן יש מצ

31 [איד]עם חוקיי לקיימה: אכנם יונה תמה:

אלבישם מלבוש רקמה: פן יש מצ

32 [אמ]ממקומה: אנחילם יום יום קדומה:

אשביעם לחם שמיימה: פן יש מצ

33 [אע]ה: אפנם מפלשת מראות מלחמה:

אצא כגיבור ברודפם להלחמה: פן יש מצ

fol. 2, recto

1 אקוממם אות[ ] אריצם מדבר שממה:

אשלח לפניהם אימה: פן יש מצ

2 אתים אומרי הב[ ]ת חכמה: אתשם באף וחימה:

אתן לבניי תשועה שלימה: פן יש מצ

3 ‹ויושע יה וגו›

4 ויושע אדיר הוגיא תעודה: ביום ההוא איביד רשעים בצול איבדא

5 ולעתיד ולוקחיי לי יירשו שיר חדש להגידה: ביום ההוא יושר השיר

[הזה] בארץ יהו[דה[93]

6 ויושע וירא בעוני עם ידידו: ביום ההוא ביטיל לחץ שיעבוד[

7 ולע ולדיו לקנות ייגלה בשכינת הודו: והיה ביום ההוא יוסיף יה

ש[נית ידו[94]:

8 ויושע אז גוי המוניי: ביום ההוא גידע כל מוניי [

9 ולע לספר על כיבואו אמוניי: ביום ההוא יקראו לירושלם כיסא [יה[95]:

[93] Isa. 26:1.
[94] Isa. 11:11.
[95] Jer. 3:17 (harmonized with the structure of the poem).

10 וי֗ו עזי דגליו מֹשאייה: ביום ההוא דיכא ברהב יפֹיפֹייא:

11 ולע בוגדים יפֹנֹם מנשֹייה: ביום ההוא יהיה ישראל שלישייה[96]:

12 וי֗ו יה הניגלה לדֹון דיניי: ביום ההוא היבעית מדייניי:

13 ולע ובאוייבֹי ללחֹום יגבֹיר רֹכֹב נֹאֹמֹניי: ביום ההוא יהיה על מצילות
הסוס קודֹש ליֹה[97]:

14 וי֗ו מרכבות ועֹודֹיו והמוניהם: ביום ההוא ויֹעֹית מרכבות צר ורוכביהם:

15 ולע נֹיבֹים ללוחֹמֹי כֹיבואו מכל פיניהם: והיה ביום ההוא תהיה מהומת
יֹה רבה בהם[98]:

16 וי֗ו תהומות זרומים גזו חלוצים: ביום ההוא זועֹם לוחצים:

17 ולע ביטויי דברו יקֹיֹם לחֹיֹיֹל אמֹוצים: ביום ההוא אשית אלפֹי יהודה
כֹכֹיֹוֹר אש [בעצים[99]:

18 וי֗ו ימינך חיסנו להבֹיעה: ביום ההוא חֹמֹוֹס בסוף השקיעה:

19 ולע יקֹבֹץ נדוחים כפץ מארבעה: ביום ההוא נאום יֹה אוספה הצוליעה[100]:

20 וי֗ו וברוב טֹובֹו היניל פדוויים: ביום ההוא טילטֹיל דעת מחֹוויים:

21 ולע רֹכֹים יפֹכֹו לשני נהרות חצויים: והיה ביום ההוא יצאו מים
[חיים[101]:

22 וי֗ו וברוח ים השכֹיך מֹירעישה: ביום ההוא יהירים בימצול ר[ ]שה:

23 ולע במינים שלושה: ביום ההוא יפקוד יֹה בחרבו הקשה[102]:

24 וי֗ו אמר כסיל להדלילה מֹיהון: ביום ההוא כופרים אֹיבֹיד ויֹהֹוֹם]

25 ולע יצמית סוס ורכב כנם בתימֹהון:
ביום ההוא אֹכֹֹה כל סוס בֹתֹימֹהון[103]:

26 וי֗ו נשפתה ליבבו בֹעֹניי: ביום ההוא לודים הישֹית גניי:

27 ולע שֹֹלים היורֹדֹת כלולה מֹמעוניי: ביום ההוא יֹגֹן יֹה[104]:

[96] Isa. 19:24. [97] Zech. 14:20. [98] Zech. 14:13.
[99] Zech. 12:6. BH³ .אשים את אלפי
[100] Mic. 4:6. [101] Zech. 14:8. [102] Isa. 27:1.
[103] Zech. 12:4. [104] Zech. 12:8.

28 ויו מי כמוך מאדיריו כנעימה ביום ההוא מצירים ביד רמה:

29 ולע בעתה יפיל על חיילי דוק וחלד במהומה: ביו הה יפקוד יה על צב
המרום במרום וע מל אד ע ה[105]

30 ויו נטיתה ניצחו אגודים: ביום ההוא ניאל רשעים רודים:

31 ולע תחתונים בהיבקעם לינדודים: והיה ביו הה יתקע בשופר ג
ובאו האובדים[106]:

32 ויו נחיתה סילסול להגיד: ביום ההוא סווינים בשחת היאיביד:

33 ולע יזכור קיים דברו להכביד: ביום ההוא אקים [את] סו[כת דויד[107]:

fol. 2, verso

1 [ויו שמ]עו ע[ ]מילל גבורה: ביום ההוא עממים בר[

2 [ולע]דר בראש ברא: ביו הה יהיה יה צב לעטרת [צבי
ול]צפירת תפארה[108]:

3 [ויו אז] פירחי ישישיי: ביום הה פיגיר בטיט יוון מבקשיי:

4 ולע חבר לכל קדושיי: והיה ביום הה שורש ישיי[109]:

5 ויו ת[פל]ה על אויבים לחצו ישרים: ביום הה צימת בזעף צרים:

6 [ולע]להרוות בחורים: והיה ביום הה יטפו ההרים[110]:

7 [ויו תביאמו]צרם כהובחד: ביום ההוא קמים ברעש היפחד:

8 [ולע]באות רום ותחת כיבואו יחד: ביום הה יהיה יה אחד ושמו
אחד[111]:

9 [ויו יה]ירות ישע: ביום הה שוסים ברוע הירשע:

10 [ולע]יגלה אדיר ונושע: הושע ויושע ויושע:›

[105] Isa. 24:21. [106] Isa. 27:13. [107] Amos 9:11.
[108] Isa. 28:5. [109] Isa. 11:10. [110] Joel 4:18.
[111] Zech. 14:9.

ויושע יה

11 [ויושע] אסונים אשל פאר ניטעם: וירא בעוניים ויושיעם:

12 [אז ג]עיית שיר ציר הינעם: עזי דאה ובעליות הירעם:

13 יה הו[ ]ר כל כלי זעם: מרכבות ורוכביהם במהלומות היפעם:

14 תהומות זרמום כיצרור אבן להטביעם: ימינך חוילה ברעץ לרועעה:

15 וברוב טחט טיבעתה לרערעם: וברוח ים נערם לייגעם:

16 אמר כסיל לרדוף עם: נשפתה לטבעו ולחיילותיו להנעם:

17 [מי כמוך] מקפיא מים במבועם: נטיתה נאדרתה צוענים ברפש לבלעם:

18 [נחית]לים כצאן להסיעם: שמעו ערילים חיל שימעם:

19 [אז]ותוארם הועם: תפול צווחה באהליהם לקלעם:

20 [עד תביא]ימו קיריית רבץ מטעם: יה ימלוך ריננו בלהג מדעם:

21]בטיו מינם אל האוהל ויוזעם: תופפו על זאת ותשר דבורה וברק בן אבינועם:

22 ›וישר אם בי[ש]ראל: כהוכנעו צרי אל אל: אומץ גבורתו גילה אל:

23 וירא ישראל

24 וירא ת[ ]מש מיודעות: אז שר הוריד חקק אצבעות:

25 עזי ראה[ ]לה בהופעות: יה קשר כובע ישועות:

26 [מרכבתו]ת צוענים הידמים בטביעות: תהומות פוררו לגלעם בשקיעות:

27 [ימינך]ה חייל ושיברה בצרים זרועות: וברוב סער אותם להעלות:

28 [וברוח] ניצבו מים בבינת דיעות: אמר מצרי ישרים מדרך להתעות:

29 [נשפ]תה להצלילו בעמקי קריעות: מי כערכך אל למושעות:

30 [נטית] ימין צרים לאסיף בבליעות: נחיתה טלאים כצאן לירעות:

31 [שמ]עו חיילי פלשת חיל שמועות: אז נחלו ואחזום זוועות:

32 [תפל ו]התתם אימות ורעות: תביאמו הר נכון בראש ונישא מגבעות:

33 [יה ימלך ד]רבו ישרים בשוועות: ויושע גגוניו שומייע שוועות:

34 [ ]מטעות: אז שוררו בפרוע פרעות:

35 [ ]לטבעם במבול קשה: שירה לאל לא מחשה:

12 TS H7:7

verso

1 טובי לב בו יזמרו ותוספת הלל יאמרו

2 יום אשר בו שמחות נעט[רו] | ולאהליהם בשלום נפטרו

3 כיתרתה מישומך עם עולם לראשם זיר | שמחת עולם
לשיש ולשמח ביום נחלם לפנות מסוכה לאהלם |

4 מלך שילח את העם שמחים בפעלם אשר נעם

5 נא בו תרומם בקהל עם | כי הדרת מלך ברב עם
שמחה על שמחה היכפלתה ויספתה לגוי ונכבדתה |

6 עמך בכבודך כיבדתה ומכבודך ניתכבדתה

7 פקודתינו שים שלומה | כיפקודת חג שלימה
צאן אדם אשר לך הושלמה תהי משכורתה משולמה |

8 קרובים ורחוקים יושלבו כי לאהליהם ישובו

9 רומימות בלב יחשובו | מים בששון עבור ישאבו
שפוט ישפוט סיפק שנה באוסף תקופת השנה |

10 [תקר]א שילומי שנה למשלישי פעמים בשנה

ובכן ביום השמיני[112] |

11 [היום תא]יך משפט מים היום תברך מפיך לחם ומים |

12 ה תיגל משפט[113] כמ ה תדרוש גבול שותה מ

[112] Num. 29:35.
[113] Zulay (1938, p. 345) reads משפטי, in my opinion wrongly.

13 ה תהגה ל[ ]הומים כמ | [ה] תודיע אות לטובה במ

ה תזכה נידונים על המ ה תחון זורעי על כל מ |

14 [ה תט מר]חפת על פני מ ה תייפה פני חשרת מ

15 ה תכ[ ]ה ותכין לסתיו מ | ה תלבש אדר מקולות מ

ה תמלא משאלות שואבי מ ה תנ[ ]ם על שטף מ |

16 [ה] תשמח לב מס כמו מ ה תענה לשופכי לך לב כמ

17 ה תפלג פלגי[114] מ | [ה תצדי]ק משוגות פחז כמ

ה תקנה לארץ נוחלי מ ה תירצה ברצונך כאשר בעב מ |

18 [ה תש]פיע בלי נחסר מ ה תתכון את מדות מ

ובכן |

19 [ונת ת]וי שיר שבחך ונרון רוממות קבע קדושתך

20 ונצניף צהל | [פ ו]נען עוז סילוד סילסולך

21 וננעים נואי נצח מיזח מלכותך | [ונל ל]כבוד כתרך

22 ונייחד יחד טוב טעמך ונחסנך חוס[ן | ז ז ד]

ונ[ ] ונודיע הוד הדרך ונדובב דייך גבורות גו[ד]לך |

23 [ונב ב]רכות אמונת אומצך: כקוראי זה אל זה כך וקרא |

24 [ ]וטרת ביו[ ]דות יום עצרת יגלה לה עתרת

25 ועים אופנים | [ ]צח אדרת לעו |

26 [ ]שלום מועדים לעם זיכרו מעידים על ביתו מידידים |

27 [ ]עדי עד מייחדים פע |

28 [ ]משמונה לחדש ישועת שושנה בחופתה ישישינה |

29 [י]שמיענה לחיות

[114] The ⟨e⟩ sign is presumably placed above the *lamed* since no space was available above the *gimel*, and ⟨palgey⟩ is intended. Cf. ⟨e⟩ ≑ *shewa* in II.8.D.

References

ALLONY, N. 1963 "A Fragment of Mishna with Palestinian Pointing," in *Sefer haYobel leRabbi Ḥanok Albek* (Jerusalem), pp. 30–40.

1965 "*Sefer haQolot—Kitāb al-Muṣawwitāt* of Mosheh ben Asher," *Leshonenu 29* (1964–65), 9–23, 136–59.

ALLONY, N. AND DÍEZ-MACHO, A. 1958a "Otros dos manuscritos 'palestinenses' de Salmos," *Sefarad 18*, 254–71.

1958b "Dos manuscritos 'palestinenses' más de la Geniza del Cairo," *Estudios Bíblicos 17*, 83–100.

1959a "A Fragment of *Pesiqta de Rav Kahana* with Palestinian Vocalization," *Leshonenu 23* (1958–59), 57–71.

1959b "Lista de variantes en la edición de los MSS 'palestinenses' TS 20:58 y 20:52," *Estudios Bíblicos 18*, 293–8.

BAR, F. 1936 *Liturgische Dichtungen von Jannai und Samuel* (Bonn).

BERGSTRÄSSER, G. 1962 *Hebräische Grammatik* (Hildesheim).

BÉT-ARYÉ, M. 1965 "The Vocalization of the Worms Maḥzor," *Leshonenu 29* (1964–65), 27–46, 80–102.

BIRNBAUM, S. A. 1954–57 *The Hebrew Scripts* (London).

BLAU, J. 1965 *The Emergence and Linguistic Background of Judaeo-Arabic* (Oxford).

DAVIDSON, I. 1924–33 *Thesaurus of Mediaeval Hebrew Poetry* (New York).

1928 *Geniza Studies in Memory of Dr. Solomon Schechter III* (New York).

1931 "The '*Seder Ḥibbur Berakot*,'" *Jewish Quarterly Review 21* (1930–31), 241–79.

DIETRICH, M. 1960 "Neue palästinisch punktierte Bibelfragmente" (Thesis, Tübingen).

1968 *Neue palästinisch punktierte Bibelfragmente* (Leiden). Same as the above. Page references are to this edition. Ms numbers are the same.

DÍEZ-MACHO, A. 1954 "Tres nuevos manuscritos bíblicos 'palestinenses'," *Estudios Bíblicos 13*, 247–65.

1956 "Nuevos manuscritos importantes, bíblicos o litúrgicos, en hebreo o arameo," *Sefarad 16*, 1–22.

1957 "Importants manuscrits Hébreux et Araméens aux États Unis," in *Supplements to 'Vetus Testamentum'* IV, 27–46.

1960 "Un Ms. de Onqelos de transición del sistema palestinense al prototiberiense," *Estudios Eclesiasticos 34*, 461–6.

1963a "Un nuevo Ms. 'palestinense' del libro de Jueces," *Sefarad 23*, 236–51.

1963b "A New List of So-called 'ben Naftali' Manuscripts...," in *Hebrew and Semitic Studies Presented to G. R. Driver* (Oxford), pp. 16–52.

1967 "Nuevo manuscrito bíblico 'palestinense' procedente de la Geniza de El Cairo," *Studia Papyrologica 6*, 15–25.

EDELMANN, R. 1934 *Zur Frühgeschichte des Maḥzor* (Stuttgart).

ELBOGEN, I. 1926 "Ḳalir Studies," *Hebrew Union College Annual 3*, 215–24.

GARBELL, I. 1959 "The Phonemic Status of *Shewa* etc.," *Leshonenu 23*, 152–5.

GINSBURG, C. D. 1867 *The Massoreth ha-Massoreth of Elias Levita* (London).

1897 *Introduction to the Massoretico-Critical Edition of the Hebrew Bible* (London).

GOSHEN-GOTTSTEIN, M. 1958 "Linguistic Structure and Tradition in the Qumran Documents," *Scripta Hierosolymitana* IV (Jerusalem), 101–37.

1963 "The Rise of the Tiberian Bible Text," in *Biblical and Other Studies* (ed. A. Altmann; Cambridge, Mass.), pp. 79–122.

HOENIGSWALD, H. M. 1960 *Language Change and Linguistic Reconstruction* (Chicago).

KAHLE, P. 1901 "Beiträge zur Geschichte der hebräischen Punktation," *Zeitschrift für die Alttestamentliche Wissenschaft 21*, 273–317.

1922 'Beitrag' (nos. 6–9) in Bauer-Leander, *Historische Grammatik der hebräischen Sprache des alten Testaments* (Halle).

1927 *Masoreten des Westens* I (Stuttgart).

1930 *Masoreten des Westens* II (Stuttgart).

1956 *Opera Minora* (Leiden).

1959 *The Cairo Geniza* (2nd ed.; Oxford).

1961 *Der hebräische Bibeltext seit Franz Delitzsch* (Franz Delitzsch Vorlesungen, 1958; Stuttgart, 1961).

KLAR, B. 1939 Review of Zulay, 1938, in *Kirjath Sepher 15* (1938–39), 287–93.

KOBER, M. 1929 *Zum Machsor Jannai* (Frankfurt a. M.).

LEVIAS, C. 1899 "The Palestinian Vocalization," *American Journal of Semitic Languages, 15* (1898–99), 157–64.

LEWIS, A. S. AND GIBSON, M. D. 1900 *Palestinian Syriac Texts from Palimpsest Fragments in the Taylor-Schechter Collection* (London).

MANDELBAUM, B. (ed.) 1962 *Pesikta de Rav Kahana* (New York).

MORAG, S. 1959 "The Vocalization of Codex Reuchlinianus," *Journal of Semitic Studies* 4, 216–37.

1963 *The Hebrew Language Tradition of the Yemenite Jews* (Jerusalem).

1965 "Remarks on the Description of the Vocalization of the Worms Maḥzor," *Leshonenu 29* (1964–65), 203–9.

MURTONEN, A. 1958 *Materials for a Non-Masoretic Hebrew Grammar* I (Helsinki).

1964 *Materials for a Non-Masoretic Hebrew Grammar* III (Studia Orientalia Ed. Soc. Or. Fennica XXIX; Helsinki).

ORLINSKY, H. M. 1966 Prolegomenon to the reprinting of Ginsburg, 1897 (Ktav, New York), pp. I-XLV.

ORMANN, G. 1934 *Das Sündenbekenntnis des Versöhnungstages* (Frankfurt a. M.).

REVELL, E. J. 1970 "Studies in the Palestinian Vocalization of Hebrew," in Wevers, J. W., and Redford, D. B., eds., *Essays on the Ancient Semitic World* (Toronto), pp. 51–100.

SCHIRMANN, J. 1954 "Hebrew Liturgical Poetry and Christian Hymnology," *Jewish Quarterly Review 44* (1953–54), 123–61.

1965 *New Hebrew Poems from the Geniza* (Jerusalem).

SONNE, I. 1944 "An Unknown Keroba of Yannai," *Hebrew Union College Annual 18* (1943–44), 199–220.

SPIEGEL, S. 1960 "On Mediaeval Hebrew Poetry," in Finkelstein, L., *The Jews* (3rd ed.; New York), vol. I, pp. 854–92.

TAYLOR, C. 1900 *Hebrew-Greek Cairo Geniza Palimpsests from the Taylor-Schechter Collection* (Cambridge).

WALLENSTEIN, M. 1956 *Some Unpublished Piyyuṭim from the Cairo Geniza* (Manchester).

1958 "A Dated Tenth Century Hebrew Parchment Fragment," *Bulletin of the John Rylands Library* 40, 551–8.

WEIL, G. 1962 "Un fragment de *Okhlah* palestinienne," *Annual of the Leeds University Oriental Society* III (1961–62), 68–80.

YEIVIN, I. 1963 "A Palestinian Fragment of Hafṭaroth and Other MSS with Mixed Pointing," *Textus* III, 121–7.

ZULAY, M. 1936 "Studies in Yannai," *Studies of the Research Institute for Hebrew Poetry* II (Berlin), 213–391.

1938 *Piyyuṭe Yannai* (Berlin).

1939 "On the History of Piyyuṭ in Eretz Israel," *Studies of the Research Institute for Hebrew Poetry* V, 107–80.

1945 "Studies in the Language of Yannai's Poems," *Studies of the Research Institute for Hebrew Poetry* VI (Jerusalem), 161–248.

ZUNZ, L. 1920 *Die synagogale Poesie des Mittelalters* (2nd ed.; Frankfurt a. M.).

PRINTED IN BELGIUM BY THE ST. CATHERINE PRESS, LTD, TEMPELHOF, 37, BRUGES.

PLATES

The following plates illustrate each of the manuscripts published. Ideally, reproductions adequate for the study of the pointing of all the texts described in chapter II should have been given here, but this would have required an excessive number of plates. Consequently it was decided, where it was impossible to reproduce the whole text, to show the layout of a page or fragment and an example of the text the size of the original for each manuscript, thus displaying as well as possible the palaeographical characteristics of the texts. Only one plate of ms 12 is included, as it does not represent a separate class.

1 Class 1, TS NS 249:2, recto.

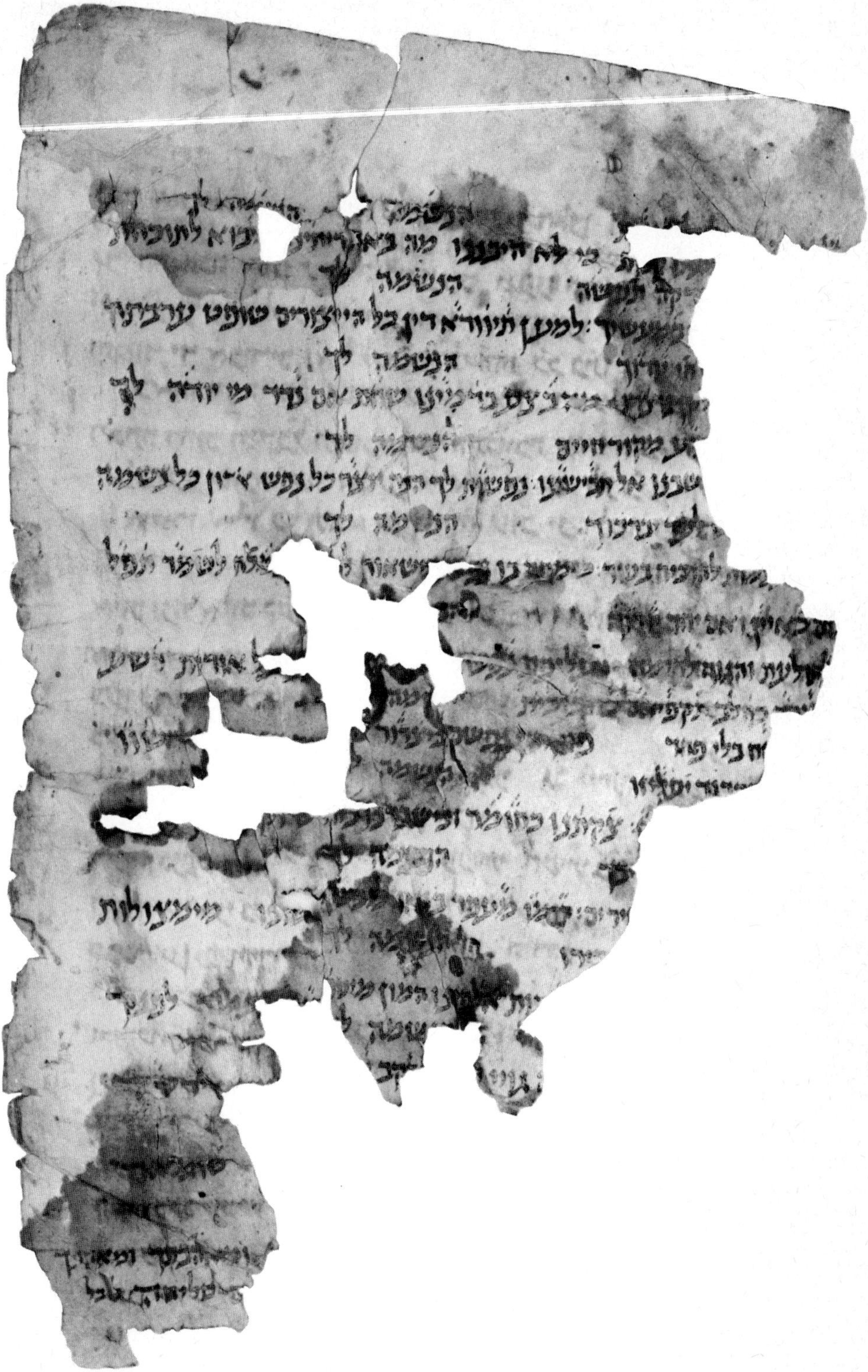

2 Class 1, TS NS 249:2, verso.

3 Class 2, TS NS 118:38, recto.

4 Class 2, TS NS 118:38, verso.

5 Class 3, TS NS 119:42 + NS 301:66, recto.

6 Class 3, TS NS 119:42 + NS 301:66, verso, lines 1–25.

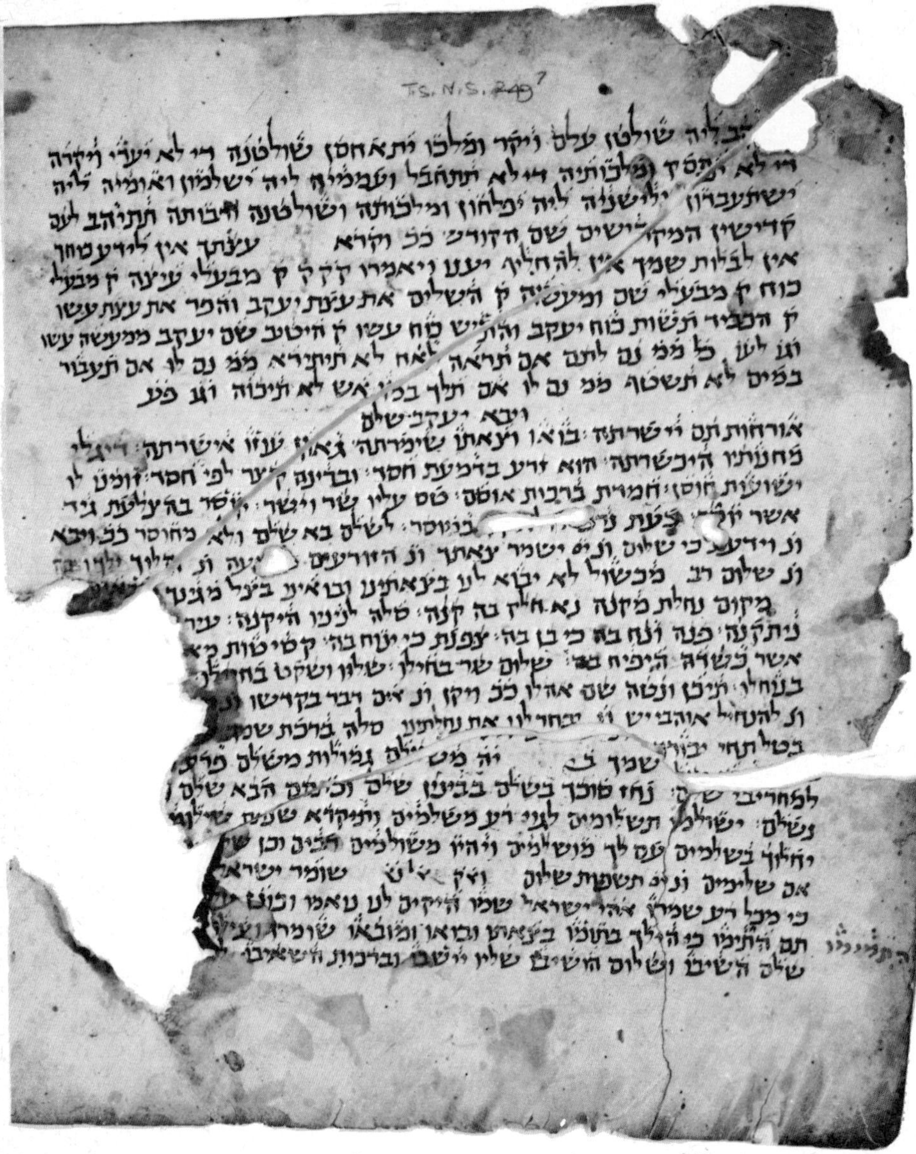

TS. N.S. 249 7

ביה שולטן עלם ויקר ומלכו ותאחסן שולטנה די לא יעדי ויקרה
די לא יתנסך ומלכותיה די לא תתחבל ועממיא ליה ישלמון ואומיא ליה
ישתעבדון ולישניא ליה יפלחון ומלכותה ושולטנה ורבותה תתיהב לעם

7 Class 4, TS NS 249:7 + NS 301:28, fol. 2, verso.

8 Class 4, TS NS 249:7, fol. 1, recto, lines 1–18.

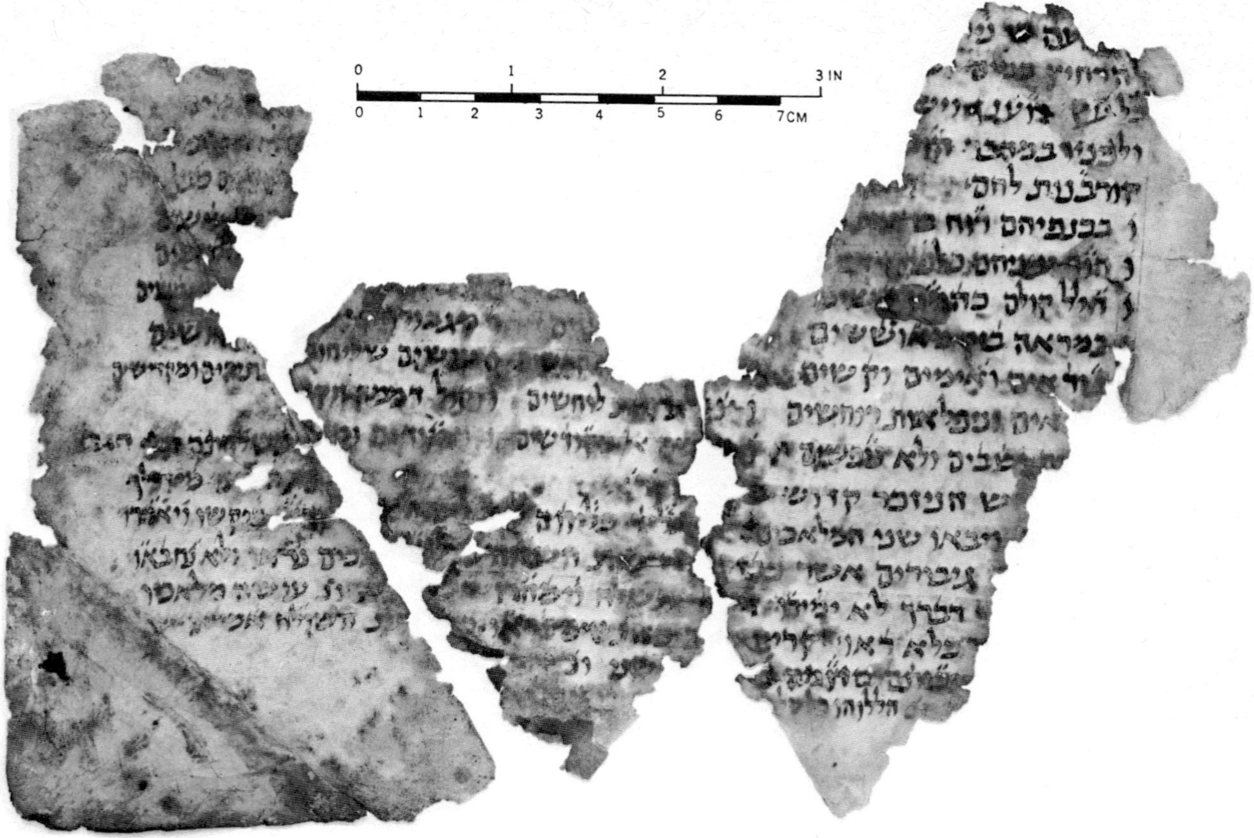

9 Class 4, TS NS 117:6 + NS 123:2, fol. 2, recto.

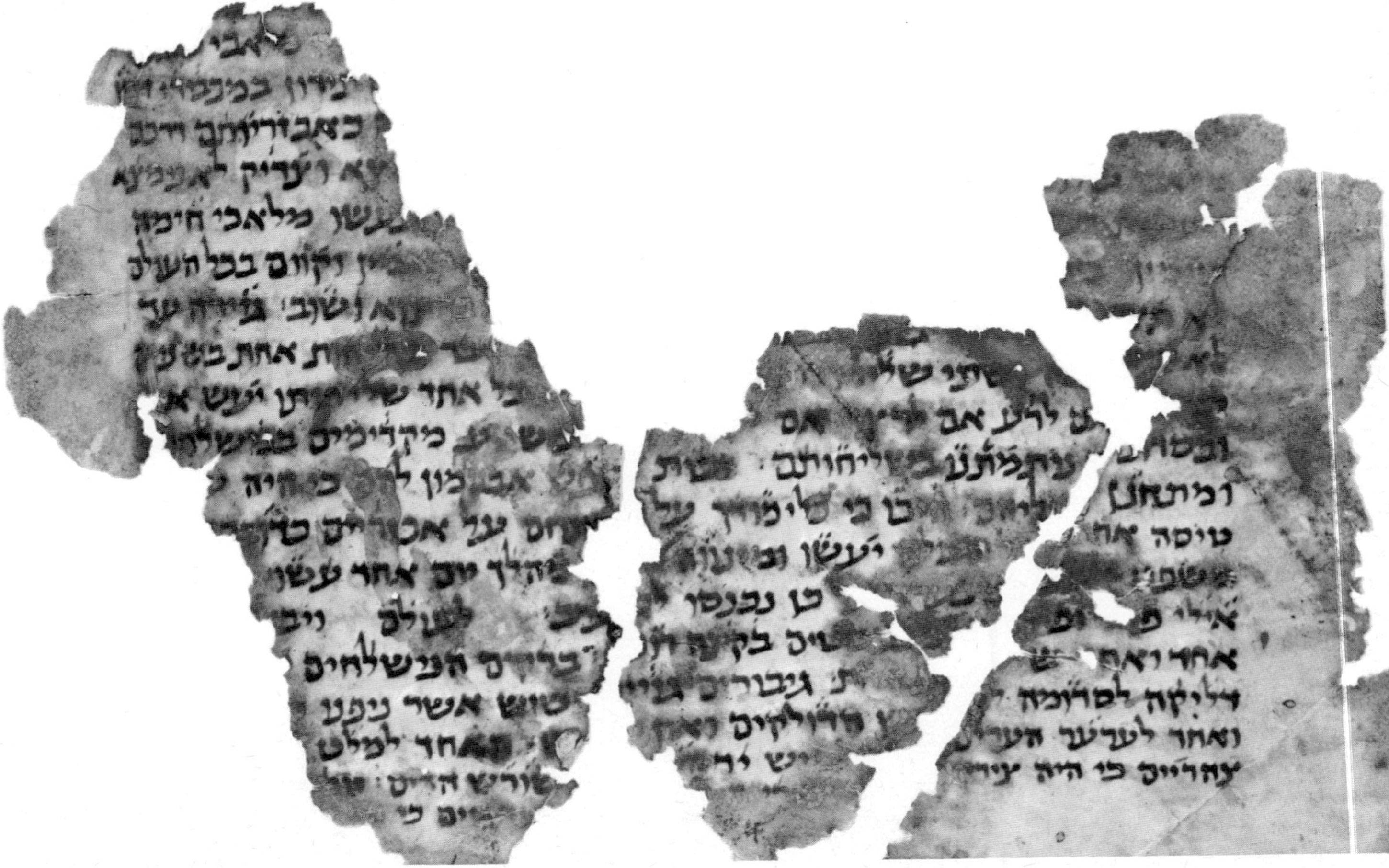

10 Class 4, TS NS 117:6 + NS 123:2, fol. 2, verso.

11 Class 5, J.T.S. MS E.N.A. 2020, fol. 23, recto.

12 Class 5, J.T.S. MS E.N.A. 2020, fol. 23, verso.

13 Class 6, TS H2:30, fol. 1, recto and fol. 2, verso.

14 Class 6, TS H2:30, fol. 1, verso and fol. 2, recto.

15 Class 7, TS NS 249:1, (a) recto, (b) verso.

16 Class 8, TS NS 249:14, verso.

17 Class 8, TS NS 249:14, recto, lines 1–16.

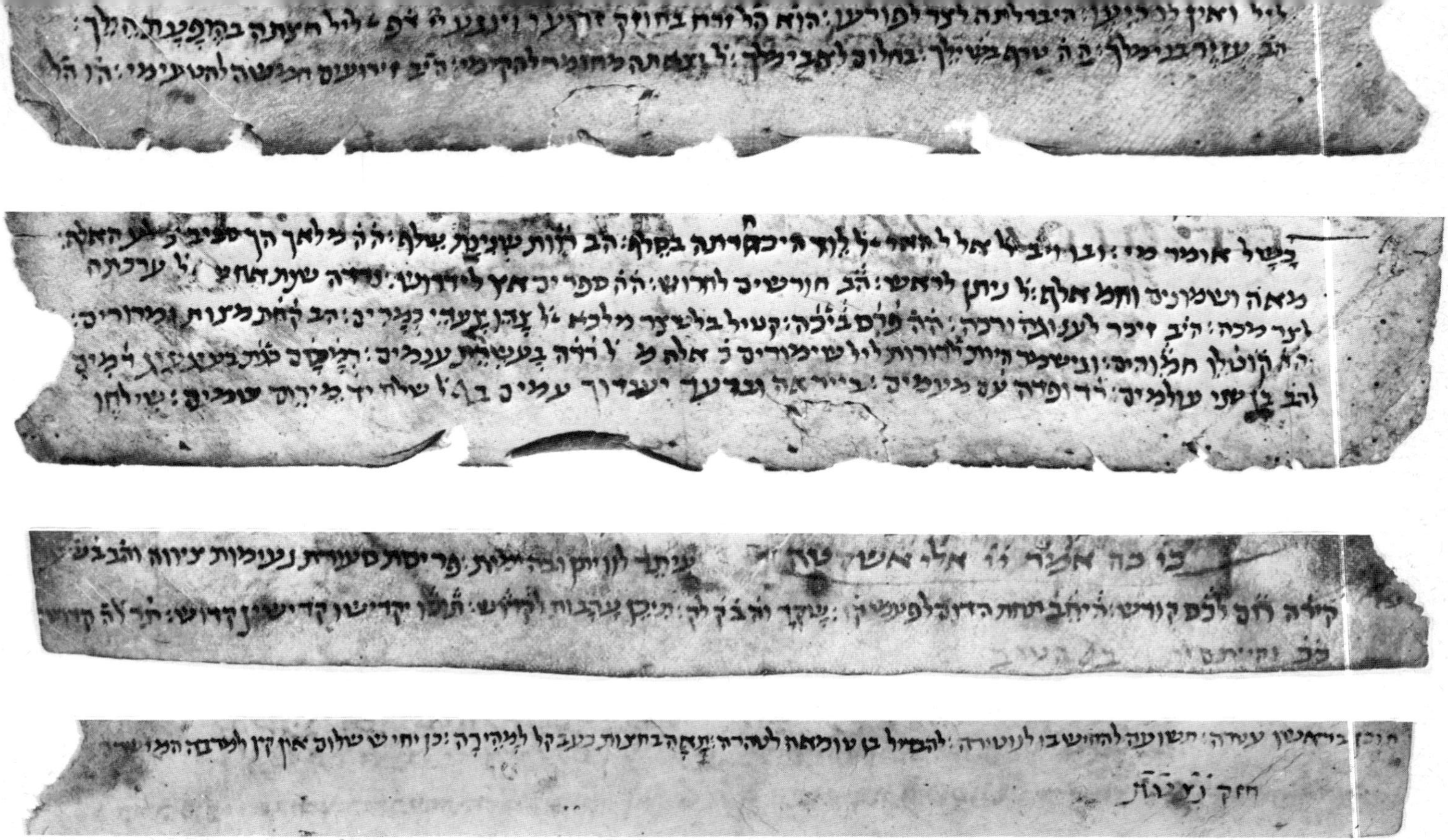

18 Class 9, (a) TS NS 249:14ª, recto, (b) TS NS 249:14ª, verso, (c) TS 12:210ª, recto, (d) TS 12:210ª, verso.

19 Class 10, TS NS 117:7 + TS H6:51, verso, lines 1–36.

20 Class 10, TS NS 117:7 + TS H6:51, verso, lines 31–66.

21 Class II, TS H2:29, fol. I, recto.

22 Class 11, TS H2:29, fol. 2, recto, lines 3–19.

23 Class 12, TS H7:7, verso.